D0394344

# Reorganizing State Government: The Executive Branch

## Other Titles in This Series

## Also of Interest

# Westview Special Studies in Public Policy and Public Systems Management

## *Reorganizing State Government: The Executive Branch*
## James L. Garnett

Although state executive branch reorganization has been surrounded by controversy and expense for more than sixty years and has been occurring at an unprecedented rate during the last thirteen, much of our knowledge of it has been anecdotal, fragmentary, conceptually imprecise, and untested, asserts Dr. Garnett. His book contributes conceptual and empirical order to the study of reorganization by analyzing competing and complementary models, evaluating research methodologies, stating hypotheses, and testing those hypotheses with data drawn from more than 150 of the state reorganizations that have taken place in this century.

Dr. Garnett addresses three basic questions: Why do state reorganizations occur? How are they conducted? What forms do the reorganized executive branches take? His specific action guidelines for governors and other state officials, agenda for further research, and extensive bibliography will be particularly useful.

James L. Garnett is assistant professor of public administration in the School of Government and Public Administration at The American University. He has also taught in the Division of Business and Public Management at the West Virginia College of Graduate Studies and has been program assistant to the governor of New York and research associate for the New York State Study and Charter Commissions for New York City.

# Reorganizing State Government:
## The Executive Branch

### James L. Garnett

Westview Press / Boulder, Colorado

*Westview Special Studies in Public Policy and Public Systems Management*

All rights reserved. No part of this publication may be reproduced or transmitted in any form or by any means, electronic or mechanical, including photocopy, recording, or any information storage and retrieval system, without permission in writing from the publisher.

Copyright © 1980 by James L. Garnett

Published in 1980 in the United States of America by
  Westview Press, Inc.
  5500 Central Avenue
  Boulder, Colorado 80301
  Frederick A. Praeger, Publisher

Library of Congress Cataloging in Publication Data
Garnett, James L.
  Reorganizing state government: the executive branch
  (Westview special studies in public policy and public systems management)
  Bibliography: p.
  1. Administrative agencies—United States—States—Reorganization.  2. State govern-
ments.  I. Title.
JK2443.G34              353.9'173              80-11882
ISBN 0-89158-835-3

Printed and bound in the United States of America

*To Petra and Erin
who make all the effort worthwhile*

# Contents

# Tables

# Figures

# Preface

The need for research of this kind was impressed upon me nine years ago when I worked in the Governor's Office in New York. One of my assignments was to devise a plan for reorganizing functions central to the governor's managerial capability. That exercise accomplished two things: (1) It triggered my interest in state executive reorganization, and (2) it demonstrated to me the need for sounder information upon which to base decisions about reorganizing. It struck me then that much of the information available to me and to state decision makers was impressionistic, anecdotal, and sketchy—hardly the kind of information that inspires confidence.

This study represents a beginning attempt to provide the sound, systematically derived information needed by state government officials and social scientists interested in state government and administrative reform. To provide more systematically derived information, I have brought to bear some of the analytical tools and orientation practiced in comparative state politics research, a body of research that, surprisingly, has avoided the long-standing issue of state executive branch reorganization.

My research encompasses all the executive branch reorganizations in forty-eight states from 1900 to 1975. In the cold of early morning I have nagging suspicions I might have overlooked some major reorganizations. But in the three years of sharing this data with state officials, state government associations, and other researchers, no one has told me, "You missed North Dakota's masterpiece of 1919." After this book is circulated, some readers will undoubtedly correct my sins of omission or commission. I welcome this, because it will help improve our knowledge of state reorganization, a historically and perennially important phenomenon. To facilitate the efforts of others to build upon this base, I have included more data in the text and appendixes than is typical.

To amass data on 151 state executive branch reorganizations required many months of wading through state archives and research library collections. Particularly valuable were the libraries and librarians of the Council of State Governments and the Institute of Public Administration.

My research effort can be understood, in large part, as an attempted meeting-of-the-minds between the state government practitioner in me and the social science researcher in me. It is my conviction that the insights of both practitioner and researcher must complement each other for significant progress to be made toward resolving the many dilemmas with which public administrators must currently cope.

There are many people to acknowledge in research of this scope. Charles Levine, Dwight Waldo, Marilyn Field, Lloyd Nigro, and James Carroll pored over an earlier manuscript. Through perceptive suggestions and tolerant education of the author, they strengthened this work immeasurably. Charles Levine deserves special mention for his conscientious efforts and many constructive contributions to my thinking. Peri Arnold, Clara Penniman, and Thad Beyle examined portions of this manuscript and also provided valuable criticism. Eric Uslaner, James Perry, David Methé, and David Krackhardt advised me on the intricacies of statistics. My thanks also go to David Walker of the Advisory Commission on Intergovernmental Relations for clarifying my sense of the (limited) role the federal government plays in stimulating state executive branch reorganization.

The Council of State Governments and the National Governors' Association provided substantial cooperation. Both organizations facilitated my research by sharing information and insights from professional staff members. The same kind of assistance was given by the Center for Social Analysis, State University of New York at Binghamton.

Three people—Luther Gulick and George Hallett of New York and James W. Martin of Kentucky—contributed greatly through their willingness to help and with their considerable insights. They have demonstrated that devoting a lifetime to the cause of "good government," in the highest sense of that term, is a noble and fulfilling contribution to society.

The West Virginia College of Graduate Studies has provided logistical and moral support for my research. Stephen Cupps, Dennis Emmett, John Breed, Richard Barnard, James Rowley, and Benjamin Perles, all of the College of Graduate Studies, have been encouraging and helpful. Deniese McBride and Frank Adams did a skillful, meticulous job of typing the manuscript. Westview's Lynne Rienner and Lynn Lloyd deserve credit for guiding author and manuscript through the publishing process.

Special appreciation goes to my wife Petra, whose tolerance, support, and encouragement enabled and motivated me to complete this book.

*James L. Garnett*

# 1
# Introduction

*Among the many serious political and economic problems, with which the American democracy is confronted, there is none in respect to which public opinion is more profoundly interested and more radically divided than in those connected with state political reorganization. More than ever before in the history of the country such problems are assuming national importance.*

— Herbert Croly, *The Promise of American Life*

## The Phenomenon

Governors and other state decision makers have turned increasingly to state executive branch reorganization as one means of gaining managerial control over state bureaucracies, coping with rising financial pressures, and installing needed management systems. Governors, following the example of former Georgia Governor Jimmy Carter, have also rediscovered the political value of reorganization as a campaign issue.

With these and other objectives in mind, twenty states underwent major executive branch restructuring between 1965 and 1975.[1] In addition to these major reorganizations, at least twenty-four other states have reorganized one or more departments since 1964.[2] The most recent series of state executive branch reorganizations has been the most active; however, it is by no means an isolated phenomenon. State executive reorganizations have come in waves, and the most recent one is the third major wave in this century. The first two waves occurred during 1914–36 and 1937–46.[3]

State reorganization activity has not ceased with these efforts. Since 1975 at least three other states have accomplished executive branch reorganizations, and a number of studies have been undertaken in other states.[4] Clearly, far from being an issue "whose time has past," state executive branch reorganization remains a perennial issue for governors, legislatures, administrative agencies, and their constituencies. The continuing tendency of governments to spawn new organizations and to disassemble and consolidate existing ones is well documented.[5]

State executive reorganizations constitute an interesting set of political and administrative phenomena apart from their significance for governmental operations. There are a number of ways in which they vary, including the date they occurred; the length and painfulness of gestation; the overall magnitude of the reform effort; the structural properties of state agencies; the degree of political competition and controversy over reorganization; the tactics pursued in the effort to adopt; the extent to which implementation is accomplished; and the roles played by administrative, legislative, and interest-group actors.

## Fundamental Research Questions

State executive reorganizations have been occurring for more than sixty years and have been of central interest to those in the field of public administration. Many of the leading contributors to public administration have been involved in the state reorganization movement as combatants or chroniclers, and the core ideas of public administration have been spawned during the ideological, political, and administrative struggles over state reorganization. Dwight Waldo, a leading observer of the development of public administration, has captured the centrality of state reorganization to this field:

> All of these phases of administrative thought and activity — academic study, personnel reform, administrative training, and organized research — have implied and eventuated in proposals to "reorganize" administration. But the Reorganization movement deserves separate consideration, for in some of its phases, particularly the movement to reorganize state governments, it has produced a characteristic and distinct literature. Moreover, it seems to be a least common denominator for a number of lesser movements . . . that have been closely related to the rise of public administration.[6]

For all of the political and administrative significance of state executive branch reorganizations, our understanding of them is very limited. To date, much of the professional literature on the subject has been personal and anecdotal in character.[7] For our understanding to be more complete, and therefore more useful, there are several basic kinds of knowledge which have to be systematically developed. This research focuses on three fundamental sets of questions:

1. *Why? Why do state reorganizations occur? What are the determinants of state reorganizations?* Unless this kind of knowledge of what determines and shapes a reorganization is available, it becomes extremely difficult to predict the outcome of a reorganization movement or the variables that can be manipulated to influence that outcome. Governors, legislatures, study commissions, and other would-be reor-

ganizers work with substantially impressionistic knowledge as to what factors are significant and how they relate to each other.

2. *What? What forms do reorganized executive branches take? How do these structures differ? What kinds of states tend to adopt what types of reorganization?* The structural dimensions of reorganizations appear to follow a limited number of models and cluster by region and time period. Understanding the diffusion patterns of these models and their dominant properties is a matter of great importance for reorganization proponents attempting to choose the most appropriate model for their objectives.

3. *How? How are state executive reorganizations conducted? What strategies and tactics are applied with regard to adoption and implementation?* Reorganizations always incur costs — costs in money, time, policy momentum, and political capital. The problem becomes one of design and implementation: knowing how to reorganize to minimize the costs and maximize the probabilities that the intended reorganization is what actually does result.

These three sets of questions are not the only ones deserving attention. A fundamental question is: Does state executive branch reorganization have any relation to state government's effectiveness in performing its task? State reorganizations are frequently promoted on the basis that they will improve governmental performance in general and service delivery in particular. But empirical support for such claims is lacking, largely because of the "failure to develop an adequate set of measures of organization performance, particularly in the public sector."[8] The answers to these three questions appear to be essential to a basic understanding of the state executive branch and prerequisite to research questions, such as the performance issue.

The primary purposes of this study are (1) to survey what is known concerning these basic questions, (2) to systematize that knowledge, (3) to establish research hypotheses drawing upon existing knowledge, (4) to gather data, through archival research, on executive reorganization in forty-eight contiguous states from 1900 to 1975,[9] (5) to examine the data and interpret the results using statistical tools, (6) to reassess the state of our knowledge, and (7) to identify directions for further research.

## Format of This Study

The next three chapters lay the conceptual foundations by surveying what is known regarding the three fundamental questions I have posed.

In Chapter 2 I examine competing and complementary theoretical perspectives on why reorganizations occur. The chapter ends with a comparison and summary of the leading perspectives.

In Chapter 3 I focus on the form or structure state reorganizations have taken. After establishing criteria for assessing typologies in the social sciences, I evaluate the major typology of state reorganization according to these criteria and present a new typology.

Strategies for adopting and implementing reorganizations are the focus of discussion in Chapter 4. Having tapped scholarly literature and government manuals and reports to identify the key strategy issues facing reorganization sponsors and opponents, I then discuss the logic behind each strategy, compare strategy alternatives, and, where possible, evaluate them on the basis of existing knowledge.

Chapter 5 opens with an assessment of the leading research methodologies applied thus far to the study of state executive reorganization. Next I develop a conceptual framework that links synthesized perspectives on why reorganizations occur (from Chapter 2) with structural variables drawn from the typology in Chapter 3 and several key strategy variables from Chapter 4. The research process followed in this study is also examined. Chapter 5 concludes with a discussion of the variables used, their operationalization, and a presentation of forty research hypotheses relating to the three fundamental research questions.

In Chapter 6 I analyze and interpret major findings of this research. A first set of findings describes overall patterns of state reorganization, showing variations by geographic region and time period. Analysis of a second set of findings—those relating to the research hypotheses—concludes Chapter 6.

In Chapter 7 I offer conclusions on each of the three fundamental research questions. A particular concern is the feasibility of developing action guidelines for reorganization decision makers. I conclude by identifying directions for further research on state executive branch reorganization.

### Notes

1. George A. Bell, "State Administrative Organization Activities, 1974–1975," *The Book of the States, 1976–77* (Lexington, Ky.: Council of State Governments, 1976), pp. 105–13. Council of State Governments, *Reorganization in the States* (Lexington, Ky.: Council of State Governments, 1972), pp. 4–9. Neal R. Peirce, "Structural Reform of Bureaucracy Grows Rapidly," *National Journal* 7 (April 5, 1975):502–8.

2. Council of State Governments, *Reorganization in the States*, pp. 10, 12–13.

3. These periods reflect the waves of state reorganization following three major federal government reorganization efforts: President's Commission on Economy and Efficiency (Taft Commission), 1910–13; President's Committee on Admin-

istrative Management (Brownlow Committee), 1937; Commission on Organization of the Executive Branch of the Government (First Hoover Commission), 1947–49. My study focuses on state *executive branch* reorganization. Judicial and legislative branch reorganizations are excluded, as are intra-agency or individual agencywide reorganizations not part of a broader reorganization program.

4. States reorganizing since 1975 include West Virginia (1977), Connecticut (1977), and New Mexico (1977). States undertaking reorganization studies include Washington, Hawaii, Mississippi, and North Dakota.

5. For discussion of reasons behind the spawning of new federal agencies, see Carl Grafton, "The Creation of Federal Agencies," *Administration and Society* 7 (November 1974):328–65, and Herbert Kaufman, *Are Government Organizations Immortal?* (Washington, D.C.: Brookings Institution, 1976), pp. 14–16, 66–68. Creation of new organizations at the state level is the focus of: Leslie Lipson, *The American Governor: From Figurehead to Leader* (Chicago: Greenwood Press, 1939), pp. 27–28, and Council of State Governments, *Reorganization in the States,* pp. 5–6, 12–13. Extensive descriptions of the disaggregation and aggregation of state organizations can be found in A. E. Buck, *Administrative Consolidation in State Governments,* 5th ed. (New York: National Municipal League, 1930), and A. E. Buck, *Reorganization of State Governments in the United States* (New York: Columbia University Press, 1938).

6. Dwight Waldo, *The Administrative State: A Study of the Political Theory of American Public Administration* (New York: Ronald Press Co., 1948), p. 34.

7. See David T. Stanley, "Sam, You Made the Frame Too Long," *Public Administration Review* 23 (July/August 1972):349.

8. Robert Backoff, "Operationalizing Administrative Reform for Improved Governmental Performance," *Administration and Society* 6 (May 1974):83. The complex performance issue is not addressed in a substantial way in this exploratory study; it remains an important next step in my research agenda. For attempts to grapple with the issue of reorganization performance impacts, see James L. Garnett and Charles H. Levine, "State Executive Branch Reorganization: Patterns and Performance" (Paper delivered at the Annual Meeting of the American Political Science Association, Washington, D.C., September 1–4, 1977); and Kenneth J. Meier, "Governmental Reorganization for Economy and Efficiency: Some Lessons from State Government" (Paper delivered at the Annual Meeting of the Midwest Political Science Association, Chicago, Illinois, April 19–21, 1979).

9. I examined state reorganizing activity over a seventy-six-year period, 1900–76. However, until 1914 no reorganization attempts meet my criteria for a state executive branch reorganization. These specific criteria are defined in Chapter 5.

# 2

# Why State Executive Reorganizations Occur: Competing and Complementary Theoretical Perspectives

---

*There was always a certain missionary attitude on the part of our crowd. We were eager to see government improved and we were convinced that we had the gospel, so we went as missionaries . . . and we showed them these texts as illustrations of what had been recommended. Then we tried to persuade the people for whom we were working that this was what they should do. This was a program they would find rewarding.*
　　　　　　　　　—Luther Gulick, Interview with James L. Garnett,
　　　　　　　　　　　　　　　　　　　　　　　　　November 30, 1976

*Enough has been said to indicate the complex pattern in the politics of reorganizations. Conflicts between Democrats and Republicans, between city and country, between reformers and bosses, colored the struggle. . . . No single factor, no simple explanation, will yield an analysis that satisfies. The ramifications and interlockings of causes are too intricate for reduction to one element. The reorganization movement was a typical fragment of the political process.*
　　　　　　　　　—Leslie Lipson, *The American Governor:*
　　　　　　　　　　　　　　　　　　　　*From Figurehead to Leader*

In social science, there is demonstrated value in examining a set of phenomena by applying different conceptual frameworks.[1] Viewing public policy decisions and actions through a variety of "conceptual lenses" can produce a variety of explanations as to what happened in a political-administrative situation and why events happened as they did.[2] "Each frame of reference is, in effect, a 'conceptual lens.' By comparing and contrasting the . . . frameworks, we see what each magnifies, highlights, and reveals as well as what each blurs or neglects."[3]

There is reason to look at state executive branch reorganization through a series of different theoretical lenses with a view toward pooling the various insights. And these lenses do focus on diverse fundamental research questions. Some deal with the structural aspect of reorganization (*what* reorganization looks like) and others the procedural facet (*how* reorganization is carried out). However, a common focus is the question: *Why* do reorganizations occur? What are the driving forces that can trigger a state executive branch reorganization?

In Figure 2.1 I have identified five theoretical perspectives. There are others, but the five have been major scholarly approaches and they can add to our understanding of reorganization. I offer a sixth approach in an attempt to synthesize the contributions of the other five.

As will be evident, these approaches also vary in the level of detail they use to "explain" reorganization, the degree to which they rely upon empirical evidence, and the level of analysis they apply. The variation in levels of analysis is crucial: varying the scope of one's lens may produce a wide range of results.

My effort here is neither to debunk certain approaches nor to tout others. Each perspective comes from a rich research tradition, and even though there is competition among approaches, each supplements and complements the contributions made by the others. And although each lens is unique it does share elements in common with the others. The result is some overlap among perspectives.

### Administrative Orthodoxy

The primary purpose of this section is to examine the contribution of orthodox writers on administrative thought to the question: Why do reor-

FIGURE 2.1

Leading Theoretical Perspectives on State Executive Reorganization

|    | Theoretical Perspective | Driving Force |
|----|-------------------------|---------------|
| 1. | Administrative Orthodoxy | correctness of administrative principles |
| 2. | Reorganization as Political Competition | political motivations and actions |
| 3. | Socioeconomic Determinants Approach | socioeconomic environment |
| 4. | Reorganization as Diffused Innovation | diffusion/emulation process |
| 5. | Reorganization as Adaptation to Modernization | modernization process |
| 6. | Reorganization as Synthesis | all of the above forces working in combination |

ganizations occur? In accomplishing this objective it will be helpful to sketch out some of the basic philosophy of Administrative Orthodoxy. (However, the major thrust is not a discourse on the political and administrative theory imbedded in the state executive reorganization movement. That task was undertaken by Waldo in 1948 and more recently by Anita Gottlieb.[4])

A number of writings in the 1920s and 1930s centered on the structural and prescriptive aspects of state executive reorganization: What *forms* should reorganization take? These prescriptions were often cast in administrative precepts that have been termed the *tenets* or *principles* of Administrative Orthodoxy. Some of the principal scholarly efforts in this tradition are by A. E. Buck, J. M. Mathews, A. N. Holcombe, Kirk H. Porter, Luther H. Gulick, and the New York Bureau of Municipal Research.[5]

Although these writers espoused no uniform set of principles of state reorganization, they did agree in large measure on what should be done in reorganizing.[6] One widely influential set of "standards" was formally articulated by A. E. Buck:[7]

STANDARDS OF ADMINISTRATIVE REORGANIZATION
These standards are no longer theoretical, but are based upon experience and supported in whole or in part by actual practice in a number of states. They may be enumerated as follows:

1. Concentration of authority and responsibility;
2. Departmentalization, or functional integration;
3. Undesirability of boards for purely administrative work;
4. Coordination of the staff services of administration;
5. Provision of an independent audit;
6. Recognition of a governor's cabinet.[8]

Considerably before the broader and heavier salvos against the tenets of Administrative Orthodoxy,[9] a lesser-known but highly vociferous opposition arose. But these early critics (Charles Hyneman, William Edwards, A. C. Millspaugh, Harvey Walker, Francis Coker, and others), like the advocates of the "principles," focused on what the reorganization ought to look like, or not look like, rather than on why reorganizations take place or how they are conducted.[10] Implicit in much of the orthodox writing is the notion that if the correct principles are followed, both the reorganization *process* and its *product* (the reform goals to be achieved) would follow almost automatically.

In spite of their preoccupation with the structural aspects of reorganization, however, orthodox theorists have afforded insights into why and how reorganizations occur. And even though Administrative Orthodoxy is by no means a homogeneous body of thought, a composite classical reform perspective of executive reorganization can do justice to that research tradition. (See Figure 2.2.)

In the classical (orthodox) reform perspective, the process was usually initiated by a sponsor who perceived a need for change in the existing organization of state government. Often the sponsor was the governor; however, it might have been one of the governor's chief aides, a legislative leader, or even a prominent business leader outside state government.[11] The perceived need for reorganization might have resulted from an event (e.g., a scandal or a change in controlling party) or from a realization that the present organization was inadequate.

Whether it was the sponsor who had the initial perception that change was needed (or demanded by constituents) or whether others felt this need first and then convinced the sponsor, it was normally the sponsor who initiated a reorganization study. The study (or "survey" as it was usually called) could be conducted by a staff composed of state government staff, local experts, or specialists from an out-of-state research bureau or consulting firm. Those nationally known research bureaus and consulting firms most active in state reorganization activities have been the New York Bureau of Municipal Research (later the Institute of Public Administration), Griffenhagen and Associates, the Institute for Government Research (later the Brookings Institution), and the Public Administration Service.[12]

Whether a local staff or outside consultants were called on to perform the reorganization study, they often influenced the sponsor's perceptions about the necessity, objectives, and methods of reform and the structures that were to result. And when working to devise reorganization plans, these people have been inclined to draw upon the body of knowledge most widely accepted — Administrative Orthodoxy.[13]

The nationally known research bureaus and consulting firms have been particularly inclined to apply the principles of administration when summoned to develop a state reorganization plan.[14] This is not surprising: some of those theorists most responsible for developing and advocating the principles were among the specialists sent by their bureau or firm to conduct the reorganization study. For example, A. E. Buck and Luther Gulick were often on the New York Bureau of Municipal Research team, Buck normally serving as the team coordinator. And W. F. Willoughby sometimes represented the Institute for Government Research.[15]

These consultants were not reluctant to spread their ideas about the most effective ways to reorganize. According to Luther Gulick,

> There was always a certain missionary attitude on the part of our crowd. We were eager to see government improved and we were convinced that we had

FIGURE 2.2

Classical Reform Perspective
of State Executive Reorganization

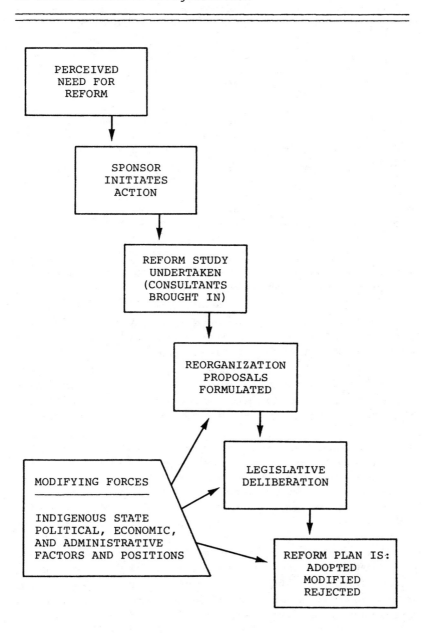

the gospel, so we went as missionaries . . . to persuade the people for whom we were working that this was what they should do.[16]

While the objectivity of these "missionaries" might be questioned by the current generation of political science and public administration scholars, their impact on government policy is rarely matched by present scholars. One illustration of the far-reaching effect of Administrative Orthodoxy comes in a statement by South Dakota Governor Richard Kneip about that state's most recent major executive reorganization, in 1973:

> The plan of organization in South Dakota contains many of the fundamental principles of classical organization propounded by such theorists as A. E. Buck and Luther Gulick. The governor's span of control is limited to a relatively small number of departments organized around broad goals, and the head of each department is directly responsible and accountable to the governor.[17]

Even if state decision makers knew what the "correct" reorganization was supposed to be (according to the principles), there was no assurance that the reorganization plan as finally adopted would embody all of this ideal. State political, administrative, economic, and other indigenous factors often modified the ideal in the interest of political feasibility. For example, while the generally held orthodox canons opposed administrative agencies independent of the chief executive, administrative tradition and political dynamics combined in a number of states to keep the education department somewhat removed from the governor's control.[18]

These reformers were basically practical men who were able to compromise in order to accomplish at least part of the ideal. However, some of these reformers considered politics a necessary evil that interfered with administrative rationality. This view is typified by Buck's contention that

> the above standards [principles] are not uniformly accepted since in every state there has been more or less of a fight between those who sought the new system and those who supported the old order of things. In some states this opposition was so strong that the consolidation plans adopted were to a large extent compromises in which *standards gave way to expediency*.[19] (Italics added for emphasis.)

In their writing, these scholars have tended to deemphasize the politics of reorganization. Accounts typically centered on the formal steps in the reorganization process and on descriptions of the existing, proposed, and adopted structural arrangements. Political opposition was sometimes noted, but rarely was there a discussion of the groups opposing or supporting reorganization, the political strategies being applied, or the political consequences for the combatants.

## Reorganization as Political Competition

Another tradition of scholarship on reorganization has sought to bring politics back into the reorganization process or, more accurately, to articulate the politics that have always been present. In this respect the Reorganization as Political Competition approach is a reaction to the orthodox perspective.

Although there is a set of literature in this tradition that focuses on state reorganization, the literature is not rich. This deficiency is explained in part by the neglect of executive reorganization politics in comparative state politics literature, a literature that dominated the study of American state politics in the 1960s and 1970s. But some state-oriented works are instructive on the politics of reorganization. And this body of literature will be supplemented with studies which have the United States federal government as their focus.

The thrust of the Reorganization as Political Competition approach is that reorganization is basically a political process aimed at political ends. Reorganizations, in this view, are undertaken to enhance a governor's power or detract from it; to insulate a governmental function from the influence of special interests or to ensure that influence; to shake up the executive branch in an effort to get rid of a "troublemaker" or to install one's own political appointees; or to boost, change, or thwart program direction. This political approach sees the orthodox principles more as a convenient rationale for reorganizing toward political ends than as important in their own right.[20]

Research questions asked by scholars in this tradition have a different focus than those asked by the orthodox theory adherents. For example, instead of asking what organizational structures are the most rational for the performance of a governmental function, Rourke, in a study of the federal employment security program, asked, "Do changes in the structural location of a government agency actually decrease the extent of influence traditionally exercised by outside groups over an area of policy with which they are concerned?"[21]

According to this perspective, reorganizations not only are undertaken to achieve political ends, but are themselves the product of political competition between the executive and legislative branches,[22] among interest groups,[23] and among parties.[24] Thus, Bosworth hypothesized that conditions for reorganization would be most favorable if "the survey is carried out under the leadership of the 'outs,' who thereupon become the 'ins' and adopt their own recommendations before new vested interests are established in the offices to be eliminated."[25]

Political control, the objective of party competitions, is another political condition Bosworth judged favorable to state executive reorganization. The ideal condition is for the governorship and both houses of the legislature to be held by the same party and for all three components to be sponsoring reorganization.

Legislative reapportionment is another political variable that has been perceived as a stimulus for state executive reorganization. George Bell, former director of research for the Council of State Governments, has listed this variable as "the most important factor" in the reorganization boom from the mid-1960s to the early 1970s.[26]

According to this view, the major actors in reorganization have political objectives and operate within political constraints. Even constitutional and judicial constraints and influences are typically the product of negotiation. The status and strength of a department after reorganization are the result of political forces and are themselves political forces (as for example in the enhancement or deflation of a program's status and resources).[27] The *objectives* of reorganization (although seldom articulated) are often political—as are the *outcomes*, both intended and unintended.

This is not to say that reorganization constraints, forms, processes, objectives, and outcomes are entirely political. The Reorganization as Political Competition perspective recognizes the economic, social, theoretical, and personal elements of reorganization. Politics, however, is seen as the primary force behind reorganization. Why does reorganization occur? It occurs because of political actions by political actors with largely political motives.

Nor is this meant to imply that the proponents of Administrative Orthodoxy approached state reorganization without regard for highly political issues. The conflict between those advocating consolidation of the state executive branch and those opposing it often hinged on very political questions: Who should be in charge here? Is it a mistake to concentrate too much power in the hands of the executive?[28]

Despite the deemphasis of the "political" in their writing, those espousing Administrative Orthodoxy were highly sensitive to political considerations and were successful in getting results from the political process. An interesting thesis advanced by Arnold holds that the reformers of the executive branch in the 1920s and 1930s used the principles of sound "scientific" and "neutral" administration as a guise for achieving their political aim: to increase the power of the chief executive.[29] Arnold's thesis has been corroborated by Luther Gulick, who admitted that the principles were essentially a "sales pitch" that reformers felt would appeal to the current strong interest in anything scientific, rational, and businesslike.[30]

By contrast, the Reorganization as Political Competition writers are concerned more with describing the realities of reorganization politics as they see them than exploring administrative or political theory.

Though the Reorganization as Political Competition perspective has made a significant contribution to our understanding of the realities of reorganization, its adherents generally have fared little better than the orthodox reformers in substantiating their conclusions or assertions with quantifiable evidence. Emphasis on quantitative evidence and methods is a hallmark of the next lens on reorganization.

### Socioeconomic Determinants

The Socioeconomic Determinants approach contrasts sharply and (in the view of some scholars) competes with the Reorganization as Political Competition approach. The points of departure are the perception of what triggers a reorganization and the modes of analysis typically applied. Instead of political actors, institutions, and processes, the most significant influence on reorganization is the impact of socioeconomic variables. This perspective in its general, and most outspoken, form has been described as "a new orthodoxy that asserted that political processes ahd little power to explain the level of expenditures and outputs of state governments."[31]

My purpose here is not to join the politics versus socioeconomic factors debate, which has been both voluminous[32] and vociferous.[33] Rather, my objective is to demonstrate the use of this conceptual lens for looking at state reorganization and to assess its strengths and weaknesses.

Despite the considerable number of research studies applying the Socioeconomic Determinants approach, it has not been used very much with reference to executive branch reorganization or even with reference to the executive branch in general. In 1968 Herbert Jacob and Michael Lipsky concluded there was a lack of useful research on state bureaucracies even though most key decisions were executive ones.[34] And since that time, bureaucratic variables have been "consistently under-represented in determinants research."[35]

One of the few determinants studies using administrative dimensions as dependent variables, rather than as intervening variables, was conducted by James Noell.[36] Among the determinants studies, his study of the influence of socioeconomic variables on the size and complexity of state and local bureaucracies is perhaps most relevant to the problem of explaining the determinants of executive reorganization. Noell's work also presents a useful illustration of the logic and method incorporated in the Socioeconomic Determinants approach. (See Figure 2.3.)

FIGURE 2.3

An Example of a Determinants Approach to State Administrative Organization

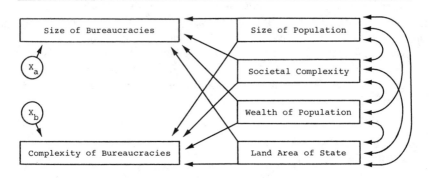

Source: James J. Noell, "On the Administrative Sector of Social Systems: An Analysis of the Size and Complexity of Government Bureaucracies in the American States," Social Forces 52 (June 1974), 556.

Note: Path diagram is arranged this way in the original article.

Drawing upon the work of other researchers, Noell formulated hypotheses regarding the relationship between (1) the size and complexity of state and local government bureaucracies and (2) a series of four socioeconomic variables: state population size, degree of societal complexity, wealth of population, and land area of state. His quest was certainly a natural one, namely, what effect do changes in underlying socioeconomic characteristics have on changes in key aspects of government bureaucracy?

Noell's conclusions are fairly representative of those found by practitioners of the Socioeconomic Determinants approach: changes in broad socioeconomic variables are statistically related (in varying degrees) to changes in characteristics of government administrative agencies.

What assessment can be made of the general Socioeconomic Determinants approach (as represented by Noell's work) in explaining why reorganizations occur? This perspective makes us conscious of the need to look beyond the often more obvious and more dramatic political and doctrinal "causes" of reorganization to a set of underlying social and economic influences that may operate more indirectly and more slowly, but which ought not to be overlooked. Socioeconomic factors have been cited in the reorganization literature, but only rarely have they been incorporated into a full-fledged determinants research design. Consequently, the full utility of this approach for studying government reorganization has yet to be realized.

Practitioners of the Socioeconomic Determinants approach generally have been careful to make explicit their assumptions, research hypotheses, operationalizations, and results toward the end that their work could be critiqued or complemented by others. This scientific spirit and allegiance to behavioralist methods is essential to the study of reorganization, a study dominated by anecdotal and impressionistic evidence.

The Socioeconomic Determinants approach itself needs to be supplemented and complemented by other perspectives. This is necessary for several reasons. First, this approach almost totally neglects the *process* of reorganization. This lens is oriented toward inputs (the socioeconomic influences) and outputs (the changes in bureaucracy), showing little regard for what happens in between — the political, administrative, social, personal processes by which reorganizations get studied, planned, adopted, and implemented. A corollary is that people are almost superfluous to the process. Broad social and economic characteristics are seen as having real impact; the actions of people (apart from their minuscule contribution to these social and economic forces), as having only marginal consequence. In this respect, the Socioeconomic Determinants perspective can produce just as much pessimism about the impact of individual and group actions as can the Reorganization as Political Competition attitude that "politics as usual will eventually carry the day."

This lack of attention to people and process is related to a second difficulty — the almost total inability of state decision makers to manipulate the key variables affecting reorganization. Even if it were known, for example, that by increasing its urbanization, changing its ethnic composition, or raising its per-capita income a state could "produce" conditions for reorganization, these variables would remain largely beyond the ability of state legislatures or governors to control in our democratic and federal system.

**Reorganization as Diffused Innovation**

The Socioeconomic Determinants approach emphasizes basic causal forces acting *within* states. The Reorganization as Diffused Innovation perspective finds this approach basically inadequate and looks instead to the diffusion of ideas, instrumentalities, policies, and even causal processes themselves *across* states. The very nature of the analytical techniques (primarily correlational analysis) employed by the Socioeconomic Determinants proponents usually requires the assumption of independence among units of analysis. This assumption reinforces a tendency to look for explanations within political boundaries, while neglecting or deemphasizing the consequences of interactions and interdependencies among states.

The Reorganization as Diffused Innovation perspective emphasizes dynamics across political boundaries, viewing state executive reorganization as a form of innovation that diffuses among governmental units.[37] While reorganization diffusion is also a key element of the orthodoxy approach, the preoccupation of that perspective is with the role of *doctrine* ("principles"). The Reorganization as Diffused Innovation lens focuses more on the diffusion-emulation *process* itself.

For the purposes of this study, I will use Gerald Zaltman, Robert Duncan, and Jonny Holbek's definition of *innovation*: "any idea, practice, or material artifact perceived to be new by the relevant unit of adoption."[38] This definition is consistent with, but more useful than, the definitions of Walker and Rogers and Shoemaker. Walker's definition limits innovations to programs and policies and does not allow for structural innovations; Rogers and Shoemaker limit the unit of adoption to an individual, rather than organization, state, or comparable unit.[39]

Most writers on the subject of diffusion of reorganization to states have taken the view that states have emulated innovations in federal executive branch reorganization. Indicative of this view is the assertion that the President's (Taft) Commission on Economy and Efficiency triggered the initial wave of state reorganization activity.[40]

> The greatest impetus to the [state] reorganization movement was given by President Taft when he appointed his Efficiency and Economy Commission of 1910. . . . True, prior to this time states had considered administrative consolidation, but the reforms had only been "piecemeal." . . . But after the creation of Taft's Commission plans were forwarded for comprehensive reconstruction of the entire state administration.[41]

A similar assertion comes from Kaufman.

> Another burst of state reorganizations was sparked by another federal commission, President Franklin D. Roosevelt's Committee on Administrative Management in 1937. Its report restated forcefully the premises and proposals by then associated with the reorganization movement and over a dozen states followed this lead.[42]

The reports of the first Hoover Commission (1947–49) were credited by some writers as having "touched off a third wave of state reorganizations."[43] Other scholars, however, have noted that emulation by states has applied more to initiating reorganization studies (often called "Little Hoover" commissions) than to emulating any federal results. In one judgment, "the late 1940s and early fifties, ironically saw the most studies and the least overall reorganization."[44]

State structures, strategies, and actors have also diffused to the federal level. For example, the President's Committee on Administrative Management (Brownlow Committee) cited state reorganizations in Illinois, Virginia, New York, and Maine as evidence that restructuring along the lines proposed in the Brownlow Committee's report had proven successful in dealing with problems similar to those the federal government faced.[45] Interest and experience in executive branch reorganization at the state level were carried on to the federal arena by Franklin Roosevelt, Senator Harry Byrd, Sr., and, more recently, Jimmy Carter.

Reorganization content and the impetus to reorganize have diffused across states as well. Illinois, with the first major state executive reorganization (in 1917), is often viewed in the literature as an innovator in state structural reform, and a number of states have emulated the Illinois example.[46] Even though the New York reorganization of 1915 was not adopted, concepts from that plan had a tremendous impact on the thinking of other states. The New York plan was widely diffused by the New York Bureau of Municipal Research.[47]

Reorganization diffusion has not only been chronological, diffusing from the first major adopter, but has also had a regional dynamics as well. While some regional diffusion dynamics can be discerned among states in the Northwest, the Midwest, the Northeast, and the Southeast, more research is needed to identify more completely the spatial patterns of reorganization diffusion.

The Reorganization as Diffused Innovation perspective has received much less attention than most of the other approaches. As a consequence, the patterns of reorganization diffusion across states have not been clearly identified. The scant literature that does deal with state reorganization diffusion has been primarily descriptive, not analytical.

Research findings on diffusion militate against overgeneralizing. These findings suggest that the types of diffusion patterns, the kinds of communication mechanisms, and the states that are innovation leaders or laggards tend to vary with time[48] and with the type of innovation.[49] Despite this caveat, I think it useful to look at a "typical" reorganization diffusion process.

The process can start in a number of ways, but typically state officials or personnel perceive a gap between what state government is doing and what state decision makers believe it should be doing. Such gaps can result from heightened or lowered performance expectations.[50] Gaps are also the product of changes in an organization's internal environment (personnel or technological changes, or shifts in power relationships) or external environment (shifts in supply and/or demand of the organization's output, broad technological changes, or shifts in the organization's relative power position).[51]

A perceived performance gap often leads to a search for ways to close that gap. This search often includes referent states with which the searching state identifies because of geographic proximity, similar characteristics, communication links, or some other reason. Walker has observed that

> [one] explanation of the adoption of innovations by the states is based on the assertion that state officials make most of their decisions by analogy. The rule of thumb they employ might be formally stated as follows: look for an analogy between the situation you are dealing with and some other situation, perhaps in some other state, where the problem has been successfully resolved.[52]

The search may even precede the perceived performance gap. Formal or informal contact with officials from other state governments may result in a discovery of some practice, policy, structural device, or program that "our state needs." There are a number of institutional forums at which state officials and personnel are exposed, both systematically and informally, to problems and developments in other states. Among such organizations are: the National Governors' Association, the National Conference of State Legislatures, the Council of State Governments, and the National Association of State Budget Officers. Typical of the official purpose of such organizations is that of the National Governors' Association, which states in part, "The functions of the Association shall be to provide a medium for the exchange of views and experiences on subjects of general importance to the people of the several states." (Article of Organization of the National Governors' Conference, p. 1.) The document *Innovations in State Government: Messages from the Governors* is an example of this kind of exchange.

The agitation for adoption of a similar organization structure, for example, can result from either a gap-first or search-first process. Throughout this process state officials and personnel, and representatives from other levels of government or from the private sector share information with each other.

The Reorganization as Innovation perspective adds several insights to our total understanding of state reorganization. More than the Socioeconomic Determinants, Administrative Orthodoxy, and Reorganization as Adaptation to Modernization perspectives, Reorganization as Innovation helps us understand the roles of legislative and bureaucratic actors in the reorganization adoption process. The Innovation approach recognizes and helps us understand the dynamics of diffusion and emulation across states, a perspective emphasized in no other approach besides the Administrative Orthodoxy perspective.

Another benefit is that much of the knowledge gained from this perspective can be intentionally manipulated by decision makers to help achieve the objectives they seek. For example, proponents can use a successful reorganization in another state as justification for undertaking the restructuring they want in their home state. And opponents can use the same knowledge. Contrast this with the Socioeconomic Determinants approach: Knowledge gained through that perspective is more difficult and sometimes impossible to utilize.

As useful as the Reorganization as Innovation framework is, it needs to be supplemented with other approaches. It is often difficult to isolate the impact of diffusion.

> Do Arkansas and Alabama adopt various policies at about the same time because they communicate with each other continuously (a diffusion or interaction explanation) or because they are so similar (in terms of problems, resources, culture, etc.) that they would do pretty much the same thing even if there was no communication between them? Doubtless the similar behavior of two states such as these is a result of both their possessing many of the same socioeconomic and political characteristics and the fact that each pays attention to what the other is doing. It is also probably true that common characteristics and a high degree of interaction are mutually reinforcing, thereby making it still more difficult to disentangle the impact of each.[53]

Another potential shortcoming of this approach is that it cannot be used as the basis for reliable generalizations. If diffusion indeed varies over time and from one area of adoption to another, knowledge of reorganization diffusion processes does not necessarily help us understand policy diffusion patterns.

In our efforts to know more about reorganization, the Diffused Innovation perspective has scarcely been utilized. However, it bears much promise.

## Reorganization as Adaptation to Modernization

Another intellectual perspective on the phenomenon of state executive reorganization centers on the process of modernization. As viewed through this lens, reorganization is primarily an attempt to adapt to actual or anticipated changes in the organizational environment.

Frederick Mosher captures the character of modernization as an explanation for reorganization when he observes,

> Herein lies a basic rationale, and often the underlying reason, for administrative reorganization: to bring up-to-date, or to permit the bringing up-to-date, of those aspects of organizational operation and relationships that have suffered from "lag"—i.e., that have failed to modify themselves through

incremental changes sufficiently to keep up with the changing context within which they operate. In fact, it may be postulated that, in a rapidly changing society, a periodic re-examination and consequent modification of organization is desirable for this purpose alone. Many organization structures, or parts thereof, originally set up in eminently rational and efficient forms in response to the needs of their times, become gradually less efficient and less in tune with the needs as the years go by. Ultimately, major modifications are necessary.[54]

The Reorganization as Adaptation to Modernization perspective can be illustrated by Samuel Beer's use of modernization to explain changes within the American federal system.[55] Of particular interest in this analysis is his treatment of the effect of modernization on the *role* of state government within the federal system and resulting implications for *structural* change.

Beer contends that modernizing forces (advances in science and technology and the continuing democratization of wants) have produced changes in the American federal system concerning type of politics deployed, policy orientation, impact on intergovernmental relations, basic character of federalism, and role of state government.[56] According to Beer, within the federal system state governments have evolved from functioning as the main instruments of social choice (during the Jacksonian period) to serving as "laboratories of experimentation" regarding regulatory policy (during the Republican era).[57] In the New Deal period the national government took the lead in innovation and experimentation and became the primary agent for social choice. The states assumed the assistant role of executing national policy through the grant-in-aid system.[58] Beer contends that the still-emerging role of state government has changed to encompass two functions: (1) planning and controlling large, typically intergovernmental programs and (2) utilizing their position as an intermediate tier between national and local governments to mobilize political consent.[59]

Implicit in Beer's framework is the idea that as the role of state government has changed at each of these stages, there has been a concomitant need to increase the state's capacity to perform its new role. A performance gap is created, and bridging this gap requires, in Beer's terms, "tools of analysis" and "reorganization."[60] Reorganization, according to this perspective, is an adaptation to a state's change in role within the federal system, a change which stems from modernization.

This is clearly a macro view of the forces behind state executive reorganizations. The level of analysis is an entire society, a nation. The driving forces are basic forces in societal development. Reorganization is less the result of actions by political groups or individual actors (Reorganization as Political Competition), the influence of values and doctrine (Administrative Orthodoxy), or the spread of ideas and instrumentalities (Reorganization as Diffused Innovation); it is more a product of broad societal forces.

As we have seen with the other perspectives, the strength of the Reorganization as Adaptation to Modernization approach is also its weakness. The major value of this perspective derives from the breadth of its scope. Those lenses that focus on more specific, narrower, explanations of reorganization (e.g., political motivations and actions) are prone to overlook more fundamental underlying forces. The modernization approach avoids this narrow focus.

On the other hand, it is extremely difficult to identify the relevant underlying forces involved in modernization and to trace the linkages through the intervening phases to the eventual reorganization. Focusing on broadly significant questions naturally reduces the degree of specificity and applicability. Even though Beer's framework incorporates coalition politics, it places less emphasis on the role of legislative, executive, bureaucratic, and interest-group actors in the reorganization process.

The Beer modernization perspective does address the influence of federal organization, policies, and procedures on state executive reorganization. Through its grant-in-aid, single state-agency requirement, and other policies, the federal government has done much to shape the recent pattern of state reorganization. The modernization perspective, like the Reorganization as Political Competition approach, posits a direct and active federal role in state reorganization.[61] The Orthodoxy and Innovation perspectives view the federal influence as operating through the more indirect processes of emulation and diffusion.

### Reorganization as Synthesis

The object of this chapter has been to demonstrate that: (1) each intellectual tradition has contributed to our understanding of state reorganization; (2) no single perspective is sufficient of itself to reveal all we need to know about reorganization; (3) each perspective brings with it strengths that aid our understanding *and* shortcomings that obstruct, limit, blur, or misdirect our inquiry; (4) the strengths of certain perspectives tend to compensate for the weakness of others. Figure 2.4 summarizes some of the fundamental distinctions and commonalities between these perspectives.

Just as Allison found that the Rational Actor Model was the dominant approach for explaining foreign-policy decisions and actions, the Administrative Orthodoxy and Reorganization as Political Competition perspectives have been the dominant conceptual lenses through which we have viewed government reorganization.

FIGURE 2.4

Some Major Distinctions Between Theoretical
Perspectives on State Reorganization

| PERSPECTIVE | (1) Administrative Orthodoxy | (2) Reorganization as Political Competition | (3) Socioeconomic Determinants | (4) Reorganization as Diffused Innovation | (5) Reorganization as Adaptation to Modernization |
|---|---|---|---|---|---|
| PRIMARY FOCUS OF INTEREST | Structure | Process | Structure | Process | Process |
| SCOPE OF CONCEPTUAL LENS | Intermediate/Organizational | Micro | Macro | Intermediate/Organizational | Macro |
| LEVEL OF ANALYSIS | Executive Branch | State Political System | State Socio-economic System | Interstate Diffusion | Societal |
| STAGE REORGANIZATION FOCUSED ON | Planning/Proposal/Adoption (minor interest in Implementation) | Adoption/Outcomes (minor interest in Implementation) | Preconditions/Adoption Performance | Planning/Proposal/Adoption | Preconditions |
| REORGANIZATION VIEWED AS | Dependent Variable | Dependent, Independent, or Intervening Variable | Intervening or Dependent Variable | Dependent Variable | Dependent Variable |
| RESEARCH ORIENTATION | Prescriptive | Descriptive | Predictive/Descriptive | Descriptive | Descriptive/Predictive |

By concentrating on only two perspectives we have restricted our ability to understand reorganization—a process about which so much is said and from which so much is expected. Only by synthesizing the contributions of all these perspectives can we take advantage of the collective strengths and compensate for the shortcomings of individual approaches.

To explore further the reasons for state reorganizations, I develop and operationalize a synthesis of these perspectives in Chapter 5. In Chapters 6 and 7 I examine the relationships between perspectives on why state reorganizations occur and the results of several reorganizations.

## Notes

1. For a general exposition of how a researcher's mental set and conceptual approach to the research question affects the nature of inquiry and the results obtained, see Thomas S. Kuhn, *The Structure of Scientific Revolutions* (Chicago: University of Chicago Press, 1970).

2. Graham T. Allison, *Essence of Decision: Explaining the Cuban Missile Crisis* (Boston: Little, Brown & Co., 1971); "Conceptual Models and the Cuban Missile Crisis," *American Political Science Review* 63 (1969):689-718.

3. Allison, *Essence of Decision*, p. v.

4. Dwight Waldo, *The Administrative State: A Study of the Political Theory of American Public Administration* (New York: Ronald Press Co., 1948), pp. 34-38, 130-55. Anita F. Gottlieb, "State Executive Reorganization: A Study of Hallucination, Supposition, and Hypothesis," Ph.D. dissertation, George Washington University, 1976.

5. A. E. Buck, *Administrative Consolidation in State Governments*, 5th ed. (New York: National Municipal League, 1930). A. E. Buck, *Reorganization of State Governments in the United States* (New York: Columbia University Press, 1938). J. M. Mathews, *Principles of American State Administration* (New York: D. Appleton & Co., 1922). A. N. Holcombe, *State Governments in the United States* (New York: Macmillan, 1926). Kirk H. Porter, *State Administration* (New York: Crofts, 1938). Luther H. Gulick, "Reorganization of the State," *Civil Engineering* (August 1933). Bureau of Municipal Research, *The Constitution of Government of the State of New York* (New York: Bureau of Municipal Research, 1915), pp. 6-16.

6. Luther H. Gulick, interview with James L. Garnett, November 30, 1976.

7. In some circles the tenets of orthodoxy even became known as "Buck's principles." See Robert H. Simmons, "American State Executive Studies: A Suggested Departure," *Western Political Quarterly* 17 (1964):777-83.

8. Buck, *Reorganization of State Governments in the United States*, pp. 14-28. Buck added the last two standards in his 1938 work, which showed an evolution of Buck's "standards."

9. The most significant critiques of the principles are generally recognized as: Waldo, *The Administrative State;* Herbert A. Simon, *Administrative Behavior: A Study of Decision-Making Processes in Administative Organization* (New York: Free Press, Macmillan, 1947), pp. 20-38; Herbert A. Simon, "The Proverbs of Administration," *Public*

Administration Review (Winter 1946):53–67; Robert A. Dahl, "The Science of Public Administration: Three Problems," *Public Administration Review* (1947):1–11.

10. Francis W. Coker, "Dogmas of Administrative Reform as Exemplified in the Recent Reorganizaton of Ohio," *American Political Science Review* 16 (August 1922):388–411. W. H. Edwards, "The State Reorganization Movement," *Dakota Law Review* 1, no. 1 (1927):13–30; 1, no. 2 (1927):15–41; and 2 (1928):17–67, 103–39. W. H. Edwards, "Has State Reorganization Succeeded?" *State Government* 2 (1938):192. Charles S. Hyneman, "Administrative Reorganization: An Adventure into Science and Theology," *Journal of Politics,* 1 (1939):62–75. A. C. Millspaugh, "Democracy and Administrative Organization," in *Essays in Political Science, in Honor of Westel Woodbury Willoughby,* John Mathews and James Hart, eds. (Baltimore: Johns Hopkins University Press, 1937). Harvey Walker, "Theory and Practice in State Administrative Organization," *National Municipal Review* 19 (1930):249–54. Harvey Walker, *Public Administration in the United States* (New York: Farrar and Rinehart, 1937), pp. 76–84.

11. For example, William Reed, a prominent tobacco-products manufacturer, played a key role in convincing Governor Harry Byrd of Virginia (who later became the sponsor) of the need for reorganizing that state in 1928. Lipson, *The American Governor: From Figurehead to Leader* (Chicago: Greenwood Press, 1939), pp. 90, 113. Gulick, interview.

12. Buck, *Reorganization of State Governments,* p. 39. Gulick, interview.

13. The reasons for Administrative Orthodoxy's pervasiveness in public and private organizations is itself a subject worthy of more extensive treatment than can be given here. For the present purpose there appear to be at least three reasons for the predominance of Administrative Orthodoxy in organizations. One, orthodox theory maintains the advantage of relative clarity and simplicity over newer theories, which are more sophisticated and complex and therefore are not as well understood by public administrators and the lay public. Harold Seidman, *Politics, Position, and Power: The Dynamics of Federal Organization* 2d ed. rev. (New York: Oxford University Press, 1975), p. 8. Two, alternative formulations about reorganization have not had the degree of exposure that Administrative Orthodoxy has had. Warwick observed in the federal bureaucracy that "for many agency heads or division chiefs it is the only operating model of organizations to which they had been exposed and the one with which they've lived. When it is necessary to expand or reorganize their own agencies, they will invoke the orthodox model almost reflexively." Donald P. Warwick, in collaboration with Marvin Meade and Theodore Reed, *A Theory of Public Bureaucracy: Politics, Personality and Organization in the State Department* (Cambridge: Harvard University Press, 1975), pp. 70–71. Three, and partly because of the other two reasons, because administrative orthodoxy has been embraced by so many actors in the public and private sectors for so long, it has a "self-confirming tendency and the classical theory is now deeply ingrained in our culture." Dwight Waldo, "Organization Theory: An Elephantine Problem," *Public Administration Review* 21 (1961):220.

14. Gulick, interview.

15. Ibid. Other scholars who espoused orthodoxy were also active as consultants on state reorganization. J. M. Mathews worked on the Illinois reorganization of

1917. Walter F. Dodd drafted the *Administrative Code for Ohio,* establishing that state's reorganization, in 1921. Buck, *Reorganization of State Governments,* pp. 190–93.

16. Gulick, interview.

17. Richard F. Kneip, "Reorganizing the Executive Branch," in *Innovations in State Government: Messages from the Governors* (Washington, D. C.: National Governors' Conference, 1974), p. 37.

18. Gulick, interview. The frequency with which the "ideal" had to be diluted before it could be accepted has been captured by Gulick with the aphorism, "The soup was always hotter than it was meant to be eaten." Gulick, interview.

19. Buck, *Reorganization of State Governments,* p. 28.

20. Harold Seidman, "The Politics and Strategies of Reorganization," Lecture at the Maxwell School of Citizenship and Public Affairs, Syracuse University, Syracuse, New York, March 3, 1977.

21. Francis E. Rourke, "The Politics of Administrative Organization: A Case History," *The Journal of Politics* 19 (1957):462. For additional discussion of the effect of reorganization on political access, see York Willbern, "Administration in State Governments," in *The Forty-Eight States: Their Tasks as Policy-Makers and Administrators* (New York: American Assembly, 1955), pp. 116–19.

22. Willbern, "Administration in State Governments," p. 118.

23. Lipson, *The American Governor,* pp. 108–15.

24. Karl A. Bosworth, "The Politics of Management Improvement in the States," *American Political Science Review* 47 (March 1953):88.

25. Ibid.

26. George Bell, "State Administrative Organization Activities, 1970–1971," *The Book of the States, 1972–73* (Lexington, Ky.: Council of State Governments, 1973), p. 141.

27. In Miles's opinion the most important criterion for judging a reorganization proposal is whether the function to be reorganized deserves a higher or lower priority. Rufus E. Miles, Jr., "Considerations for a President Bent on Reorganization," *Public Administration Review* 37 (March/April 1977):156.

28. Hyneman, "Administrative Reorganization," pp. 71–73, and Waldo, *The Administrative State,* pp. 130–55, provide excellent discussions of these issues.

29. Peri E. Arnold, "Executive Reorganization and Administrative Theory: The Origin of the Managerial Presidency" (Paper delivered at the Annual Meeting of the American Political Science Association, Chicago, Illinois, September 2–5, 1976).

30. Gulick, interview. Charles Beard, Gulick's mentor, wrote, "There is tactics as well as wisdom in seeking principles for the reconstruction of state governments in institutional experience in its broadest sense—in public and private enterprise." Charles A. Beard, "Reconstructing State Government," *New Republic* 4 (August 1915):5.

31. Herbert Jacob and Kenneth N. Vines, "Epilogue," in *Politics in the American States: A Comparative Analysis,* 2d ed. rev., Herbert Jacob and Kenneth N. Vines, eds. (Boston: Little, Brown & Co., 1971).

32. For excellent synopses of this extensive literature, see Herbert Jacob and Michael Lipsky, "Outputs, Structure and Power: An Assessment of Changes in the Study of State and Local Politics," *The Journal of Politics* 30 (1968):510–38. John H.

28 *Why State Executive Reorganizations Occur*

Fenton and Donald W. Chamberlayne, "The Literature Dealing with the Relationships between Political Processes, Socioeconomic Conditions, and Public Policies in the American States: A Bibliographic Essay," *Polity* 1 (1969):388–404. Richard I. Hofferbert, "State and Community Policy Studies: A Review of Comparative Input-Output Analysis," *Political Science Annual* 3 (1972):3–72. George W. Downs, Jr., *Bureaucracy, Innovation, and Public Policy* (Lexington, Mass.: Lexington Books, 1976): especially 1–13, 46–63.

33. There has been a significant body of criticism pointing out, among other things, the atheoretical nature of much of this research, the lack of attention to intergovernmental policies and processes as determinants of state policy outputs, the neglect of administrative variables, and the preoccupation with fiscal outputs. For theoretical and methodological critiques of state policy determinants research, see Jacob and Lipsky, "Outputs, Structures, and Power," Ira Sharkansky, "Environment, Policy, Output, and Impact: Problems of Theory and Method in the Analysis of Public Policy" in *Policy Analysis in Political Science*, Ira Sharkansky and Richard I. Hofferbert, eds. (Chicago: Markham, 1970). Phillip M. Gregg, "Units and Levels of Analysis," *Publius* 4 (Fall 1974):59–86. Douglas D. Rose, "National and Local Forces in State Politics: The Implications of Multi-Level Policy Analysis," *American Political Science Review* 67 (December 1973):1162–73. Bernard H. Booms and James R. Halderson, "The Politics of Redistribution: A Reformation," *American Political Science Review* 67 (September 1973):924–33. Brian R. Fry and Richard F. Winters, "The Politics of Redistribution," *American Political Science Review* 64 (June 1970):508–22. R. Kenneth Godwin and W. Bruce Shepard, "Political Processes and Public Expenditures; A Re-examination Based on Theories of Representative Government," *American Political Science Review* 70 (December 1976):1127–35.

34. Jacob and Lipsky, "Outputs, Structures, and Power," p. 523.

35. Downs, *Bureaucracy, Innovation, and Public Policy*, pp. 10–11.

36. James J. Noell, "On the Administrative Sector of Social Systems: An Analysis of the Size and Complexity of Government Bureaucracies in the American States," *Social Forces* 52 (June 1974):549–58.

37. The literature on diffusion of innovations is already massive and is mushrooming. For general keys to this literature, see Everett M. Rogers and Patricia C. Thomas, *Bibliography on the Diffusion of Innovations* (Ann Arbor, Mich.: Department of Population Planning, University of Michigan, 1975). Public Affairs Counseling (A Division of Real Estate Research Corporation), *Factors Involved in the Transfer of Innovations: A Summary and Organization of the Literature* (Washington, D.C.: U.S. Department of Housing and Urban Development, 1976). Gerald Zaltman, Robert Duncan, and Jonny Holbek, *Innovations and Organizations* (New York: John Wiley & Sons, 1973). Everett M. Rogers, *Diffusion of Innovations* (New York: Free Press, 1962). Everett M. Rogers and Floyd Shoemaker, *Communication of Innovations: A Cross-Cultural Approach* (New York: Free Press, 1971). For specific application to states, see Irwin Feller, Donald Menzel, and Alfred J. Engel, *Diffusion of Technology in State Mission-Oriented Agencies* (University Park, Pa.: Center for the Study of Science Policy, Pennsylvania State University, 1974). R. K. Yin, K. Heald, and M. Vogel, "Tinkering with the System: Technological Innovations in State and Local Governments," R-1870-NSF (Draft) (Washington, D.C.: National Science

Foundation, 1975). Jack L. Walker, "The Diffusion of Innovations among the American States," *American Political Science Review* 63 (September, 1969):880–99. Virginia Gray, "Innovation in the States: A Diffusion Study," *American Political Science Review* 67 (December 1973):1174–85. James A. Robinson, ed., *State Legislative Innovation* (New York: Praeger Publishers, 1973). Robert Eyestone, "Confusion, Diffusion, and Innovation," *American Political Science Review* 71 (June 1977):441.

38. Zaltman, Duncan, and Holbek, *Innovations and Organizations*, p. 10.

39. Walker, "Diffusion of Innovations among the American States," p. 881. Rogers and Shoemaker, *Communication of Innovations*, p. 19.

40. Buck, *Reorganization of State Governments*, p. 7. Edwards, "The State Reorganization Movement," p. 22. Kaufman, *Politics and Policies in State and Local Governments*, p. 42.

41. Edwards, "The State Reorganization Movement," p. 221.

42. Kaufman, *Politics and Policies in State and Local Governments*, p. 42.

43. Ibid.

44. Council of State Governments, *Reorganization in the States*, p. 1. Bosworth, "Politics of Management Improvement in the States," p. 84.

45. W. Brooke Graves, *Reorganization of the Executive Branch of the United States: A Compilation of Basic Information and Significant Documents* (Washington, D.C.: Library of Congress, 1949), p. 140.

46. Kaufman, *Politics and Policies in State and Local Governments*, p. 42. Gulick, interview. John C. Bollens, *Administrative Reorganization in the States Since 1939* (Berkeley: University of California Bureau of Public Administration, 1947), p. 2.

47. Gulick, interview.

48. David Collier and Richard Messick, "Prerequisities versus Diffusion: Testing Alternative Explanations of Social Security Adoption," *American Political Science Review* 69 (1975):1299–1315.

49. Gray, "Innovation in the States," pp. 1179–80.

50. James March and Herbert Simon, *Organizations* (New York: John Wiley & Sons, 1958), p. 183. Anthony Downs, *Inside Bureaucracy* (Boston: Little, Brown & Co., 1966), pp. 171–93.

51. Zaltman, Duncan, and Holbek, *Innovations and Organizations*, pp. 55–58.

52. Walker, "Diffusion of Innovations among the States," p. 889.

53. Downs, *Bureaucracy, Innovation, and Public Policy*, p. 30. This position is consistent with the finding of Collier and Messick that, for adoption of social security policies among nations, ". . . a combination of hierarchical diffusion and a prerequisites explanation appear to be the most satisfactory means of accounting for the pattern of adoption among the latest adopters." Collier and Messick, "Prerequisites versus Diffusion," p. 1314.

54. Frederick C. Mosher, ed., *Governmental Reorganization: Cases and Commentary* (Indianapolis: Bobbs-Merrill, 1967), p. 494.

55. Samuel H. Beer, "The Modernization of American Federalism," *Publius* 3 (Fall 1973):53.

56. Ibid., pp. 54–57.

57. Ibid., p. 81.

58. Ibid., p. 74.

59. Ibid., pp. 81–87.
60. Ibid., p. 91.
61. For a discussion of the utilization of federal "single state agency" and "sole agency" requirements to affect state administration, see Seidman, *Politics, Position, and Power,* pp. 166–70.

# 3
# Toward a New Typology of
# State Executive Reorganization

*Types and typologies are ubiquitous, both in everyday social life and in the language of the social sciences. Everybody uses them, but almost no one pays any attention to the nature of their construction.*

— John C. McKinney,
"The Process of Typification"

*There are sciences to which eternal youth is granted . . . all those to which the eternally onward flowing stream of culture brings new problems. At the very heart of this task lies not only the transiency of all . . . types, but also at the same time the inevitability of new ones.*

— Max Weber, *The Methodology of the Social Sciences*
(translated and edited by E. A. Shils and H. A. Finch)

## Typologies in Social Science:
## Definition, Utility, and Criteria

Typological classification is a subdivision of the broader study and practice of classification called taxonomy. A *typology* is "a system of groupings . . . usually called types, the members of which are identified by postulating specified attributes that are mutually exclusive and collectively exhaustive — groupings set up to aid demonstration or inquiry by establishing a limited realtionship among phenomena."[1] A further distinguishing characteristic of typologies is that they are "inductively arrived at rather than formally deduced a priori."[2] Social scientists often derive typologies from types constructed by participants in the social system, whose behavior the social scientist observes. The leading typology of state executive reorganizations, the primary focus of this chapter, is an example of types derived from concepts of practicing government officials.

The primary value of any typology lies in its ability to illuminate the set of phenomena under investigation. Tiryakian holds that typologies serve two basic functions: *codification* and *prediction*.

A typology goes beyond sheer description by simplifying the ordering of the elements of a population, and the known relevant traits of that population into distinct groupings; in this capacity a typological classification creates order out of the potential chaos of discrete, discontinuous, or heterogeneous observations. But in so codifying phenomena, it also permits the observer to seek and predict relationships between phenomena that do not seem to be connected in any obvious way.[3]

Sociologists, who along with psychologists have done the most work with typologies in the social sciences, have often found typologies to be an essential methodology. In the words of Jerald Hage, "Sociologists, following the examples of biologists, have felt that until we can classify, we do not have any hope of analysis."[4] Whether or not one accepts Hage's uncompromising position, there is widespread recognition of the value of typologies. Typologies are often useful for simplifying complexity in order to see relationships more clearly and to generate further hypotheses for exploration.

Two sets of criteria, one developed within the discipline of sociology and the other by political scientists, are useful in assessing the adequacy of a typology. The sociologist Edward Tiryakian has put forth one set of criteria.

The typological procedure requires that:
a.  each and every member of the population studied may be classified in one and only one of the major types delineated, which is the equivalent of saying that the typological classification must be comprehensive and its terms mutually exclusive;
b.  the dimension(s) which is (are) differentiated into types must be explicitly stated;
c.  this dimension must be of central importance for the purpose of the research.[5]

Political scientists Herbert Jacob and Michael Lipsky delineated their own set of criteria for assessing typologies. Their purpose was to encourage the development of more rigorous and useful typologies in political science.

The classification systems used by state and local scholars are often untested as to their reliability, validity and utility. Their *reliability* depends on the existence of operational guides for placing phenomena in exhaustive and mutually exclusive categories. Their *validity* depends on our knowing what they represent by applying them to actual data. *Utility* is related to the problem(s) and question(s) under investigation. To be useful, a classificatory scheme must distinguish on theoretical grounds between empirically different phenomena. Both *theoretical relevance* and *empirical differentiation* are characteristic of a successful classificatory scheme, but are criteria which are rarely met in state and local studies.[6] (Emphasis added.)

Even though they are stated differently, there is a high degree of commonality between the two sets of criteria and I have merged them into a single list. (See Figure 3.1.) I will use these merged criteria to evaluate the leading typology of state executive reorganization.

## The Prevailing Typology of
## State Executive Branch Reorganization

The most widely recognized typology of state executive reorganization is that developed by Dr. George Bell when he was director of research for the Council of State Governments. In one statement of this typology Bell said, "Comprehensive reorganizations of state government appear to fall in three general categories."[7] However, Bell did not define a *comprehensive* reorganization. This omission has created typological problems that I discuss in the next section. Bell's three types are the *Traditional*, the *Cabinet*, and the *Secretary-Coordinator*. There is no written statement of the derivation of these labels, but it is reasonable to assume that at least the latter two were adopted from terms used by the states themselves in reorganization reports and legislation.[8]

Figure 3.2 relates one version of Bell's types and the state reorganizations he has placed in each type.

## Applications of the Bell Typology

It is primarily this statement of Bell's typology that other writers have recognized and utilized. Joan Ehrlich used Bell's typology verbatim to compare reorganizations in California (Secretary-Coordinator), Massachusetts (Cabinet), Colorado (Traditional), and Kentucky (hybrid). Her intent was to point out lessons relevant to the Virginia reorganization being considered in 1975.[9]

Reporting on reorganization developments in a number of states, Neal Peirce also used Bell's typology to describe the variations in state executive reorganization. Peirce's account of Bell's typology differed from Bell's 1974 written statement, however. Peirce added more detail. His account specified that in the Cabinet type the department heads not only serve at the pleasure of the governor, but also exercise "complete or substantial authority over all the former agencies consolidated into their departments."[10] Referring to the Traditional type, Peirce added that *minor* agencies are usually transferred into *major* ones.[11] These discrepancies probably resulted because Peirce obtained much of his information from Bell through interviews and may well have gotten a slightly different version through that process.

FIGURE 3.1

Some Criteria for Evaluating Typologies

1. SPECIFICITY:  the degree to which dimensions (operational guides) used for placing a member into types are made explicit.

2. COMPREHENSIVENESS:  the degree to which each member of the population under consideration can be appropriately "typed" within the classification scheme.

3. EXCLUSIVITY:  the degree to which a member of the population being considered can be appropriately placed in only one type, the types being mutually exclusive.

4. RELIABILITY:  the degree to which members are placed in the same types by independent observers (that is, the degree to which typing can be replicated).

5. PREDICTABILITY:  the degree to which accurate predictions can be made from utilizing the typology.[a]

6. INSIGHTFULNESS:  the degree to which use of the typology facilitates the discovery of new empirical entities or new relationships among the phenomena under study (similar to Tiryakian's fruitfulness).

7. THEORETICAL RELEVANCE:  the degree to which the underlying dimension(s) and the types themselves are germane to the purpose of the research and the phenomena being studied.

Source:  Edward A. Tiryakian, "Typological Classification," p. 178; Herbert Jacob and Michael Lipsky, "Outputs, Structure, and Power," pp. 530-531.

Note:  [a]Prediction was mentioned before by Tiryakian as an objective of typological classification.

FIGURE 3.2

Types of State Executive Reorganization:
Bell Typology Version I

1. TRADITIONAL TYPE

"[With the Traditional type] the reduction of
the number of agencies is accomplished to some
degree within the existing pattern of agencies
headed by elected officers, boards and commissions."

States classified as having Traditional
reorganizations (and the years they reorganized)
are:  Michigan (1965), Wisconsin (1967), Colorado
(1968), Florida (1969), Montana (1971), Arkansas
(1971), North Carolina (1971), Georgia (1972).

2. CABINET TYPE

"[Cabinet type is that type] whereby heads of
reorganized departments are all appointed by and
responsible to the governor."

State reorganizations typed in this category
are:  Massachusetts (1969), Delaware (1969-70),
Maryland (1969-70), Maine (1971), South Dakota
(1973).[a]

3. SECRETARY-COORDINATOR TYPE

"[Secretary-Coordinator reorganizations are
those in which the] structure and authority of
agencies is unchanged and the secretaries have
primarily a coordinating function."

The states with Secretary-Coordinator type
reorganizations are:  California (1968) and
Virginia (1972).[a]

Source:  George Bell, "State Administrative Activities,
1972-1973," pp. 138-139.

Note:  [a]The reorganization in Kentucky (1972-73) was
a combination of Cabinet type and Secretary-
Coordinator type.

Writing in 1976, Anita Gottlieb also referred to these three types. Her objective was to demonstrate that many states reorganized into what is termed the Traditional type even though "this type of reorganization, in many instances, is in direct contradiction to the stated objectives of the reorganizers."[12] In addition, Gottlieb made the point that even though states in the Cabinet type "have come closer to achieving complete integration of the states' administrative agencies under the governor than have the states which attempted the Traditional type of reorganization," a number of state reorganizations classified as Cabinet type have still not realized the ideals of administrative orthodoxy.[13] Gottlieb's only criticism of the Bell typology centered on the fact that Bell (and Peirce) included Massachusetts in the Cabinet type; Gottlieb contended that Massachusetts had not yet attained that classification.

Bell's typology also has been used in state reorganization reports, as well as in research articles.[14] With the exception of Gottlieb's disagreement over the typing of Massachusetts, no questions have been raised about the adequacy or utility of Bell's typology. His typology has been used to help elucidate the issue of reorganization in at least two states (Oklahoma and Virginia) and has received wide exposure through the *National Journal* via Peirce. Yet the Bell typology in its various forms is not an adequate classificatory scheme and may result in more confusion than illumination.

## A Critique of the Bell Typology

A substantial problem with the Bell typology (which also raises problems in critiquing the typology) is the fact that it offers no one consistent definition of the three types. There are at least two published versions, and it appears likely that Peirce received yet another version from Bell. The less widely recognized statement of the typology is set forth here as Figure 3.3. Again, the exact language of the original statement is preserved for maximum accuracy.

The more widely recognized first version of Bell's typology will be assessed first in terms of the criteria established earlier.

### Criterion 1: Specificity

John McKinney observed, "One of the most persistent problems in typologizing has been the lack of specification of the operations performed in the construction of the types."[15] Much of the trouble with the Bell typology stems from its inadequate specification of operations. Thus, difficulty has arisen over what constitutes a "comprehensive reorganization." If a state reorganization was "comprehensive," Bell included it in his typology; if it was partial or piecemeal, he did not.[16] But labeling a reorganization "comprehensive" did not mean that all agencies had been

FIGURE 3.3

Types of State Executive Reorganization:
Bell Typology Version II

1. STANDARD TYPE[a]

"[The standard reorganization involves the] regrouping of existing departments into something like 20 or 25 departments, maintaining much of the existing types of top structure like boards and commissions and elected officers, with various degrees of authority transferred to the heads of these new departments from having very strong management control to very little of it."

2. CABINET TYPE[b]

"[These reorganizations are] cabinet in the sense that all the department heads are responsible to the governor, usually serving at his pleasure. In the cabinet type states you tend to have agencies grouped into broader functional groupings than under the so-called standard one. There may be 10 to 15 departments."

3. SECRETARY-COORDINATOR TYPE[b]

"[This type of reorganization occurs when] existing departments are grouped into very broad functions, four to six maybe; with no change in authority, however. The existing department heads maintain the authority that they have had before. The secretaries are appointed by the governor and serve primarily in a coordinating role."

Source: George Bell, "Executive Reorganization and Its Effect on Budgeting," Proceedings of the 29th Annual Meeting of the National Association of State Budget Officers, August 1973, pp. 90-91.

Notes: [a]States classified in version II as having Standard type reorganization are the same as those classified as Traditional type in version I.

[b]Kentucky was classified as Secretary-Coordinator for the present, with likelihood it would be Cabinet type eventually. Otherwise, members of the Cabinet and Secretary-Coordinator types in version II are the same as of the respective types in version I.

reorganized; many of the state reorganizations included in the typology left one or more units as they were. For example, even though the Arkansas (1971) reorganization did not extend to the secretary of state, the attorney general, the auditor, the Fish and Game Commission, the Highway Commission, or the professional licensing boards, Arkansas is included in the typology.

The inclusion rule undoubtedly involves the *number* of departments reorganized, but again there is no indication of a cutoff point. State officials in Utah have disagreed with Bell's exclusion of that state's 1967 reorganization from the "comprehensive" or "major" classification and therefore from the typology altogether.[17] When trying to replicate Bell's typification, a Council of State Governments' staff specialist in state reorganization found no substantive reason for excluding Utah from the typology. The Utah 1967 executive branch reorganization resulted in only three newly created major departments (not enough by whatever standard Bell used), but the three departments were a consolidation of nineteen units of state government most of which had independent status before reorganization.[18] Whether the "comprehensive" distinction hinges on the proportion of agencies affected by reorganization, the total number of agencies affected by reorganization, the total number of new agencies created, or some combination of these criteria is not clear. It appears that the criterion — total number of new agencies created — is applied, but this is not explicit.[19] There is ambiguity at the start of the typification process, in determining which states to type.

The dimensions on which the Bell typology is based are also unspecified. Figure 3.4 attempts to make explicit those dimensions implicit in Bell's typology (version I) and to indicate how the three types fall along these dimensions.

If the dimensions for Bell's typology had been specified, it would have been apparent that the dimensions are not uniformly applied to each type. For example, Dimension I.2 (role and authority of head of department after reorganization) is applied only to the Traditional type. The Cabinet type is based on only one dimension (I.1, the process by which the department head is selected after reorganization). The other two types are based on two dimensions, but not the same two dimensions.

The same lack of specification of operations is also evident in Bell's version II where some, but not all, dimensions are the same as in version I. Not only are more dimensions implicit in version II, but there is also greater internal uniformity in applying these dimensions to the three basic types. (See Figure 3.5.)

The specificity criterion has been violated in a number of ways. There is not one operationally specified typology; rather, there are at least two versions with little explicit statement of underlying dimensions.

FIGURE 3.4

Typological Dimensions:   Bell Version I

---

DIMENSION I.1:   Process by which head of department
                 is selected after reorganization.
  Traditional:   elected
  Cabinet:   all appointed by governor
  Secretary-Coordinator:   not specified

DIMENSION I.2:   Role and authority of head of
                 department after reorganization.
  Traditional:   not specified
  Cabinet:   not specified
  Secretary-Coordinator:   secretary performs
    coordinating role

DIMENSION I.3:   Degree of management authority retained
                 by those departments transplanted into
                 other agencies.
  Traditional:   not specified
  Cabinet:   not specified
  Secretary-Coordinator:   structure and authority of
    transplanted departments is unchanged

DIMENSION I.4:   Degree to which reduction in number of
                 agencies is done through consolidating
                 into existing or new departments.
  Traditional:   consolidation is accomplished to some
    degree within the existing pattern of agencies
  Cabinet:   not specified
  Secretary-Coordinator:   not specified

---

Summary:   Bell Version I

| Type | Dimensions Applied |
|---|---|
| Traditional | I.1,I.4 |
| Cabinet | I.1 |
| Secretary-Coordinator | I.2,I.3 |

FIGURE 3.5

Typological Dimensions:  Bell Version II[a]

---

DIMENSION II.1:  Number of departments after
                reorganization.
  Standard:  "something like 20 or 25"
  Cabinet:  "may be 10 to 15"
  Secretary-Coordinator:  "4 to 6 maybe"

DIMENSION II.2:  Breadth in which agencies are
                grouped by function.
  Standard:  not as broad as with Cabinet type
  Cabinet:  broader than with Standard type
  Secretary-Coordinator:  very broad

DIMENSION II.3:  Method by which department head is
                selected after reorganization.
  Standard:  appointed or elected if board or
    commission, elected if single head
  Cabinet:  single head usually appointed by governor
  Secretary-Coordinator:  single head appointed
    by governor

DIMENSION II.4:  Type of department head after
                reorganization.
  Standard:  plural or single executive
  Cabinet:  single executive
  Secretary-Coordinator:  single executive

DIMENSION II.5:  Degree of management control held
                by heads of departments after
                reorganization.
  Standard: very little control to very strong control
  Cabinet:  not specified
  Secretary-Coordinator:  little control, secretary
    serves primarily a loose coordinating function

DIMENSION II.6:  Degree of management control held
                by heads of transplanted departments.
  Standard:  not specified
  Cabinet:  not specified
  Secretary-Coordinator:  no diminution of previous
    authority

---

| Type | Summary: Bell Version II Dimensions Applied |
|---|---|
| Standard | II.1,II.3,II.4,II.5 |
| Cabinet | II.1,II.2,II.3,II.4 |
| Secretary-Coordinator | II.1,II.2,II.3,II.4,II.5,II.6 |

---

[a]In version II, Bell uses the term "Standard" in
place of "Traditional" from version I.

## Criterion 2: Comprehensiveness

This criterion is satisfied if there are no gaps in typological coverage, that is, if all members of the population being considered can be typed appropriately.

The most obvious lack of comprehensiveness stems from application of Dimension II.1 in Bell's version II. In several respects this dimension is one of the most useful: because the number of departments after reorganization can be counted without much difficulty, the state reorganization can be typed on that basis. This dimension comes as close as any to being an explicit operational guide. However, Bell's guides are imprecise: "something like 20 or 25"; "may be 10 to 15 departments"; "4 to 6 maybe."[20] Based on Bell's guide for this dimension, how should reorganizations in Colorado (18 departments), Florida (23 departments), Michigan (19), or Montana (19) be typed?[21] Bell placed all four in the Standard (Traditional) type, demonstrating that the number ranges are not exact.

## Criterion 3: Exclusivity

The typing of Kentucky's 1972–73 reorganization as a "combination of Cabinet and Secretary-Coordinator" according to Bell's first version breaks the rule that types are to be mutually exclusive. If types are properly constructed, there should be only one way to type any member of the population being considered. Bell's version II typing of Kentucky as Secretary-Coordinator at the time of typification, but evolving to Cabinet after phase two of reorganization, is more consistent with the methodology of typological classification. (One of the features of typologies is that they can be used to study transitional situations.)

Kentucky is not the only state difficult to place in a single type. The Council of State Governments has found "considerable overlap" between the Cabinet and Traditional types, making it difficult to type state reorganizations that have occurred since 1973.[22]

## Criterion 4: Reliability

The ambiguities in the reliability requirement have very dysfunctional effects. Because Bell's operational guides are inadequate, replication of his typification is an extremely uncertain task. As with Utah or with Gottlieb's dissent over the typing of Massachusetts, it has often proven difficult to determine why a particular typing decision was made rather than an alternative one.

## Criterion 5: Predictability

Since prediction is a fundamental purpose of a typology, an evaluation of that predictability warrants special emphasis. "Typologies must be understood as representative of a pragmatic research methodology and thus subject to evaluation in terms of the accuracy of predictions which result from their utilization."[23]

If the predictability criterion is met, it would be possible to predict certain characteristics about a state reorganization by knowing its type. This is because "a good typology is not a collection of undifferentiated entities but is composed of a cluster of traits which do in reality 'hang together.'"[24]

In order to make an assessment, however crude, of predictability, I randomly selected one state of each type. The *predicted* characteristics (the stated dimension values for that type) were then compared with the *actual* characteristics of that state's reorganization to test for degree of congruence.[25] The results of these comparisons are shown in Table 3.1. Bell's version II was used for this test because it has fewer unspecified dimensions or dimension values.

The overall prediction rate (50 percent) would have been higher except for the number of predictions (5 out of 18) defaulted because a dimension value was not specified or was so broad as to be virtually meaningless. The high degree of prediction on California is to be expected, because California is the leading example of its type and was the model for the Secretary-Coordinator type. The extremely low predictability of Wisconsin's 1967 reorganization is explained in part by Wisconsin's having some characteristics more consistent with a Cabinet type than with a Standard (Traditional) one. The faultiness of the Standard type itself is probably even more responsible for the low score.

These results show that the Bell typology version II could be tightened considerably if all dimensions were unambiguously specified for all types. Even after better operationalizations have been constructed, however, the typology's utility for prediction is still relatively confined to legal-structural aspects of reorganization, an emphasis characteristic of the Administrative Orthodoxy approach to reorganization.

*Criterion 6: Insightfulness*

The Bell typology concentrates heavily on structural and legal dimensions. For this reason, the capacity of the typology to spark insights is more limited than if the typology had also captured the *strategy dimension* (e.g., kind of tactics applied, sources of political support and opposition), *difficulty dimension* (length and competitiveness of campaign to promote reorganization), and other dimensions that complement and supplement the legal and structural.

However, Bell typology does facilitate the generation of new research questions and the discovery of new entities and relationships. Gottlieb's utilization of the types in assessing deviation from the orthodox reform

TABLE 3.1

Ability of Bell Typology (Version II) to Predict Characteristics of Three Reorganizations

Standard (Traditional) Type

| Predicted Characteristics | Actual Characteristics: WISCONSIN (1967) |
|---|---|
| II.1 "something like 20 or 25 departments" | II.1 28 departments (14 executive departments plus 14 independent agencies) |
| II.2 functional grouping not as broad as with Cabinet type | II.2 broad functional areas (e.g. Natural Resources, Health, and Social Services) |
| II.3 department head appointed or elected if plural executive, elected if singular | II.3[a] majority of heads of executive departments and independent agencies are elected officials or elected or appointed plural executives |
| II.4[b] department head can be plural or single executive | II.4 there are both plural and single department heads |
| II.5 degree of managerial control held by post-reorganization department head ranges from very little to very strong | II.5 degree of managerial control held by secretary varies: where transplanted agencies are integrated into the post-reorganization departments the secretary holds program coordinator, planning, and budgeting authority; for transplant agencies with authority intact, these functions are done under supervision of the secretary |
| II.6[b] degree of managerial control held by head of transplanted department is not specified | II.6 discussed under II.5 |

Prediction Score = 1 out of 6; Prediction Rate = 16.7%

44

TABLE 3.1 (cont.)

Cabinet Type

| Predicted Characteristics | Actual Characteristics: DELAWARE (1969-70) |
|---|---|
| II.1 "may be 10 to 25" departments | II.1[a] 10 post-reorganization departments |
| II.2 functional groupings broader than with Standard (Traditional) type | II.2[a] broad functional areas |
| II.3 department head usually appointed by governor | II.3[a] all 10 department heads appointed by governor |
| II.4 single executive as department head | II.4[a] single executives (called secretaries) head each department |
| II.5[b] degree of managerial control held by post-reorganization department head is not specified | II.5 secretaries have considerable power to rearrange structure within their departments, to appoint and remove division heads (with governor's approval) |
| II.6[b] degree of managerial control held by head of transplanted department is not specified | II.6 division heads, which are comparable to heads of transplanted agencies, assist secretaries with budget preparation, some staff specialists lost to secretary's staff; overall management control is moderate |

Prediction Score = 4 out of 6; Prediction Rate = 66.7%

TABLE 3.1 (cont.)

## Secretary-Coordinator Type

| Predicted Characteristics | Actual Characteristics: CALIFORNIA (1968) |
|---|---|
| II.1 number of departments is "4 to 6 maybe" | II.1[a] 4 departments ("super-agencies") |
| II.2 very broad functional groupings | II.2[a] very broad functional groupings: Human Relations, Resources, Business and Transportation, Agriculture Services |
| II.3 department head appointed by governor | II.3[a] heads of all departments appointed by governor |
| II.4 single executive department head | II.4[a] all department heads are single executives (secretaries) |
| II.5 degree of managerial control held by post-reorganization department head is slight, primarily coordination | II.5 secretaries have managerial authority to review and approve budgets, review program operations, and evaluate performance in addition to their coordinating and communications responsibilities |
| II.6 degree of managerial control held by head of transplanted department is the same as before | II.6 heads of transplanted departments now have secretarial budget review and program evaluation that were not there before reorganization |

Prediction Score = 4 out of 6; Prediction Rate = 66.7%

Overall Prediction Score = 9 out of 18; Prediction Rate = 50%

[a]Scored as being predicted correctly.

[b]Default on prediction, because dimension either is not specified or is so broad as to be meaningless.

ideal is a good example. Bell scrupulously avoids trying to make value judgments regarding the superiority of one type over the other. But strongly implicit in his typology, and in his other writing from the Council of State Governments, is the notion that the Traditional type least approximates the reform ideal, the Cabinet type best approximates it, and the Secretary-Coordinator type falls somewhere in between, closer to the Cabinet type.

Carrying this idea a step further, one could speculate whether those state governments whose latest reorganization most closely approximates the reform ideal achieve better results than those states whose structures are further from that ideal. In other words, is there any difference in measurable results between the higher reform types (Cabinet and Secretary-Coordinator) and the lower reform type (Traditional)?

*Criterion 7: Theoretical Relevance*

The Bell typology *is* relevant to the phenomena it attempts to represent. The structural-legal dimensions are of interest to social science researchers. And they are even more germane to state government officials, who are vitally interested in concepts such as power of appointment, degree and kind of managerial authority over departments, and the number of department heads reporting to the governor. Evidently Bell directed his typology to state officials, orienting the dimensions toward the concerns of that group rather than toward those of university researchers.

The most telling flaw of Bell's typology is not that it failed to pass muster on a set of standards devised by scholars of typologies. Rather (because those standards were not sufficiently observed), the principal flaw is that the typology has limited utility for state government administrators, legislators, and staff analysts — people who want a typology that will increase their understanding through simplification, that will not confuse or mislead them. Recognizing the shortcomings of the Bell typology, a research specialist for the Council of State Governments has begun work to revise the typology. She said, "I could not use this [Bell typology] as a working document for making distinctions between reorganizations. . . . But it is the only one there is. Dr. Bell's work is the first in this area and should be appreciated for giving others a typology from which to work and from which to build."[26]

## Toward a New Typology

A modified typology of state executive reorganization is presented in Figure 3.6. This typology draws heavily from both of Dr. Bell's versions and takes into account some of the strengths and shortcomings discussed in this chapter. Operationalizations have been made explicit to facilitate

FIGURE 3.6

Modified Bell Typology
of State Executive Reorganization[a]

DIMENSION 1: Number of agencies after reorganization.

Traditional: (High) $\geq 17$
Cabinet: (Medium) 9-16
Secretary-Coordinator: (Low) 1-8

DIMENSION 2: Degree of functional consolidation.

Traditional: (Low Consolidation) over 50% of all consolidation is into single-function agencies, narrowly defined (e.g., Water Supply, Highways)

Cabinet: (Moderate Consolidation) over 50% of all consolidation is into single-function agencies, broadly defined (e.g., Environmental Protection, Transportation)

Secretary-Coordinator: (High Consolidation) over 50% of all consolidation is into very large multiple-function or broad single-function agencies (e.g., Human Resources, Natural Resources)

DIMENSION 3: Proportion of post-reorganization department heads appointed by governor

Traditional: (Low) <50%
Cabinet: (Moderate) $\geq 50\%$ $\leq 66\%$
Secretary-Coordinator: (High) $\geq 67\%$

FIGURE 3.6 (cont.)

---

DIMENSION 4:   Proportion of post-reorganization
               agencies with plural executives
               (e.g., boards or commissions).

Traditional:  (High)  ≥25%

Cabinet:  (Moderate)  ≥10% ≤24%

Secretary-Coordinator:  (Low)  ≤9%


DIMENSION 5:   Degree of management authority retained
               by transplanted agencies.

Traditional: (High)  most (>50%) of the
    reorganization transplants involve transplant
    of agencies into other units, with the
    transplanted agencies primarily retaining
    their statutory authority, structural identity,
    and control over management support services
    (e.g., budgeting, purchasing)

Cabinet: (Low)  most (>50%) of the reorganization
    transplants involve transplants into other
    units, with the transplanted agencies primarily
    relinquishing statutory authority, structural
    identity, and control over management support
    services

Secretary-Coordinator: (Moderately High)  most
    (>50%) of reorganization transplants involve
    the transplant of agencies into super-agencies,
    with the transplanted agencies primarily
    retaining their structural identity and much
    of their statutory authority while relinquishing
    some control over management support services
    (e.g., submitting to budget review by the
    super-agency)

---

[a]This modification draws from both published
versions of Bell's typology.

replication. The types have been made mutually exclusive on Dimension 1 (number of agencies after reorganization) and on Dimension 3 (proportion of postreorganization department heads appointed by governor). Dimensions 5 and 6 have been combined because they are essentially two sides of the same issue of managerial control.

All dimensions are specified for each type to aid typing on comparable dimensions. This eliminates the possibility that a prediction of type will be defaulted because of unspecified dimensions. However, there may still be a default on predicting type because data are missing from some of the dimensions. This modified typology is tighter in its construction, but it is still basically confined to structural and legal dimensions until other refinements are made.

Drawing on the work of Bell and Gottlieb, I use this modified typology in Chapters 5 and 6 as an operationalization of the variable Degree of Reorganization Reform (i.e., the extent to which a state's executive branch reorganization approximates the reform ideal articulated by administrative orthodoxists). In this context the Traditional type represents a low degree of reform and the Cabinet type a high degree of administrative reform. The Secretary-Coordinator type represents moderate reform but is closer to the Cabinet type than to the Traditional type. Application of the modified typology facilitates the exploration of relationships between reorganization type and determinants of reorganization and between reorganization type and adoption strategies.

## Notes

1. *The New Encyclopedia Britannica, Micropedia*, vol. 10 (Chicago: Encyclopedia Britannica, 1974), p. 221.

2. Edward A. Tiryakian, "Typological Classification," in *International Encyclopedia of the Social Sciences* (New York: Macmillan, 1968), p. 178.

3. Ibid.

4. Jerald Hage, *Techniques and Problems of Theory Construction in Sociology* (New York: John Wiley & Sons, 1972), p. 10.

5. Tiryakian, "Typological Classification," p. 178. Tiryakian includes the additional criteria of *fruitfulness* (the degree to which the typology "facilitates the discovery of new empirical entities") and *parsimony* (keeping to a minimum the number of major types necessary to cover the largest number of observations). Tiryakian has noted that parsimony is not always helpful if the number of types is so small that the variance within each type or subtype is unduly increased.

6. Herbert Jacob and Michael Lipsky, "Outputs, Structure, and Power: An Assessment of Changes in the Study of State and Local Politics," *The Journal of Politics* 30 (1968): 530–31.

7. George Bell, "State Administrative Activities, 1972–1973," *The Book of the States, 1974–75* (Lexington Ky.: Council of State Governments, 1974), p. 138.

8. For example, "cabinet structure" is focused on in Office of Planning and Program Coordination, Commonwealth of Massachusetts, *Modernization of the Government of the Commonwealth of Massachusetts,* December 1968. The California Reorganization Plan No. 1 of 1968 (*Reorganization of the Executive Branch of California State Government,* February 1, 1968) establishes *Secretaries* as the heads of the four statutory agencies. Among the duties prescribed for secretaries are assisting in setting of goals and exercising "the authority of the Governor in *coordinating* activities with other federal, state or local jurisdictions." Reorganization Plan No. 1 of 1968, pp. 7–8. (Emphasis added.)

9. Joan E. Ehrlich, "State Executive Branch Reorganizations," *University of Virginia Newsletter* 51 (March 1975):26–27.

10. Neal Peirce, "Structural Reform of Bureaucracy Grows Rapidly," *National Journal* 7 (April 1975):505–6.

11. Ibid., p. 505.

12. Anita F. Gottlieb, "State Executive Reorganization: A Study of Hallucination, Supposition, and Hypothesis (Ph.D. dissertation, George Washington University, 1976), pp. 127–128.

13. Ibid., p. 128.

14. One state report that draws heavily on the Bell typology is Volunteer Executives, *Reorganization* (Report to the Oklahoma Special Commission on the Reorganization of State Government, February 5, 1976), p. 32.

15. John C. McKinney, "The Process of Typification," in *Theoretical Sociology,* John C. McKinney and Edward A. Tiryakian, eds. (New York: Appleton-Century-Crofts, 1970), p. 257.

16. George Bell, "Executive Reorganization and Its Effect on Budgeting," in *Summary of the Twenty-Ninth Annual Meeting of the National Association of State Budget Officers* (Lexington, Ky.: Council of State Governments, 1973), p. 91.

17. Judith Nicholson, research associate, Council of State Governments, telephone interview, May 18, 1977.

18. Utah Legislative Council, *Selected Organizational Studies in Utah State Government,* December 1970, pp. 2, 11–14.

19. Nicholson, interview.

20. Bell, "Executive Reorganization and Its Effect on Budgeting," pp. 90–91.

21. Council of State Governments, *Reorganization in the States* (Lexington, Ky.: Council of State Governments, 1972), p. 6.

22. Nicholson, interview.

23. McKinney, "The Process of Typification," p. 247.

24. Tiryakian, "Typological Classification," p. 178.

25. The *actual* characteristics are post-reorganization observations noted in the Council of State Governments, *Reorganization in the States.* These characteristics do not reflect administrative changes up to the present.

26. Nicholson, interview.

# 4
# Reorganization Strategies: How Much Is Known?

*Reorganization movements have sufficient hazards without raising the question of the legitimacy of their progeny.*
　　　　　　　　　 — Karl Bosworth, "The Politics of Management
　　　　　　　　　　　　　　　　　　Improvement in the States"

*Strategy is a system of make-shifts.*
　　　　　　　　　 — Helmuth von Moltke, *Essay on Strategy*

## The Importance of Strategy Considerations

Cautions·about the difficulty of achieving reorganization or attaining administrative reform in the broader context come from the diverse literatures of political science, public administration — public policy, organization theory and social change, and organizational innovation. Some accounts of failures to adopt and implement reorganizations are contained in the literature, although unsuccessful attempts rarely receive as much attention as full-blown or even moderate successes.[1] From such accounts I have identified the following major obstacles to reorganization: (1) the negativistic, conservative attitude of legislative bodies toward major reform;[2] (2) bureaucratic resistance to administrative reform;[3] (3) the high political risk involved;[4] (4) constitutional-legal constraints on reorganization;[5] (5) inadequate knowledge and understanding of reorganization objectives and processes;[6] (6) resistance of clientele groups affected by reorganization;[7] and (7) resource limitations.[8] These barriers represent the general set of constraints proponents of reorganization must overcome to achieve adoption.

Given the obstacles, risks, and costs involved, it is incumbent upon reorganizers to avoid errors in adoption and implementation strategy that might increase these hazards. To provide practical guidance for governors, legislators, bureaucrats, and other state officials engaged in reorganization, I have pulled together much of the existing thinking on state reorganization strategy. To increase the usefulness of this information, I have concentrated on strategy variables within the command of state decision makers rather than on variables over which they have limited control.

These strategy choices center around questions of *timing* (Which is the most advantageous time to attempt reorganization?), *tactics* (Should the reorganization be pushed all at once or incrementally?), *adoption mechanism* (Does the choice of legal instrumentality inhibit or facilitate adoption?), *role of governor* (Does the governor's role in the campaign to adopt reorganization make any difference in the outcome?), and *promotion campaign* (In what forums and in what manner is promotion of reorganization most effective?).

There have been some other state reorganization strategy issues (e.g., whether to rely on "big-business interests" to support reorganization and which type of reorganization study to conduct),[9] but the above issues have remained the most salient according to both the early and the recent literature.

## Adoption Strategies

### Timing

There appear to be two distinct types of timing issues: *cycle-oriented timing* and *circumstance-oriented timing*. *Cycle-oriented timing* revolves around recurring time periods, such as the governor's term of office or the legislative session. I will pose this strategy question from the governor's point of view because governors are typically most concerned with executive branch reorganization. Is the beginning of a gubernatorial administration the best time to launch an executive reorganization or is it wise to wait until later in the administration? There are rationales for both options.

One school of thought contends it is more advantageous to attempt reorganization early, before political credits are used up and before post-honeymoon opposition sets in. This opposition can even come from the governor's own party if failures on other policy issues have created disillusionment. According to Theodore Lowi, tendencies to preserve the status quo are likely to consolidate over time. New departures in policy are therefore more likely to occur at the initial stages of a new administration, particularly when a minority party gains control of government.[10]

Even though the National Governors' Association does not endorse a particular timing strategy, it has implied that executive reorganization, if it is to be done at all, should at least be considered during the early portions of a governor's tenure. This is especially true for new governors. Implicit in the association's *Handbook for the New Governor* is the need to consider reorganization early because "sorting out . . . alternatives, checking for statutory restrictions, drafting changes to those statutes and mobilizing political support for change are all time-consuming, frequently requiring several months and often longer."[11]

According to this handbook, one problem results from a governor's desire to change organizational structure and appoint personnel at the beginning of a new administration. A governor cannot always wait until reorganization has crystallized before making appointments to get the machinery of state government in place. On the other hand, prereorganization appointees, particularly at the cabinet level, may find themselves in a different structure and with different working relationships than the governor envisioned. The National Governors' Association suggests two strategy options for dealing with this particular problem of timing.

> One solution to this problem is for the Gubernatorial candidates to start the reorganization process during the [election] campaign by initiating the staff work and task forces required to put a reorganization package together. . . . An alternative solution is for the Governor and his advisors to decide on the general outlines of probable reorganization before starting to recruit cabinet members. Accomplishing this will allow the Governor to bring cabinet members into the existing structure with some knowledge of what he expects to do with them in a reorganized structure, and will permit him to take holding actions (continuing an incumbent in office or appointing someone on a temporary basis) at the outset of the administration while the details of the reorganization plan are being completed.[12]

Not all the evidence favors undertaking reorganization early in an administration. Some authorities contend that executive reorganization proposals take time to be properly conceived and prepared. They reason that it is better to take the time necessary to propose a carefully and thoroughly developed plan than to risk a hastily conceived plan, the defects of which might expose it to defeat. An outstanding example of this kind of strategy error is the Louisiana reorganization act of 1940, which was later declared unconstitutional.

> The reorganization act and the accompanying fiscal code provided for a vastly improved organization; however, it was attempted in too short a time with the consequent omission of the deliberate consideration to which such far-reaching legislation was entitled. The result was almost disastrous for the [Governor Sam H.] Jones administration.[13]

*Circumstance-oriented timing* is usually independent of timing within a fixed administrative term or legislative session. It is based on the assumption that conditions for reorganization are especially favorable after certain kinds of actions have dramatized the need for reform or during conditions in which reorganization is viewed as less of a risk.

Bosworth contended that the timing of reorganization, and of other major changes, must take into consideration the general mood of the public. His reasoning starts with the postulate that legislatures are basically "negative toward proposals for either moderate-scale or major changes in the formal allocation of influence in their governments."[14] Legislative conservatism can be overcome during conditions that reduce inhibitions to risk-taking. These conditions occur during periods of general "deep despair" or "high optimism."[15]

> When horizons are low because of despair, it is easy to reason that any change is unlikely to worsen conditions and may improve them (e.g., Nebraska's shift to unicameralism and other depression changes in important state policy). When horizons are wide with general optimism, the risks of any change seemed lessened (e.g., the many changes in the period from the late 1890's to World War I).[16]

So crucial is this question of timing for Bosworth that he contends periods not conducive to change will override other strategy considerations (e.g., alignments of legislatures, scope and presentation of survey findings) and result in defeat of reorganization proposals.

Even though more than twenty years old, Bosworth's conceptualization of the timing issue is useful for understanding some growth-oriented state reorganizations of the 1960s and some retrenchment-focused reorganizations of the 1970s.

Circumstance-oriented timing strategies are often more powerful in their impact on reform efforts, but they are not as much within the control of reorganization sponsors or opponents. These strategy options depend upon events or conditions that are seldom predictable.

### Tactics

The choice of adoption tactics involves the decision to achieve reorganization in one major effort (most often referred to as *comprehensive* tactics) or to attempt reorganization by applying phased or *incremental* tactics over a longer period. Harvey Walker made the same distinction between *comprehensive* and *piecemeal*.

> *Comprehensive* reorganizations are those in which the whole administrative structure of the state (with certain exceptions) . . . is reconstituted along new lines by a single legislative act, usually known as an administrative code. *Piecemeal* reorganizations are those in which the legislature takes up each func-

tion of the state government separately and provides a new administrative structure for each by a separate legislative act. Such reorganizations are usually spread out over several sessions, so that only one to three functions can be dealt with at any particular legislative meeting.[17] [Emphases added.]

Walker weighed the advantages and disadvantages of each adoption tactic and concluded that the piecemeal (incremental) approach is preferable. For Walker the telling disadvantage of the comprehensive, all-eggs-in-one-basket tactic was that some parts of the reorganization package might be unsatisfactory even though the plan as a whole might be sound. Whether or not there were weak spots, interest groups opposed to different sections could combine to defeat the entire proposal.

Writing two years later, Leslie Lipson arrived at a different conclusion. He allowed that Walker's arguments were "not without merit" but said that Walker's primary objection could be countered with the knowledge that those supporting reorganization were often just as heterogeneous as the opponents. Some support for the whole plan could then be gained by groups that emphasized only one element. To repeat Lipson's example: "Would the energetic advocates of the short ballot in New York have lent all their force to a 'piecemeal' bill for merely reorganizing the department of public works?"[18] Lipson concluded, "One cannot advocate a particular set of tactics as applicable to all states. Techniques should vary with political necessity."[19] Under ideal circumstances more incremental tactics might be pursued to allow for careful trial, error, and adjustment. This is not always possible under all conditions or with all legislatures. Lipson determined that incremental tactics phased over time would not have been appropriate for Democratic New York Governor Al Smith, who had to contend with a largely Republican legislature in the 1920s. "The fight would only have flared up anew at each proposal."[20]

Although governors and other state decision makers are naturally guarded about publicly revealing their preferred reorganization tactics, former Georgia governor and current president Jimmy Carter is on record as advocating comprehensive tactics for state reorganization.

The most difficult thing is to reorganize incrementally. If you do it one tiny little phase at a time, then all those who see their influence threatened will combine their efforts in a sort of secretive way. They come out of the rat holes and they'll concentrate on undoing what you're trying to do. But if you can have a bold enough, comprehensive enough proposal to rally the interest and support of the general electorate, then you can overcome that special-interest type lobbying pressure.[21]

However, Jimmy Carter appears to follow Lipson's contingency strategy more than this statement would indicate.[22] Carter's efforts to reorganize the federal executive branch have followed a more phased function-by-function approach. An April 6, 1977, White House press announcement on reorganization stated that no single master plan would be put forth for reorganization, that a series of incremental steps would be taken using a "bottom up" approach to agency restructuring.[23]

The literature on adoption tactics raises some issues important to reorganizers and opponents. But the prescriptions for either comprehensive or incremental tactics have been based largely on personal preference or on observations of a limited number of reorganizations.

### Adoption Mechanism

One reorganization-strategy issue that has received considerable attention from scholars is the type of legal mechanism employed to adopt a reorganization. The principal focus has been the relative merits and drawbacks of *constitutional* versus *statutory* mechanisms.

*Adoption by Statute or Constitutional Provision.* The general assessment has been that reorganization by statute is more feasible politically than reform via constitutional change, but that really thoroughgoing restructuring normally requires constitutional revision. Walter Dodd, John Mathews, Arthur Bromage, A. E. Buck, Leslie Lipson, John Bollens, Karl Bosworth, and Austin MacDonald all took this general position after observing the results of state reorganization attempts.[24] In 1924, Dodd observed that "substantially all of the changes so far accomplished have been achieved by legislation without much aid from constitutional change."[25] Dodd also noted that all the major state reorganizations up to that time had been achieved through statute, except in Massachusetts, where a 1918 constitutional amendment ordered state executive reorganization by legislative act. Rejection of constitutional changes that would have installed reorganizations in New York (1915) and Missouri (1921) also contributed to Dodd's conclusion that the statutory mechanism was a more effective adoption device.

A 1930s assessment concurred on both the political limitations of the constitutional device and the reform limitations of the statutory mechanism.

> A number of elective administrative officers in the American states are provided for by the respective state constitutions. They have a constitutional status, and *constitutional amendments supplanting them are not easily passed.* This explains why from 1917 to 1925 twelve of the states reorganized their administrations by statute. Reorganization of administration by statute has been logical enough in view of the difficulties and delays which constitutional amendment entails in various states.[26]

Bosworth's analysis of state reorganization efforts in the late 1940s and early 1950s supports these earlier findings. Bosworth found that, "Constitutional proposals were made in all the states . . . in which the legislative response was negative. . . . Of the fifteen states in which there was significant legislative accomplishment, only six of the reorganization proposals included constitutional amendments."[27]

Both statutory and constitutional adoptions have been viewed as mixed blessings. Reorganization by statute has been regarded as more feasible but also as easier for opponents and new political regimes to reverse or eliminate. In addition, major state officials and departments were often entrenched in constitutional provision and could not be touched by statute, which limited the overall impact of such a reorganization. Conversely, adoption of reorganization by constitutional amendment has been considered more difficult to get approved, but once in place has been regarded as more permanent. The greater durability of constitutionally installed state reorganization was thought necessary by some proponents who feared their work might be prematurely overturned. But this permanence can also be dysfunctional if it decreases administrative flexibility by constitutionally "locking-in" certain positions or agencies or by setting a ceiling on the number of departments.

The "win some–lose some" nature of this strategy choice is illustrated by the debate over constitutional limitations. Some authorities have advocated a specific constitutional limitation on the number of departments. (A limit of twenty major departments has been the most common.[28]) Others have viewed this constitutional strategy in contingency terms.

If there is no constitutional restriction, the legislature can play havoc; and if there is a limitation, new functions may be jumbled up with old ones where they do not belong. One is caught between the Scylla of legislative irresponsibility and the Charybdis of expanding governmental activities. Neither device can be generally advocated as the better for all states without exception. Each state must choose according to its own political conditions. Given the traditions and habits of the legislature in Illinois and New York, it would seem better to specify the maximum even at the risk of rigidity.[29]

*Adoption by Executive Reorganization Plan.* A third kind of legal instrumentality grants the governor reorganization authority through executive order or reorganization plan. There have been state variations of this mechanism; basically, however, the reorganization-plan device grants the initiative for making reorganization proposals to the executive branch subject to veto by the legislature.[30] In most cases the procedure calls for "the governor to present reorganization proposals to the legislature, and, after an allotted time has elapsed, the proposals go into effect unless the legislature takes action to disapprove them."[31] The executive reorganization plans as instituted by states have been patterned after the president's reorganization authority with regard to the federal executive branch.[32]

The following is a typical assessment of the reorganization plan in state government:

> The device embodied in the federal reorganization enabling acts of authorizing a chief executive to submit reorganization plans to the legislature, with the plans going into effect unless the legislature takes positive action to veto them, has had very slight use in the states. This attempt to put inertia and indecision on the side of change has been considered in a number of states but has been rejected, apparently generally in fear of adverse decisions on constitutionality.[33]

Bosworth's appraisal was no doubt influenced by the fact that New Hampshire dropped its executive reorganization-plan device in 1950. An advisory opinion of the New Hampshire State Supreme Court questioned the constitutionality of legislative delegation of reorganization powers to the executive. The reorganization-plan procedure has been suspect in some circles because it reverses the usual legislative process in which the legislature acts, subject to executive veto. Thus, when a 1975 law in Oklahoma gave the governor power to implement reorganization-commission recommendations by executive order subject to legislative veto, the attorney general ruled that this procedure violated the separation of powers doctrine. The governor instead submitted reorganization proposals in bill form.[34]

Another difficulty with this mechanism is related to legislative prerogative. Most state provisions for adoption by executive reorganization plan do not allow the legislature to modify the plan, only to accept or reject it in toto. It is not surprising that "this problem has been troubling state legislators in states which have considered the executive reorganization procedure."[35]

In terms of an overall assessment of the reorganization plan mechanism, Lynn Eley concluded,

> The executive reorganization plan procedure has had only a limited success where it has functioned *under legislative authorization alone.* Indeed, it may be questioned whether in a majority of the states which have had the statutory plan, the cause of executive reorganization had been helped or hindered. Although no effort has been made at direct comparison, it appears that states without the plan have done as well as those that have it, and some have done a good deal better.[36]

Findings in a 1972 report by the Council of State Governments support Eley's assessment. The council found that most states have scarcely used their executive reorganization authority, that they have tended to use legislation to enact major executive reorganizations even when the reorganization-plan device was available.[37]

To summarize: The literature on legal mechanisms for adopting executive reorganization has generally pointed out both the positive and negative attributes of each device, but the general assessment favors the statutory mechanism as proving most effective. Lipson is in the minority in contending that the choice of adoption mechanism is contingent upon political conditions in each state.

## Role of the Governor

Another strategic factor is the role of the governor in adopting reorganization. Does the governor's role influence the passage of reorganization? State governors are often in a position to affect other, more particularistic strategy options, such as timing of the adoption effort, tactics, or legal mechanism. There is evidence, however, that the overall role the governor plays in the adoption process is an important strategy variable apart from the governor's influence on any other single strategy or set of strategies.

There is not much scholarly literature discussing a governor's role during the adoption process. This kind of topic usually is conveyed by word of mouth or via in-house memorandum and is largely confined to those involved in reorganization decision making. Certainly the topic has received scant attention from scholars of state reorganization and the governorship.

Lipson did compare the governor's presence in reorganization efforts in four states (Illinois, New York, Massachusetts, and Virginia) during the first two decades of this century. He also analyzed the impact of that presence, or lack of it, on adoption outcome. Lipson stated his informal hypothesis this way:

> First, how important was the governor in achieving reorganization? A priori one would suppose that the governor had great influence. The object of the movement was to instill better principles of organization into his branch of the government. He knew existing defects firsthand, and the proposed reforms would increase his power. There was every incentive for him to be a vigorous leader in the [reorganization] movement. To a large extent this a priori hypothesis is confirmed by the facts. In many states the governor exerted his influence, but not in all.[38]

Lipson observed that in the Massachusetts reorganization of 1919 the governor was "relatively indifferent." The proposed amendment for reorganization was introduced by a Harvard University professor and a Harvard graduate at their own initiative. It was not introduced at the request of Governor McCall, who "lent scarcely any help to those who favored reorganization."[39] McCall's successor, Calvin Coolidge, "gave his passive approval, but was not the energetic leader who pushed the passage of the Administrative Consolidation Act."[40] Lipson concluded that "a chief characteristic of the Massachusetts reorganization was that it was a reorganization of the executive, for the executive, but not by the executive."[41] In Massachusetts the legislature and interested citizens led the campaign to get reorganization adopted. If lack of support from the governor did not scuttle passage, was there any other impact? Lipson concluded there was. He doubted that a governor playing a forceful role in reorganization would have allowed the Commission on Administration and Finance to hold such a degree of independence and even be able to "check [the governor] in certain administrative acts."[42]

In these early reorganizations Lipson found that the governors of Illinois, Virginia, and New York were more activist. They made reorganization a campaign issue and vigorously supported passage in the legislature. The active support of the governor greatly facilitated adoption, and in New York, Governor Al Smith proved crucial to passage. In all three states the governor became the chief sponsor and moving force behind the campaign to adopt reorganization.

Bosworth took a different approach in his study of the results of thirty state "Little Hoover" commissions from 1948 to 1953. Instead of focusing on the office of governor per se, he looked at the broader question of who *sponsored* reorganization. Was it the governor, key legislative leaders, interest groups, or others, and what difference did reorganization sponsorship make in the results? Bosworth does not define sponsorship, but it can be inferred from context that initiating the adoption campaign, leading the political support for adoption, and being identified with reorganization are key components.

Bosworth found that certain sponsors were more highly associated with adoption. He found that sponsorship of the governor was more vital to passage than was legislative sponsorship. In fifteen states where Bosworth found some notable adoption, governors participated in the initiation of ten and legislators were the apparent initiators in four. In one state a private agency took the initiative. In Bosworth's estimation, "Even more striking evidence of the significance of governors in these movements is seen in the fact that governors were active in the sponsorship of the movements in eight of the nine states adopting more than 40 percent of the proposals."[43]

Just as active gubernatorial support was highly associated with adoption or partial adoption, legislative sponsorship did not relate highly with passage. Bosworth found that legislatures initiated five of the eight reorganization attempts where there was not significant adoption of recommendations. The other three, initiated by the governor, failed totally, one after the governor had withdrawn support.

Bosworth's research supports Lipson's less-structured research regarding the importance of the governor's role in adopting reorganization. As insightful as Lipson's conclusions are, his basic sample of four states is extremely limited and includes no adoption failures for comparison. Bosworth's sample is larger (thirty states) and includes reorganization adoptions and failures to adopt. However, there are some internal inconsistencies in his data, and the methodology and results are not fully reported. These limitations detract from the overall usefulness of Bosworth's work.

A more recent discussion of the governor's role in adopting reorganization is included in the National Governors' Association's *The Critical Hundred Days: A Handbook for the New Governor*. The *Handbook* does not contain a self-conscious analysis of the governor's role, nor is there any attempt to associate role with adoption or failure to adopt. Neither is there any suggestion that the more active the governor's general role, the better. There are, however, some points that add to our understanding of this strategy variable. The *Handbook* is also important because of its sources and audience.

Several role-types can be inferred from the *Handbook*. One strategy role the governor might play is that of reorganization *initiator*, especially during the election campaign. According to the *Handbook*, this option is rarely taken because research and planning for reorganization is "not the most pressing order of business in a campaign." It is conceivable that Jimmy Carter's success in using executive branch reorganization as a presidential-campaign issue may stimulate more governors to follow suit by initiating studies to back up campaign pledges.

Another gubernatorial role implicit in the *Handbook* is that of *mission control center*. The governor and his or her advisors are not only the focal point for basic reorganization planning; they are also the clearinghouse for information and advice on strategies, structural changes, and the political and administrative ramifications of these. It is especially important, according to the *Handbook*, that agency heads be consulted on such issues before any public announcements are made. This action is thought to be "essential to understanding details and predicting reaction."[44]

Related to the role of *mission control center*, but not explicit in the *Handbook*, is the role of *lobbyist*. If the governor supports reorganization, the governor and governor's staff often bear the brunt of lobbying for passage of reorganization proposals. This lobbying can take the forms of publicizing reorganization via the news media or "town meetings," assembling a coalition supporting reorganization, educating and persuading legislators, and defending proposals against attack.

Governors are not always pro-reorganization. Legislators, employee organizations, citizens' groups, and others may advance reorganization proposals that the governor cannot accept or that compete with the governor's own proposals. Missouri's Governor Christopher Bond, for example, vetoed a legislator-sponsored proposal that he thought conflicted with the State Reorganization Commission's proposals (which took effect in 1974).

For all the interest governors typically have in executive branch reorganization, their role in adopting reorganization remains inadequately defined.

### Promotion Campaign

Promotion-campaign strategy encompasses the other strategic considerations, namely, timing, tactics, adoption mechanism, and role of governor. All these strategy choices are oriented toward adoption, but the promotion campaign is so crucial to adoption that it deserves discussion in its own right.

There are special problems involved in getting reorganization proposals approved. These problems heighten the need for careful attention to promotion strategy. One of the most fundamental and most often overlooked problems has been identified by the U.S. Advisory Commission on Intergovernmental Relations.

> Any particular reorganization plan submitted to referendum is typically competing for public favor not merely against the status quo ("this particular change versus no change at all"), but potentially also against alternative ways of dealing with the problems that give rise to the proposal. The difficulty of this assignment may be suggested by analogy: it is as if, in order to replace the incumbent of an elective office some one opposing candidate had to obtain more votes than the total cast for the incumbent *and* all other candidates combined, in a single election open to any number of candidates and without any primary or run-off arrangement.[45]

The burden of proof is clearly on the sponsors and supporters to demonstrate that their proposals are superior to existing conditions *and* to competing alternatives, even though some of these alternatives may be unarticulated.

Despite the sometimes crucial nature of promotion strategy, there has been comparatively little about it in the literature. There have been no major systematic research efforts to determine whether any particular promotional methods or uses of media have been more highly associated with adoption.

Even though written, self-conscious examination of state reorganization campaign strategy has been sparse, some knowledge can be drawn upon. A number of promotion strategies have been catalogued in Table 4.1. For the most part, these strategies are based on the experience of one state or a few states and therefore lack generalizability beyond those small samples. One source for these strategies is the Council of State Governments' 1949 National Conference on State Reorganization Problems reported on by Hubert Gallagher. Gallagher's report does not attribute promotion strategies to individual states; rather, it synthesizes discussion at the conference. Because he made no systematic attempt to link promotion strategies with adoption results, it is impossible to assess accurately the effectiveness of the strategies he recommends.

Even though these stratagems primarily represent unvalidated conventional wisdom, there is some value in identifying them so that they can be assessed systematically. The promotion strategies summarized in Table 4.1 also represent part of the bag of tricks available to reorganization backers and indicate leverage points that can be utilized by opponents of reorganization. For example, by recognizing the stratagem of appointing a representative study commission, opponents can take advantage of built-in opposition on the commission itself.

The following discussion attempts, not to elaborate upon each strategy enumerated in Table 4.1, but only to discuss points that might be unclear or warrant further comment.

*Target Populations.* In the state reorganization literature, two kinds of target populations are emphasized: *influentials* and the *general public*. Influentials are reported to include the governor, legislators, and key lobbyists and the lobbies they represent. The direct inference here is that these key lobbies are private sector groups. That the state bureaucracies constitute a key lobby in their own right is only indirectly implied. In addition, neither Bosworth nor Gallagher, the two primary writers on promotion strategy, attributes special power over reorganization to any particular committees or legislative leaders. They treat all legislators as "influentials" who warrant a specialized approach.

These target populations are to be approached differently. Table 4.1 shows there are some approaches more appropriate to a particularistic than to a general audience; however, there appears to be more of a difference in emphasis than in kind of strategy. For example, briefings and hearings are recommended for both specific and general audiences. There is an implied suggestion that great care should be taken to assure that influentials are briefed about reorganization proposals and that they have given their ideas and recommendations. However, in more complex states, where power configurations are not as readily discernible, selective promotion may need to be decreased in favor of reaching a more general target population.

*Study-group–Oriented Promotions.* One subject that merits elaboration is the

TABLE 4.1

Strategies for Promoting State Executive Reorganization

| PROMOTION STRATEGIES | TARGET POPULATION | | | |
| --- | --- | --- | --- | --- |
| | I. INFLUENTIALS | | | II. GENERAL PUBLIC |
| | Governor | Legislators | Key Lobbies | |

**Study-Group-Oriented**

| PROMOTION STRATEGIES | Governor | Legislators | Key Lobbies | General Public |
| --- | :---: | :---: | :---: | :---: |
| (1) Allow representation on study group[a,b,c] | X | X | X | X |
| (2) Give special briefing for[a,b] | X | X | X | |
| (3) Testify before[a,b] | | X | | |
| (4) Take testimony from[a,b,c] | X | X | X | X |
| (5) Conduct open forum to present findings and recommendations[a,b] | | | X | X |
| (6) Keep promotion in mind when conducting research[b] | X | X | X | |
| (7) Keep part of study group around for follow-up[b] | X | X | X | |

**Study-Report-Oriented**

| PROMOTION STRATEGIES | Governor | Legislators | Key Lobbies | General Public |
| --- | :---: | :---: | :---: | :---: |
| (8) Make report readable and attractive[a,b] | X | X | X | X |
| (9) Prepare summary document for wide distribution[b] | | | X | X |
| (10) Consider issuing periodic reports to sustain interest[a] | X | X | X | X |
| (11) Avoid "boners" in report. Be certain examples are necessary and not politically unwise[b] | X | X | X | X |
| (12) Documentation need only be adequate, not excessive[a] | X | X | X | X |
| (13) Do not exceed authorized scope of study[b] | X | X | X | |

TABLE 4.1 (cont.)

| | TARGET POPULATION | | | |
|---|---|---|---|---|
| | I. INFLUENTIALS | | | II. GENERAL PUBLIC |
| PROMOTION STRATEGIES | Gov-ernor | Legis-lators | Key Lobbies | |
| (14) "Prime the pump" to pave way for acceptance of key proposals[a] | | X | | |
| (15) Make some non-controversial proposals to allow opportunity for saving face[a] | | X | X | |
| **Timing-Oriented** | | | | |
| (16) Allow sufficient time for discussion of report[a] | | X | X | X |
| (17) Consider type of legislative session (special or regular)[b] | | X | X | X |
| **Leadership in Promotion** | | | | |
| (18) Promotion campaign coordinator must be chosen carefully[a] | X | X | X | X |
| (19) Introduction to public should be done by locals[b] | X | X | X | X |
| **Media-Oriented** | | | | |
| (20) Utilize governor's press conferences and releases[b] | X | X | X | X |
| (21) Media (newspaper, radio, television) can be utilized[b] | X | X | X | X |

Sources: [a]Karl Bosworth, "The Politics of Management Improvement in the States," pp. 95-97.

[b]Hubert Gallagher, "State Reorganization Surveys," pp. 255-256.

[c]National Governors' Association, The Critical Hundred Days: A Handbook for the New Governor, pp. 18-22.

synchronization of research and promotion. Gallagher insists that one should not wait until reorganization proposals have been developed to start gathering support. The job of "selling" the report must be kept in mind throughout the research process. Those doing the research must be in contact at all times with the organizations that stand to be affected by the studies.[46] If the proposals and supporting documentation are not developed with a view towards marketability, the final product will be more difficult to promote.

The importance of having expertise available to explain the study group's recommendations and to counter criticisms is also emphasized by Bosworth and Gallagher. This may be accomplished by retaining members of the study group after the final report has been transmitted or by utilizing staff members from executive departments or legislative committees who have worked on the reorganization planning.[47] One risk of using consultants to conduct the bulk of reorganization research and planning is that they may be transferred to another project and not be available for follow-up.

*Study-report-Oriented Promotions.* Some steps can be taken with study reports to gain support for the reorganization proposals. Certainly it helps to have an attractive, readable report. Of perhaps more importance is to exclude from the report a political or technical "boner."

> Often entire reports have failed because of some minor recommendation that was politically unwise. . . . Opposition has been aroused by examples that were not at all necessary to the substance of the report. Pointed examples can add strength to a report, but they must be wisely chosen.[48]

For supporters, the defensive value of a sound study report is greater than its value as a means of recruiting support for reorganization. Opponents may scrutinize study reports and proposals for political or technical mistakes they can turn to their advantage.

Another strategy decision involves how wide or narrow a research scope the reorganization study will encompass. There are a number of factors to be considered in determining research scope. Some relate to general environmental conditions and are not directly manipulable by decision makers. These include the issues that precipitated the reorganization study and the present health of the state administration. Other factors may be beyond the control of the study group but can be manipulated by the governor and legislature. These factors include legal mandate for the study, time allotted, and research budget.

Even after these factors have been taken into account, the study group has some latitude for determining the scope of its work. Factors to be considered in this context are research feasibility, the authorized limits set by the research sponsor, and the degree of specificity.

Both Gallagher and Bosworth have pointed out that surveys not attempting to cover the "waterfront" have a greater probability of acceptance. Bosworth warns against developing a research program "stretching beyond that understood by the authorizing body."[49] If the legislature or the governor find that the study group's research spills over into areas not initially agreed upon, then both the study group and its proposals are likely to be suspect.

Regarding the level of specificity, the relevant literature generally advocates concentrating on major issues, keeping detail to a minimum.

> The surveys should . . . be concerned with top-level problems of organization and administration — they should not be distracted by specific tax and fiscal problems and they should not become involved in the minutiae of organization or the details of procedures. A report concerned with the larger problems and principles of organization and management has a better chance of adoption than a report concerned with details.[50]

This posture appears to be most widely accepted, but there may be situations where minor, more-detailed analyses and proposals are constructive. One reason for including detail is strategic, another methodological.

The strategic reason, about which there is much disagreement, espouses the *pump-priming* approach: getting the legislature (or other decision forum) to act on minor or moderate-scale reorganization proposals enhances receptivity toward other moderate-scale and major proposals. The risk is that attention might be drawn away from the most significant proposals, damaging their chances for approval.

Minor and moderate-scale proposals might also be useful to the study group and to primary supporters of reorganization as *face-saving* devices. Saving face can be very important. In Bosworth's words, "Some accomplishment, even though it be not of a first order, is a great solace to the participants and avoids the reputation of a fiasco, so that the state of future efforts may be easier."[51] Face-saving can be used to the advantage of both opponents and proponents of reorganization. For example, a legislature basically opposed to broad reorganization may take a convenient "out" by adopting a few minor proposals. This can give a legislature some accomplishment, lessening the pressure to act on major recommendations.

Another exception to the rule of not including organizational procedures and structural details in the research scope is based on methodological considerations of organizational analysis. Waldo has made a distinction between problems that call for an *organizational* (i.e., structural) response. According to Waldo, an organizational analyst ought to be alert to which of the two kinds of problems is at issue. If a problem is amenable to solution by both organizational and procedural remedies, then according to Bosworth, "a change in procedure, as the less drastic remedy, is nearly always to be preferred."[52] In addition, Dwight Waldo contended that *"measurable* economies can be shown much more easily and frequently through procedural than through organizational [structural] changes."[53] Such nuances may be overlooked if the scope of the reorganization study does not include an examination of detailed operating procedures.

Another consideration in promotion strategy is whether reorganization proposals are more likely to be approved in regular or special sessions of the legislature. Conferees of the 1949 Conference on State Reorganization Problems favored regular sessions.

> Both methods have been tried successfully. A special session may attract too much attention to the report, giving "snipers" a chance to concentrate their fire at a time when there are no other issues before the legislature to command attention. If the report is considered at the same time that the budget and state policies generally are examined, the legislatures will have a better balanced picture of the state's needs and resources.[54]

This assessment gives us an idea of why our knowledge of reorganization-adoption strategies is not more advanced than our present understanding, which is dominated by hearsay and personal anecdote. Writers like Hubert Gallagher who have focused on strategy issues have not been inclined toward systematic analysis. Gallagher reports that introducing proposals into both regular and special legislative sessions has been "successful." But there is no indication of the number of "successes" or "failures" for each strategy option, the ratio of successes to failures, or any other measure upon which an informed strategy decision might be based. Gallagher's rationale for rejecting the special session in favor of the regular session seems plausible but is hardly conclusive.

In the absence of systematic evidence, one could argue just as forcibly that introducing reorganization proposals during a regular legislative session runs the risk of the legislators' attention being diverted by other issues, particularly budget, appointment, taxation, and other decisions that must be made if state government is to function. Following this line of reasoning, a special session might afford less distraction and provide a better forum for discussing the strengths and weaknesses of reorganization proposals. Thus, the issue of regular versus special sessions has yet to be systematically tested.

## Implementation Strategies

For purposes of this study, implementation of state executive branch reorganization is defined as "the process of setting into place and putting into routine operation the reorganization program adopted by legislation, constitutional provision, reorganization plan, executive order, or other means." Several points need to be made about this definition. First, as a reorganization program is being implemented, it rarely stays the same as when it was adopted. Additional pieces of legislation or executive orders often are needed to carry out the intent of an adopted reorganization package. Administrative discretion, exercised through formal or informal devices, further changes the reorganization program during the implementation phase. So does the action or inaction of state government employees, consultants, and contractors involved in implementation. Thus, although implementation typically is viewed as putting an adopted reorganization package into effect, the process is by no means automatic or mechanical. The reorganization program is itself modified during its implementation.

A second point relates to when the implementation occurs. According to Donald Van Meter and Carl Van Horn, implementation "takes place after legislation has been passed and funds committed (or after a judicial ruling and accompanying decree)."[55] This temporal sequence would appear to leave implementation out of the policy-decision process that produces the legislation, ruling, or decree. But just as adoption strategy considerations cannot be ignored until the formal campaign to promote reorganization is under way, neither can implementational strategy be conveniently left until after the reorganization program has been approved. This is consistent with the observations of Jeffrey Pressman, Aaron Wildavsky, and Erwin Hargrove that implementation is already shaped to some extent by the policy design itself.[56] In Hargrove's words, "Strategy and plan affect execution. . . . The process of setting the strategy of implementation overlaps in time with the policy decision process."[57] This link is readily apparent in state executive reorganization. The implementation schedule and the provisions for personnel and other administrative support for implementation are often written into the reorganization plan itself. The scope of the reorganization plan and the controversial nature of its proposals are just two of several design elements that can affect implementation. Thus, even though most of the implementation process occurs after adoption, some of the process, particularly that concerned with implementation strategy, almost necessarily occurs in the earlier phases of problem definition, research and planning, and adoption.

## Salience of Implementation Strategy
## for State Executive Reorganization

At the beginning of this chapter I pointed out that considerable barriers to reform have produced a number of casualties — reorganization programs that began with high optimism and much fanfare but were scuttled, lost, or dissipated. Because the crippling blow can occur after adoption, attention to implementation strategy is just as essential to the overall success of reorganization as is actual passage of the program. Increasingly evident in many spheres of public policy and administrative reform is the understanding that legislative passage may be only the prelude to the processes determining success or failure.

The reorganization of Massachusetts government in the late 1960s vividly illustrates how crucial implementation is for executive branch reorganization. In August 1969 Massachusetts Governor Francis Sargent signed into law House Bill No. 5202 — An Act to Form a Cabinet Level Government. Enactment of the "Modernization Act," as it was called, was hailed by Governor Sargent as "one of the most significant events in the history of Massachusetts government." An administrative specialist involved in reorganization planning wrote these words about the Massachusetts "modernization" in 1971:

> Massachusetts . . . has elected to meet its challenges by a massive restructuring of its 50,000-man Executive Department and a reshaping of the decision and control processes. . . . Massachusetts at the moment has everything going for it in tackling this task — more perhaps than any state in recent memory.[58]

Writing two years later the same author lamented,

> The great idea did not survive. What looked so hopeful, so logical, so absolutely necessary to more sane operation of government is now largely a collection of reports and some wistful memories left with a few people who knew what the whole thing was about.[59]

Robert Marden, director of the Office of Planning and Program Coordination and one of the architects of the modernization program, felt that "despite the fact that Massachusetts is listed by the Council of State Governments as a reorganized state, reorganization never occurred in Massachusetts."[60]

What happened in just two years to transform the Massachusetts executive reorganization from breakthrough to failure? The answer lies primarily within the sphere of implementation — implementation that was already partly shaped by the adoption process itself. I will draw from this Massachusetts reorganization experience in illustrating some of the following implementation-strategy issues.

## Reorganization Implementation Strategies: How Much Is Known?

Some aspects of the adoption strategies discussed above have their parallels in the implementation of reorganization — timing, tactics, and role of the governor. In addition, the issue of adequacy of resources devoted to implementation is raised in the form of budget strategy. Only a small group of scholars, journalists, and officials have been writing about reorganization-adoption strategies, but attention to reorganization implementation has been even more limited. As with reorganization adoption, implementation-strategy issues are seldom discrete. Thus, for example, one strategy decision might very well involve tactics, budget, and role of governor.

*Implementation Timing Strategy*

Implementation timing errors are basically of two kinds: (1) rushing implementation, not allowing adequate time for putting reorganized structures, programs, and procedures in motion, and (2) delaying reorganization implementation so that momentum is dissipated and extra problems set in.

Delayed implementation was one that inhibited the Massachusetts reorganization. A Democrat-controlled legislature amended the reorganization act to postpone appointment of department secretaries for twenty months, from 1969 to 1971. Perhaps they thought that if incumbent Republican Governor Sargent were defeated, a Democrat would be able to make the top appointments to the new cabinet departments. There was no consensus that delaying the appointment of cabinet secretaries would be harmful to reorganization. Robert Casselman saw the twenty-month delay in appointments as a constructive amendment, one that allowed a transition staff to prepare the management systems for the changeover to the cabinet departments.

In retrospect we can see that this delay in implementation resulted in lost momemtum. "Sargent could do little for the present but wait. It would be twenty months before he could begin to name the secretaries and move the plan into action."[61] And another result of the delay was that the legislature was even more heavily Democratic when implementation began.

Degree of preparation often has to be weighed against the factor of momentum, as illustrated by the case of Massachusetts. Premature changeover to the new departments and new management systems can create difficulties, but so can delayed installation, which creates the risk of losing momentum and the interest of the public and key officials. The need to maintain the governor's interest and active involvement is a particularly important factor in the decision of when to begin implementation and when to complete it.

*Role of the Governor in Implementation*

The importance of the governor's active participation in gaining passage

of a reorganization program was stressed earlier. Keeping the governor involved during implementation appears to be just as critical and usually
more difficult. Part of this difficulty lies in the tendency to assume that the
battle has been won with adoption, that "once a policy has been 'made' by a
government, the policy will be implemented and the desired results of the
policy will be near those expected by the policy-makers."[62]

Another element affecting the governor's role during implementation is
the fact that higher managerial sophistication often is required of an effective participant in implementation. A governor, even an experienced and
capable one, is less likely to be interested in, or knowledgeable about, the
highly specialized budget, accounting, personnel administration, logistical
planning, and other work commonly involved in implementing an executive branch reorganization. Such particularized administrative tasks are
generally delegated to staff or agency specialists, who then may lose touch
with the governor. Writing about the Massachusetts reorganization,
Casselman has forcefully articulated this point:

> To [Governor Sargent] reorganization meant primarily the chance to have
> a few able, carefully selected top administrators handling for him and with
> him the incredibly complex policy and "management" problems that confront
> a governor daily. He was aware that some "very fine work" was in progress to
> develop new methods (Program-based Management System and others) to
> help the secretaries do their jobs, but he could not have described those
> methods and still cannot. He took on faith the fact that they would be good
> and helpful, but that faith was not backed with any visceral conviction that
> they could indeed be made to work. He could not have explained why two-
> thirds of the cost of operating the new cabinet was chargeable to those
> systems. And because he could not, he did not. . . . In fairness to him (and
> other good governors like him) how could he be expected to know these
> things? His experience nowhere included the management of an operation in
> which information critical to decisions was routinely and systematically
> available. He was not a student of PPBS in any deep sense, or even a careful
> analyst of his own Massachusetts budget process. In short, he knew too little
> about what he was missing or why he was missing it. . . . How many gover-
> nors have similar backgrounds, and would have done the same?[63]

Kaufman and Van Meter and Van Horn have emphasized the implementation problems created when communication to subordinates (implementors) is faulty. Policy directives or performance standards can be
ambiguous, inconsistent, or simply misunderstood.[64] But, as evidenced by
the Massachusetts experience, the upward communications gap can be just
as serious. If governors and other superiors do not have a clear idea of what
is taking place during implementation, their effective involvement is limited.

A governor is in a more familiar role during the adoption phase — cultivating public support and assembling votes to pass a proposal or series of proposals. Promoting reorganization is more analogous to campaigning for election or gathering support for the governor's legislative program. Both of these are activities governors, as a rule, have had more experience with. Most governors are not as comfortable with the tasks of directing or monitoring reorganization implementation or serving as advocate for those reforms being installed. Nor is much written to guide a governor in implementing reorganization.

*The Critical Hundred Days: A Handbook for the New Governor* contains two pointers for governors involved in reorganization implementation. The first is a recommendation to make gubernatorial appointments with a view toward the roles of these appointees in implementing reorganization.

> In contemplating reorganization by consolidating existing departments, a new Governor may find it is important that one person be appointed to a group of departments who would likely become the head of the consolidated groups and that other appointees in that group be individuals who would facilitate reorganization.[65]

The *Handbook* also cautions governors not to appoint department heads who may later oppose the implementation of reform.

Judging by the very limited literature on the role of the governor in implementing reorganization, it is evident that this role has not been well defined and is in many respects an awkward one for governors. Several elements of a governor's role have been suggested, but there is nothing available that would enable a governor to select a role or set of roles with any confidence that they will be appropriate given the political, administrative, and financial situation in his or her state. Nor are there any findings that associate a governor's rate of activity and the degree of implementation completed. A tentative list of role options available to a governor includes the following:

*Student* — becoming as well informed about the structures, systems, and procedures to be reorganized as his or her experience and capacities allow. The governor needs to be a student of the implementation process itself and of the objectives and constraints of implementing reorganization.

*Advocate* — supporting the cause of reorganization by fighting for implementation funds and other resources and explaining and defending implementation progress to the legislature, the general public, and those interest groups affected by the reorganization. To be an effective advocate, the governor must have done the required homework as student.

*Strategist* — resolving the strategy issues that surround reorganization implementation. How much time is needed for thorough implementation? Should implementation be launched at one time in all agencies or should it be attempted sequentially, agency by agency? Who should be in charge of implementing reorganization—the governor? a top aide? the director of administration? the budget director? the planning director? area (e.g., human services) coordinators? These and other strategy questions must be answered. If the governor is not involved in such strategy decisions, he or she may be held responsible for the end result anyway. It should be emphasized that some decisions about implementation cannot wait until after a reorganization plan has passed. Some implementation strategies need to be considered in the earliest phases before a study report has been prepared.

*Guardian*—guarding against undesirable alternatives during implementation. A governor may need to guard the prerogatives of the governorship in the face of bolstered power centers in other parts of state government, to guard against the elevation of a political rival through the reorganization process, or to guard the authority and resources of weaker but vital agencies or programs that otherwise might be swallowed up or plundered by stronger departments or programs. A governor may also need to guard against having the mission of an agency or program misdirected or thwarted by a dominant mission. For example, budgeting typically is dominant whenever budgeting and planning are combined in the same agency.

*Enforcer*—exercising the power of the governor's office to enforce compliance with implementation directives. Sometimes noncompliance can come from bureaucratic or political actors who oppose reorganization.

*Delegator*—delegating to the governor's personal staff, to a transition team, or to agency heads or functional coordinators the primary responsibility for implementing reorganization. As is true with other types of administrative delegation, a governor may need to have a solid grasp of the tasks involved before delegation can be effective.

*Observer*—remaining aloof from the process of implementing reorganization. A governor may remain aloof because of the assumption that implementation will be routine following adoption. A governor may also choose the role of observer because of reluctance to become entangled in bureaucratic (and perhaps legislative and interest-group) warfare. There may be times when a governor's most prudent course is to "remain above the fray." On the other hand, a governor must also consider that in a number of states and in a number of situations the governor will be held responsible whether directly involved or not. Under such circumstances a governor may want to reject the observer role in favor of others that allow more control over the process and the outcomes.

These roles are not necessarily mutually exclusive, although some are. A governor could be a delegator and an enforcer, for example, but not an enforcer and an observer. It would appear that the choice of proper role is a complex function of the governor's personal characteristics and the situational variables affecting reorganization implementation. Research to identify the most viable roles given particular situations has yet to be undertaken by scholars of the American governor or scholars of administrative reform.

*Implementation Tactics*

Implementation tactics will be viewed in a manner analogous to the earlier treatment of adoption tactics. The basic strategy option is whether implementation is to be primarily *incremental* (multiple stages phased over a longer period of time) or *comprehensive* (done in one basic step over a shorter period).

Tactics for implementing reorganization in a state may echo the tactics for adoption, but this is not automatically the case. It is conceivable for a state to make a comprehensive adoption with one major constitutional or legislative package, but to implement that reorganization in stages over a longer period. The Massachusetts executive reorganization adopted in 1969 is an example of this. A rarer occurrence would be incremental adoption and comprehensive implementation. The Michigan reorganization enacted in 1921 approaches this combination. Six separate pieces of adoption legislation were implemented in a comparatively short time. Figure 4.1 shows some of the possible combinations of adoption and implementation tactics.

The strategy issue I call implementation tactics is referred to as *timing* by Peirce and Gottlieb. Robert Backoff uses the term *sequence of change* to mean "how many properties or components are being affected during some time period of implementation. . . . A 'comprehensive' sequence would be one in which all affected units were being changed during all time periods of implementation. 'Selective' sequences would refer to changes in different properties during different phases of the implementation process."[66]

Peirce has identified three basic implementation tactics: one-step, phased "umbrella" plan, and one function at a time. He briefly describes these, going from most comprehensive to most incremental.

> Such states as Georgia, Delaware and South Carolina abolish all or most of the old agencies in one step and reconstituted state government from the ground up.
> Others established "umbrella" type super-cabinet posts, and then, over a period of years, reorganized the old-line agencies below them. Massachusetts and North Carolina have followed this type of timetable.

A third strategy reorganizes one functional area after another. Arizona and Kentucky are typical examples.[67]

Peirce has also summarized the advantages and handicaps of these tactics:

> A one-step approach may be more than a state government can digest immediately, and many details are left unattended. But in a long drawn-out process, enthusiasm may lag so that the job is never really complete.[68]

Not all those who have written about reorganization implementation tactics are as even-handed in their assessment. Joan Ehrlich and Gottlieb both concluded that the two-phased tactics (Pierce's umbrella-type) was less

FIGURE 4.1

Reorganization Adoption and Implementation Tactics:  Combinations of Polar Types

|  |  | ADOPTION | |
|  |  | Incremental | Comprehensive |
|---|---|---|---|
| **IMPLEMENTATION** | **Incremental** | I.<br><br>Incremental Adoption;<br><br>Incremental Implementation | III.<br><br>Comprehensive Adoption;<br><br>Incremental Implementation |
|  | **Comprehensive** | II.<br><br>Incremental Adoption;<br><br>Comprehensive Implementation | IV.<br><br>Comprehensive Adoption;<br><br>Comprehensive Implementation |

likely to result in completed implementation of the reorganization program. Both of these authors drew heavily from the Massachusetts experience in making their conclusion. For them, one of the problems with the two-phased tactic is that the actions taken in the later phases tend to deviate from the standards set by the reorganization plan and by the first implementation efforts.

To illustrate this problem Gottlieb used the example of the most recent North Carolina reorganization, which was adopted in 1971 and implemented in stages in 1973, 1974, and 1975. She observed that

> The four departments reorganized in 1973 followed the principles of the original reorganization act. The remaining thirteen departments, which were reorganized in 1974 and 1975, left the agencies in the departments relatively independent and the department head powerless in many areas.[69]

Assessment of the two-phased approach has not been entirely negative. The Massachusetts two-phased approach, for example, was seen to have the advantage of postponing some of the difficult decisions and political fights until after the reorganization was adopted and implementation was under way. In phase one, cabinet departments based on broad functional groupings (e.g., transportation, education, and environment) were created and existing administrative units assigned to each department. The secretaries in charge of cabinet departments were to recommend more detailed internal organizational changes in the second phase two years later. Both Berkley and Casselman concluded that postponing the "bureaucratic bloodshed" was responsible for the high level of adoption and implementation. It may have been that strong political resistance would have frustrated reorganization in Massachusetts no matter what tactics were applied. But in a climate hostile to reorganization it is even more imperative that such strategy choices be carefully weighed.

The Massachusetts case illustrates that tactics advantageous for adoption are not necessarily most effective for implementation. The distinction between adoption and implementation tactics and the nature of their interdependence is not fully understood by some of those engaging in reorganization or by some of those writing about it. There is a tendency to view adoption and implementation tactics as a single strategy choice. Adoption may well be emphasized to the detriment of implementation if this distinction is not recognized.

### Budget Strategy and Reorganization Implementation

The uses of budgets as strategy tools to abet or inhibit state reorganization are but variations of general budgetary strategies.[70] As with the other implementation strategy issues, little of the literature explicitly discusses the use of budgeting in state reorganization strategy. The topic is included here because the budget tool is a powerful one that has been used effectively by reorganizers and opponents alike. Omission of this strategy issue would constitute a failure to recognize a major factor in state executive reorganization.

One strategy utilized by opponents of reorganization is to approve legislation for a new program but to thwart it by underfunding. In Massachusetts, in spite of the fact that the two-phased reorganization plan was approved by the General Court in 1969, legislative opponents of reorganization were able to hamper the reorganization effort by appropriating insufficient funds for implementation, particularly for the management-control systems. Casselman considered the most damaging blow to be the House's 1971 elimination of the budget for the Program-based Management System staff for the following fiscal year. "By that action they wiped out the entire staff that had been trained in the new systems, and destroyed most of the remaining hopes that the goals of the modernization effort might someday be achieved."[71]

Budget fattening can be as effective an opposition weapon as budget starvation. By providing a reorganization effort with a conspicuously fat budget, opponents can sometimes curse it with advantages. A reorganization conducted with great fanfare and lavish spending can attract opposition from other state agencies that resent this favored treatment, from cost-conscious taxpayers' organizations, and from state officials and clientele groups who expect more than the reorganization is able to deliver.

A strategy that proponents can use in implementation and adoption is to use federal planning grants to finance much of the cost of reorganization research and planning and the printing of reports and brochures. This strategy does not just add to the funds available for state use. By financing at least a portion of often-controversial reorganization research with non-state revenues, the strategy reduces the potential for criticism. Likewise, brochures promoting or explaining reorganization are less vulnerable to charges of "wasting state taxpayers' money" if they are financed by federal grant money. States that have utilized Section 701 Planning Grants from the U.S. Department of Housing and Urban Development for reorganization studies include Montana, Massachusetts, North Carolina, Maine, and Oklahoma.

## Implementation Strategies: Why Is So Little Known?

In the absence of good comparative data on the failures of state reorganizations, it would only be speculation to contend that more reorganizations have been thwarted by implementation shortcomings than by defeat in the legislature or at the polls. Certainly implementation problems have the potential to thwart reorganization, and they have done so. Moreover, because it is only through effective implementation that adopted reorganization proposals can bring about results, implementation is a crucial part of the reorganization process. A logical question thus arises: If implementation is so vital to the reorganization process and implementation strategies can make or break an executive reorganization, why hasn't there been more effort to know more about reorganization implementation?

Van Meter and Van Horn have asked essentially the same question with regard to policy implementation in general. In response, they offer four reasons for the neglect of policy implementation.

1. There is the naive assumption that implementation follows automatically after policy formulations and that results do not deviate from expectations.
2. The implementation process is assumed to be a series of mundane decisions and interactions unworthy of the attention of scholars seeking the heady stuff of politics.
3. The focus on analysis of policy alternatives and rational policy making (as exemplified by Planning Programming Budgeting Systems and similar analytic techniques) has excluded attention "of the lower echelons of agencies responsible for implementation."
4. The enormous difficulties involved in studying implementation (due to complex methodological problems, data inadequacies and research costs) have "discouraged detailed analysis of the process of policy implementation."[72]

These same reasons appear valid for explaining the neglect of state reorganization implementation. Certainly the methodological, data, and resource constraints are formidable. Some of these research problems will be examined further in Chapters 5 and 7.

In spite of the general neglect of implementation issues in the literature on state reorganization, there is some cause for optimism. A resurgence of scholarly interest in policy implementation in general was in evidence in the 1970s, so perhaps this interest will spill over into state reorganization implementation.

### Reorganization Strategies: An Epilogue

Our knowledge of state reorganization strategies has been limited by the paucity of writing on the subject and by the lack of systematic, comparative, and longitudinal research on a large scale. It may be that social-science scholars find such strategy issues theoretically uninteresting, too normative in flavor, or too applied. Whatever the reason, reorganization strategy issues have not received the research attention that appears warranted by the number of state governments that have undertaken and continue to undertake reorganization for a variety of objectives. What scholarly attention there has been has not kept pace in the 1970s.

In the next chapter I will attempt to lay an overall conceptual framework for the rest of our discussion. This framework relates three theoretically and tactically important adoption strategies with synthesized perspectives on why reorganizations occur (information drawn from Chapter 2) and with structural types of reorganization (developed in Chapter 3).

### Notes

1. Accounts of state reorganization failures are contained in: Robert C. Casselman, "Massachusetts Revisited: Chronology of a Failure," *Public Administration Review* 33 (March/April 1973):129–35. Karl Bosworth, "The Politics of Management Improvement in the States," *American Political Science Review* 47 (March 1953): 84–99. William H. Edwards, "A Factual Summary of State Administrative Reorganization," *Southwestern Social Science Quarterly* 19 (June 1938):53–67. George Berkley, "Reorganizing Administration in Massachusetts," in *The Craft of Public Administration* (Boston: Allyn and Bacon, 1975). A. E. Buck, *Reorganization of State Governments in the United States* (New York: Columbia University Press, 1938). Harlan W. Gilmore, "Louisiana Clings to Reform," *National Municipal Review* 33 (April 1944):165–67.

2. Donald P. Warwick, *A Theory of Public Bureaucracy: Politics, Personality and Organization in the State Deparment* (Cambridge: Harvard University Press, 1975), p. 104. Bosworth, "The Politics of Management Improvement in the States," pp. 85–86.

3. Gerald E. Caiden, *The Dynamics of Public Administration: Guidelines to Current Transformations in Theory and Practice* (New York: Holt, Rinehart and Winston, 1971), p. 122. Herbert Kaufman, *The Limits of Organizational Change* (University, Ala.: University of Alabama Press, 1971), pp. 36–38. Harold Seidman, *Politics, Position and Power: The Dynamics of Federal Organization,* 2d ed. (New York: Oxford University Press, 1975), p. 108. Warwick, *A Theory of Public Bureaucracy*, pp. 192–93. Leslie Lipson, *The American Governor: From Figurehead to Leader* (Chicago: Greenwood Press, 1939), pp. 106–8. Timothy W. Costello, "Change in Municipal Government: A View from the Inside," *The Journal of Applied Behavioral Science* 7 (March/April 1971):131–45. Victor A. Thompson, "Bureaucracy and Innovation," *Administrative Science Quarterly* 10 (June 1965):1–20, presents a classic discussion of problems of innovation in general within a bureaucratic context. York Willbern, "Administration in State Governments," in *The Forty-Eight States: Their Tasks as Policy-Makers and Ad-*

*ministrators* (New York: American Assembly, 1955), p. 115.

4. Avery Leiserson, "Political Limitations on Executive Reorganization," *American Political Science Review* (February 1947):69-84. Warwick, *A Theory of Public Bureaucracy*, p. 104. Neal R. Peirce "Structural Reform of Bureaucracy Grows Rapidly," *National Journal* 7 (April 5, 1975):506. Seidman, *Politics, Position and Power*, pp. 95, 101-3.

5. Joseph P. Harris, *Congressional Control of Administration* (Washington, D.C.: Brookings Institution, 1954), pp. 16, 24. Seidman, *Politics, Position and Power*, pp. 57-60. Lipson, *The American Governor*, pp. 122-24. Walter F. Dodd, "Reorganizing State Government," *Annals* 113 (May 1924):167-68. Austin F. MacDonald, *American State Government and Administration* (New York: Thomas Y. Crowell Co., 1955), p. 353. Arthur W. Bromage, "State Reorganization," *National Municipal Review* 24 (December 1935):667. Kaufman, *Limits of Organizational Change*, pp. 31-34.

6. Casselman, "Massachusetts Revisited," pp. 129-35. Frances Pennell Bish contends that the barrier of inadequate understanding is the most fundamental. *"How we conceptualize organizational problems and their solutions, and how we use available data and information to alter these conceptions when relevant, represent the 'ultimate' limits on our capacity to achieve desired ends through organization reform."* Frances P. Bish, "The Limits of Organizational Reform" (Paper presented at the 1976 Annual Meeting of the Southern Political Science Association, Atlanta, Georgia, November 5, 1976).

7. Willbern, "Administration in State Governments," pp. 115-16. Lipson, *American Governor*, pp. 109-11. Peirce, "Structural Reform of Bureaucracy Grows Rapidly," p. 505.

8. Kaufman, *Limits of Organizational Change*, pp. 23-29. Berkley, "Reorganizing Administration in Massachusetts," p. 68. In "Massachusetts Revisited," p. 134, Casselman reinforces the point that resource limitations may be imposed by political opposition to reorganization as well as by an actual resource shortage.

9. Lipson discusses the strategy question of involving big business in *American Governor*, p. 112. For an extensive treatment of the strategy issues surrounding the reorganization study, see James L. Garnett, "State Executive Branch Reorganization: Perspectives, Structures and Strategies" (Ph.D. dissertation, The Maxwell School, Syracuse University, 1978), pp. 145-60.

10. Theodore Lowi, "Toward Functionalism in Political Science: The Case of Innovation in Party Systems," *American Political Science Review* 57 (September 1963):570-83.

11. National Governors' Association, *The Critical Hundred Days: A Handbook for the New Governor* (Washington, D.C.: National Governors' Association, 1975), pp. 20-21.

12. Ibid., pp. 18-19.

13. Gilmore, "Louisiana Clings to Reform," p. 165.

14. Bosworth, "The Politics of Management Improvement in the States," p. 85.

15. Bosworth's perceived acceptance of greater change during perods of "fat" and "lean" is consistent with Allison's conclusion that greater organizational learning and change occurs during periods of: (1) "budgetary feast," when resources are available for experimentation, possible failure, and resultant learning, (2) "prolonged

budgetary famine" where major changes in the form of retrenchment are enforced, and (3) "dramatic performance failures" which result in drastic change (usually initiated externally) but with less internal resistance to change. Allison, "Conceptual Models and the Cuban Missile Crisis," *American Political Science Review* 63 (September 1969):701.

16. Bosworth, "The Politics of Management Improvement in the States," p. 85.

17. Harvey Walker, *Public Administration in the United States* (New York: Farrar and Rinehart, 1937), pp. 81–82.

18. Lipson, *The American Governor*, p. 125.

19. Ibid.

20. Ibid.

21. James E. Carter quoted in Peirce, "Structural Reform of Bureaucracy Grows Rapidly," p. 506.

22. According to Argyris and Schön, a person's "espoused theory" is that theory of action to which one gives, or claims to give, allegiance. This is contrasted with one's "theory in use" which actually governs one's actions and is based on actual behavior rather than pronouncements. Chris Argyris and Donald A. Schön, *Theory in Practice: Increasing Professional Effectiveness* (San Francisco: Jossey-Bass, 1974), p. 7. Based on this distinction it might be noted that there is either a discrepancy between Carter's "espoused theory" and "theory in use" or that his "espoused theory" has changed since becoming president. Federal executive branch reorganization may call for a different set of strategies than does state reorganization.

23. Charles Mohr, "President Signs Bill to Permit Government Reorganization; First Effort Would Be in His Own Office," *New York Times*, April 7, 1977.

24. Dodd, "Reorganizing State Government," pp. 167–68. John M. Mathews, *American State Government* (New York: D. Appleton and Co., 1922), pp. 283–84. Bromage, "State Reorganization," p. 667. Buck, *Reorganization of State Governments in the United States* p. 34. Lipson, *American Governor*, pp. 122–25. John C. Bollens, *Administrative Reorganization in the State since 1939* (Berkeley: Bureau of Public Administration, University of California, 1947), p. 7. Bosworth, "The Politics of Management Improvement in the States," pp. 92–93. MacDonald, *American State Government and Administration*, p. 353.

25. Dodd, "Reorganizing State Government," p. 167.

26. Bromage, "State Reorganization," p. 667.

27. Bosworth, "The Politics of Management Improvement in the States," pp. 92–93.

28. Mathews, *American State Government*, pp. 283–84. National Municipal League, *Model State Consitution*, 6th ed. (New York: National Municipal League, 1963), p. 70.

29. Lipson, *American Governor*, p. 124.

30. For a more extensive treatment of the background and application of this type of the reorganization plan mechanism see Lynn W. Eley, *The Executive Reorganization Plan: A Survey of State Experience* (Berkeley: Institute of Governmental Studies, University of California, 1967).

31. Ibid., p. 1.

32. Presidential reorganization authority is discussed in detail in: W. Brooke

Graves, *Reorganization of the Executive Branch of the United States: A Compilation of Basic Information and Significant Documents, 1912-48* (Washington, D.C.: Library of Congress Legislative Reference Service, 1949). Barry D. Karl, *Executive Reorganization and Reform in the New Deal: The Genesis of Administrative Management, 1900-1939* (Cambridge: Harvard University Press, 1963), pp. 190ff. Herbert Emmerich, *Federal Organization and Administrative Management* (University, Ala.: University of Alabama Press, 1971), pp. 162-65, 245-66.

33. Bosworth, "The Politics of Management Improvement in the States," p. 97.

34. Judith Nicholson, "State Administrative Organization Activities, 1976-1977," in *The Book of the States, 1978-79* (Lexington, Ky.: Council of State Governments, 1978), p. 106.

35. Eley, *Executive Reorganization Plan,* pp. 18-19.

36. Ibid., p. 26.

37. Council of State Governments, *Reorganization in the States* (Lexington, Ky.: Council of State Governments, 1972), p. 10. The report listed California's use of a reorganization plan in its 1968 reorganization to "super agencies" as an exception to this tendency.

38. Lipson, *American Governor,* pp. 99-100.

39. Ibid., p. 100.

40. Ibid.

41. Ibid.

42. Ibid.

43. Bosworth, "The Politics of Management Improvement in the States," pp. 88-89.

44. National Governors' Association, *The Critical Hundred Days,* p. 18.

45. U.S. Advisory Commission on Intergovernmental Relations, *Factors Affecting Voter Reactions to Governmental Reorganization in Metropolitan Areas* (Washington, D.C.: U.S. Advisory Commission on Intergovernmental Relations, 1962), p. 27.

46. Hubert R. Gallagher, "State Reorganization Surveys," *Public Administration Review* 9 (Autumn 1949):256.

47. Ibid.

48. Ibid.

49. Bosworth, "The Politics of Management Improvement in the States," p. 92.

50. Gallagher, "State Reorganization Surveys," p. 255. This stance is consistent with the charge of the President's Committee on Administrative Management. At the organizational meeting of members and staff May 9 and 10, 1936, the staff was told not to be distracted by substantive operational or internal problems in the bureaus being investigated. Staff members were to analyze on the basis of factual research that was sufficient to prevent only "egregious errors." Minutes of the President's Committee on Administrative Management collected in the papers of Louis Brownlow, as cited in Karl, *Executive Reorganization and Reform in the New Deal.*

51. Bosworth, "The Politics of Management Improvement in the States," p. 94.

52. Dwight Waldo, "Organizational Analysis: Some Notes on Methods and Criteria," *Public Administration Review* 7 (Autumn 1947):240.

53. Ibid. Harvey Walker has made substantially the same assertion: "It is to them [improved management procedures in budgeting, purchasing, personnel, etc.]

rather than to [structural] reorganization per se that most of the financial advantages from reorganization schemes should be credited." *Public Administration in the United States*, pp. 83-84.

54. Gallagher, "State Reorganization Surveys," p. 256.

55. Donald S. Van Meter and Carl E. Van Horn, "The Policy Implementation Process," *Administration and Society* 6 (February 1975):448.

56. Jeffrey L. Pressman and Aaron B. Wildavsky, *Implementation* (Berkeley: University of California Press, 1973), p. xiii. Erwin C. Hargrove, *The Missing Link: The Study of the Implementation of Social Policy* (Washington, D.C.: Urban Institute, 1975), pp. 2-3.

57. Hargrove, *Missing Link*, p. 3.

58. Robert C. Casselman, "An Old State Takes a New Look at Public Management," *Public Administration Review* 31 (July/August 1971):427.

59. Casselman, "Massachusetts Revisited," p. 129.

60. Anita F. Gottlieb, "State Executive Reorganization: A Study of Hallucination, Supposition, and Hypothesis" (Ph.D. dissertation, George Washington University, 1976), p. 132.

61. Berkley, "Reorganizing Administration in Massachusetts," p. 69.

62. T. B. Smith, "The Policy Implementation Process," *Policy Sciences* 4 (1973): 197-98.

63. Casselman, "Massachusetts Revisited," p. 133.

64. Herbert Kaufman, *Administrative Feedback* (Washington, D.C.: Brookings, 1973), p. 2. Van Meter and Van Horn, "The Policy Implementation Process," pp. 448-50.

65. National Governors' Association, *The Critical Hundred Days*, p. 21.

66. Robert Backoff, "Operationalizing Administrative Reform for Improved Governmental Performance," *Administration and Society* 6 (May 1974):87.

67. Peirce, "Structural Reform of Bureaucracy Grows Rapidly," p. 506.

68. Ibid.

69. Gottlieb, "State Executive Reorganization," p. 131.

70. For discussion of budget strategies in general, see S. Kenneth Howard, *Changing State Budgeting* (Lexington, Ky.: Council of State Governments, 1973), pp. 55-57. Aaron Wildavsky, *The Politics of the Budgetary Process*, 2d ed. (Boston: Little, Brown & Co., 1974), pp. 167-76.

71. Casselman, "Massachusetts Revisited," p. 132.

72. Van Meter and Van Horn, "The Policy Implementation Process," pp. 450-51.

# 5
# Methodologies for Studying Reorganization: A Next Step

*A good catchword can obscure analysis for 50 years.*

— Wendell W. Willkie

*One frequently has the impression that a student of administration would like as little to be caught consorting with a Theory as a member of the Anti-Saloon League to be photographed in the back room of the White Rose.*

— Dwight Waldo, *The Administrative State:*
*A Study of the Political Theory*
*of American Public Administration*

Despite the centrality of state executive branch reorganization to both the academic and practicing spheres of public administration, our knowledge about this phenomenon has not come very far. Part of the reason for our lack of knowledge is the awesome complexity of large-scale administrative, political, and economic reform. Another reason is that the catchwords of state reorganization dogma have served to delay and obscure analysis. Charles Hyneman, Dwight Waldo, Anita Gottlieb, and others have called attention to gaps between the dogma of state reorganization and administrative reality.

A third reason for our very tentative knowledge lies in the limited nature of the research methods applied thus far to the study of state executive reorganization. This methodological "state of the art" has been limited by three problems: (1) the narrow range of research methods used, (2) the fact that those methods have had limited power, and (3) the fact that the methods usually have been applied with less rigor than they are capable of.

This chapter begins with a review of the dominant research methods applied to state reorganization and closes with a description and discussion of methodological approaches I have taken in my research. Just as different theoretical perspectives are useful for understanding distinct facets of a phenomenon, different methods of inquiry also enable us to uncover different kinds of knowledge, to see different relationships, and to verify existing knowledge gained through other methods.

## Dominant Research Methods
## Applied to State Reorganization

The most prevalent approaches for studying state executive reorganization have been the single case study and the comparative case study. In addition, there has been limited use of quantitative, comparative research.

### Single Case Study Method

The most frequently applied method has been the case study of a single
state executive branch reorganization. This has been the predominant approach both in the earlier studies of reorganization[1] and in the more recent
investigations.[2] These single-state studies predominantly report such information as structural changes, the legal process used in adoption, major efforts of study commissions, and occasionally the roles of the governor and
the legislature. Most of these case studies concentrate on the adoption process and either take implementation for granted or neglect to discuss this
phase. More recent case studies have been more likely to discuss implementation problems and the interest-group politics involved in both the adoption and the implementation phases, but they are essentially as atheoretical
as the earlier single-case accounts.

In fact, the notions of observing and comparing general variables, of
drawing generalizations, or of testing hypotheses are alien to many writers
in this case-study tradition. Because there has been almost no attention
paid to hypothesis formulation and testing and to generalizing from one
case and state to another, there has been little cumulative quality to this
state reorganization research.

The same basic criticism could be made about the single-case state
reorganization studies as a group as has been made about single case
studies of state policy in general:

> All too often in the literature of state politics one or another state has been
> selected to illustrate a point; this allows colorful description, but it introduces
> biases into the analysis; for such casual selections can hardly serve as a valid
> basis for generalizations.[3]

The tendencies for case studies (1) to encompass a set of events occurring
in a relatively discrete period and (2) to concentrate on institutional actors
operating within a task environment generally have had the effect of em-
phasizing proximate variables and explanations more than antecedent, environmental variables. Other problems with the single-case approach are:
"unclear specification of dimensions, inability to make precise statements
about the impact of individual variables,"[4] and the potential lack of objec-

tivity on the part of researchers reporting on a state reorganization in which they were involved.[5]

In summary, some methodological shortcomings of single-case state reorganization studies have been a result of basic limitations in the method itself (e.g., lack of generalizability) and others (e.g., lack of hypothesis testing and unclear specification of variables) appear to be more the function of the writers' application of the single-case method.

## Comparative Case Study Method

The potentially more powerful comparative case study has been underutilized in studying state executive reorganization. The most notable comparative case studies on reorganization are by Joan Ehrlich, Leslie Lipson, and Frederick Mosher.[6]

Ehrlich's is a comparison, not of detailed, historical cases, but of major elements of reorganization in four states in order to draw generalizations about reorganization type and tactics that would be relevant to the reorganization in Virginia. While Ehrlich does attempt to draw modest generalizations, there is no rationale for the choice of cases other than that they each represented a major type of reorganization (Kentucky representing a hybrid type). With such a small sample, the generalizations run a high risk of being biased.

As James Keeley has observed,

A single-case study is quite vulnerable to the peculiarities of its particular case; a comparative case study, unless the number of cases used is quite large relative to the total population of relevant cases, may only marginally be less vulnerable to its cases, in the absence of some strategy of case selection.[7]

Lipson's study has essentially the same methodological strengths and weaknesses as Ehrlich's. Lipson has done a commendable job of comparing state reorganizations on a series of variables, including role of the governor in achieving reorganization, importance of patronage, type of opposition to reorganization, tactics utilized, and type of agencies involved. While Lipson's basic case sample is also four reorganizations, he does provide better theoretical justification for his selection of cases by specifically noting characteristics of the states he chose.

In neither of these comparative case studies is there a deliberate attempt to develop or test hypotheses. Mosher's edited volume of reorganization cases, about half of which relate to state agency reorganization, does attempt to develop hypotheses. Among his objectives were to "develop new hypotheses as to regularities and variables in reorganization processes in governmental agencies" and "to explore the applicability and the validity of the participation hypothesis in public administration."[8] Although this particular hypothesis is tested, no set of hypotheses has been formally generated for further research.

In terms of case selection, there was no control by randomization, but Mosher did attempt to control by selecting cases similar in all relevant variables except for those under investigation. The random-sampling method would have reduced bias in case selection, but the latter method served to "minimize the variance in background factors while maximizing the variance in the independent and dependent variables."[9] The Mosher study has been the most rigorous of the comparative case studies on state reorganization. He paid more attention than most to definitional issues, selection of cases, and hypothesis formulation and testing. This study could perhaps have been even more useful had the hypothesis-generation objective been realized and the participation hypothesis subjected to statistical tests. Despite some limitations inherent in the case-study method, there is a growing realization that the case approach, particularly the comparative case method, holds more potential for rigorous analysis and theory building than previously recognized.[10]

### Quantitative, Comparative Research on State Executive Reorganization

Despite the behavioral revolution in the study of state politics, the quantitative, comparative method has rarely been used to study state reorganization. Karl Bosworth's survey of thirty state "Little Hoover" reorganization attempts between 1948 and 1953 has been the major attempt at quantitative, comparative research on state executive branch reorganization.[11] The ambitious scope of his research, which was conducted more than twenty years ago, has not yet been duplicated — even after the surge of research activity in comparative state politics. However, there are many limitations as well as insights in Bosworth's work. Some of the limitations were mentioned in Chapter 4, but I will summarize them here.

1.  Bosworth's failure to present his raw data makes it difficult to replicate or intelligently interpret his results.
2.  The narrow six-year time span covered makes it extremely risky to make inferences about state reorganization during other periods or about historical trends in state executive reorganization.
3.  There is no attempt at a priori hypothesis formulation, although a number of hypotheses are implicit in the way the research was structured.
4.  Bosworth's conclusions and generalizations are sometimes made on

the basis of inadequate empirical evidence. For example, his conclusion that the use of national consulting firms is not strategically sound was based on the experience of only two states — the only two on which he had postwar data.[12]

## Research Process Used for This Study

The research that went into this book was designed to draw upon the many insights developed in earlier studies, to translate some of these insights into hypotheses to be tested, to collect empirical data for testing the hypotheses, and to test the hypotheses using statistical techniques. The purpose of this section is to give the reader an understanding of that research process. Toward this end, a few variables, hypotheses, and indicators are discussed to illustrate techniques or problems it involved. A complete list and fuller discussion of variables, hypotheses, and indicators appears in a later section of this chapter.

### Literature Search and Interviews

The scholarly literature on state reorganization was combed to identify issues, constructs, implicit propositions, variables, methods, and data sources that could be utilized for my own study. In addition, I conducted interviews with researchers and state officials to identify those issues deemed most salient and to produce further leads. A list of interviews can be found in the bibliography.

### Development of Conceptual Framework

The next phase centered on developing a conceptual framework that would tie together the fundamental research questions posited in Chapter 1. It should be noted that these first two phases did not take place in strict temporal order. What did happen was more of an iterative process that went through several cycles of idea gathering and concept formulation.

To explore empirically my conceptual framework, I devised a research design that incorporates both cross-sectional and longitudinal analysis. The period 1900 to 1975 was examined for executive branch reorganizations or attempts to reorganize in the forty-eight contiguous states. The first recorded attempt at large-scale state executive branch reorganization occurred in 1914. For my purposes an executive branch reorganization was defined as meeting the following criteria: (1) there is typically a reorganization study group of some type that examines a *range* of functional areas and management issues; (2) one or more reports or sets of research proposals are developed and circulated, and (3) there is *proposed* the creation, abolition, or reorganization of at least four discrete agencies that involve four or more functional areas (e.g., health, transportation, environment, education, labor) or administrative support services (e.g., audit, budget, personnel, purchasing, and planning).

There are both theoretical and methodological reasons for establishing such cut-off points. Theoretically, there is justification for believing that executive and legislative policy makers respond differently to moderate- and broad-scale administrative reform efforts than to more limited efforts. Methodologically, there is nothing mystical about the number of four as a cut-off; however, reorganizations smaller than this tend to be too numerous and too difficult to obtain information for on a systematic basis.

### Search for Variables

I used several techniques for developing variables. Some variables were directly suggested by statements found in the literature. For example, the variable Timing of Adoption Effort — that stage in a governor's tenure in office in which reorganization is attempted or adopted — is derived from Theodore Lowi's discussion of considerations in the timing of reform.[13]

Another technique involved the conversion of types into variables. Jerald Hage has advised, "By reading the discussion of a typology or by finding an implicit one, . . . we discover not only a few general variables but some implied hypotheses as well."[14]

Implicit in George Bell's typology of reorganization is the notion that certain types approach the reform ideal more closely than do other types. The variable Degree of Reorganization Reform is based on Bell's three major types of reorganization. Likewise, Harvey Walker's distinction between comprehensive and piecemeal tactics for reorganizing suggested the variable Comprehensiveness of Adoption Tactics.

### Hypothesis Formulation

Once again, Hage's techniques were followed, this time for developing theoretical statements. I examined the existing literature for explicit and implicit propositions relating to state reorganization. In all but one instance, where there were data limitations, these statements were then converted into simple continuous theoretical statements. Continuous theoretical statements were derived because of their greater precision, greater capacity for reflecting complexity, and greater information potential.[15]

For example, Bosworth reasoned that the optimal political condition for reorganization existed when the governorship and both houses of the legislature were held by the same party with all three components sponsoring reorganization.[16] If the party of the governor, typically the party sponsoring reorganization, also held one house, or preferably both houses, chances for adopting a reorganization would be improved. To test this implicit proposition, I devised the variable Governor's Party Control of Legislature in stage three. The general hypothesis then became: The higher the degree of governor's party control of the legislature, the higher the probability of reorganization adoption.

Some hypotheses came from constructs in the literature that could not be tested because there were insufficient data. An example is the following: The greater the governor's role in a reorganization adoption campaign, the greater the probability of adoption. This hypothesis was derived from Lipson's case-study comparisons.[17]

### Finding Operational Indicators

Two basic procedures were used for finding indicators. Some indicators became almost self-evident after close examination of the theoretical definitions of each variable and the hypotheses themselves. Governor's Party Control of the Legislature is a case in point. Information drawn from the hypothesis can be added to that obtained from the theoretical definition of that variable: the degree to which the governor's party also has majority control over legislative houses at the time reorganization is attempted. Based on these cues, an index of governor's party control was constructed such that: 1 = governor's party controls governorship when reorganization is attempted; 2 = governor's party also holds majority control of one house of the legislature; 3 = governor's party holds majority control of both houses.

Indicators for still other variables were derived from literature search. The prolific literature on comparative state politics yielded several indicators. For example, State Government Innovation Capacity was operationalized as Jack Walker's Composite Innovation Score, and Richard Hofferbert's State Industrialization Rank is a proxy for Level of Modernization.[18]

### Data Collection

Almost all data used in this study were obtained from archival records — state statutes; constitutions; executive orders; governor's reorganization plans; official and unofficial reorganization study reports; consultant reports; and newspaper, journal, and monograph accounts of reorganization. In addition, two documents proved invaluable as sources of archival information: *The Book of the States,* compiled biennially by The Council of State Governments, and the *Guide to U.S. Elections,* compiled by the staff of the *Congressional Quarterly.*[19] Besides these sources, I used two data sets for reasons of data availability and comparability. Both Walter Dean Burnham's *Partisan Division of American State Governments, 1834–1974* and Richard Hofferbert's *Socioeconomic, Public Policy, and Political Data, 1890–1960* had the advantage that many of the "bugs" had already been worked out.[20] The indicators taken from both of these data sets were developed from archival records, as were the indicators for my other variables.

I used archival records for two basic reasons. First, it is doubtful whether other means of data collection, such as interview or questionnaire, could have supplied the data necessary for so extensive a longitudinal study of state reorganization. Many people who were knowledgeable about earlier reorganizations are either difficult to identify or, if known, are no longer living. Second, executive branch reorganization is often a highly charged emotional issue: there are winners and losers. The danger of distortion is high when reactive measures are applied in such a sensitive setting. Eugene Webb and others have "argued strongly for the use of archival records" in social science research to prevent some of the problems asociated with reactive measures used in survey research.[21] Of course, archival data on state reorganization are by no means immune to the problems of distortion. "When records are seen as sources of vulnerability, they may be systematically altered."[22] Such distortion is a possibility with regard to a consultant's report on a reorganization for which he was engaged or a governor's staff report on an embarrassing failure. To guard against such distortion, I used multiple sources of data where they were available. For example, information from consulting reports was checked against information in case accounts, state documents, or interviews.

An illustration of this validity problem is the Council of State Governments' emphasis on "positive" information on reorganization. In order not to embarrass members of the Council, unsuccessful attempts to reorganize are not routinely reported in *The Book of the States* or other Council documents.[23] This is one example of *selective deposit,* the likelihood that certain kinds of information will be recorded more adequately than other kinds. It is plausible to assume that, because most accounts on reorganization are written by study commissions, consultants, or other proponents, information favorable to reorganization is more likely to be recorded. *Selective survival* also appears to favor pro-reorganization information even though state legal codes and case accounts are likely sources of data on reorganization failures.

Despite the potential for distortion in some of the nonreactive archival measures used in this study, such records remain the best sources of data on state reorganization. The purpose of the interviews used in my research was to generate ideas rather than to collect data, although interviews were also used to validate archival data.

It would appear appropriate to say here that my original research plan called for collecting data on political, administrative, and economic performance in order to assess the *impacts* of state executive reorganization. Some such indicators were obtained, but a more comprehensive assessment of reorganization performance must await more and better data.

### Data Analysis

After data were collected and coded, analysis was performed using the *Statistical Package for the Social Sciences.*[24] Discussion of the analytical techniques applied can be found in Chapter 6 along with the findings of data analysis.

## A Conceptual Framework on State Reorganization

My purpose in Chapter 2 was to emphasize the varied understandings that different theoretical perspectives could bring to the study of state executive branch reorganization. For that reason, several perspectives were included because they brought to bear additional insights and different shades of understanding even though their basic theoretical thrust was similar. For example, the Socioeconomic Determinants approach was set apart by its particular logic and its methodological contributions. Yet the underlying socioeconomic variables dealing with changes in population, affluence, urbanization, industrialization, and so forth are consistent with a perspective that views these as forces in the modernization process. Likewise, the Administrative Orthodoxy approach highlights the important role of administrative principles in state reorganization, yet the missionarylike way in which those principles have been spread amounts to diffusion of innovation.

A synthesized conceptual framework on state executive branch reorganization is presented in Figure 5.1. While this synthesis loses something in degree of detail and shades of emphasis, it has the advantage of greater theoretical parsimony, and it lends itself to operationalization. The Reorganization as Adaptation to Modernization and Reorganization as

FIGURE 5.1

A Conceptual Framework on State Executive Branch Reorganization

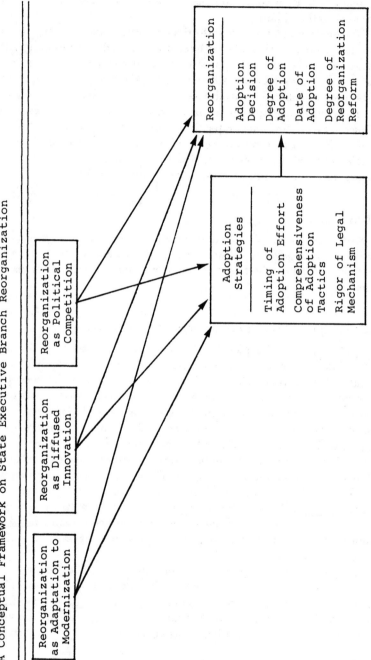

Diffused Innovation perspectives, respectively, retain the theoretical thrust of the Socioeconomic Determinants and Administrative Orthodoxy approaches.

It should be strongly noted that my intent in Figure 5.1 is to show relationships among perspectives, reorganization strategies, and reorganization characteristics. Both the complexity of the reorganization phenomenon and the limitations in the data, much of which is ordinal level, inhibit a strict causal interpretation. Statistical techniques for identifying causal patterns, such as path analysis or regression analysis, are generally thought to require at least interval-level data in order not to overtax the assumptions behind these techniques.[25] Another school of thought allows or even encourages the use of interval-level statistics on ordinal data in most circumstances.[26]

I am not at all opposed to statistical experimentation and development of new techniques for analyzing lower-level data, but it would appear judicious to be cautious about analyzing a phenomenon where there is little prior analysis to go on. Application of causal modeling techniques at this stage of research on state reorganization may give the impression that more exactitude exists than is actually the case.

As conceived in the framework of this study, variables that involve reorganization characteristics — such as whether a reorganization is adopted or not (Adoption Decision), how much of a reorganization is adopted (Degree of Adoption), and how extensive its reforms are (Degree of Reorganization Reform) — are influenced by factors inherent in the political, diffusion, and modernization perspectives. Part of the influence of these perspectives factors is thought to be reflected through the intervening strategy variables — Timing of Adoption Effort, Comprehensiveness of Tactics, and Rigor of Legal Mechanism. These key strategy variables are also thought to have a direct influence on reorganization outcomes, as the literature strongly suggests. The strategy applied is thought to be influenced in turn by the political, socioeconomic, and diffusion variables.

As shown in Figure 5.1, these three perspectives range from proximate (Reorganization as Political Competition) to distant (Reorganization as Adaptation to Modernization) in terms of their anticipated influence on state executive reorganization.

### Variables and Indicators

The variables used in this research and their theoretical definitions, operational indicators, and sources for indicators are summarized in Table 5.1. Explanatory notes and comments about particular variables are included in the notes to Table 5.1.

TABLE 5.1

Variables, Theoretical Definitions, Indicators, and Sources

| Variable | Theoretical Definition | Indicator | Sources for Indicator |
|---|---|---|---|
| REORGANIZATION AS POLITICAL COMPETITION: | | | |
| Degree of Electoral Competition for Governorship | The degree of electoral competition for gubernatorial election. | Index of Competitiveness for Gubernatorial election preceding reorganization. Index of Competitiveness is calculated as two times the percent of vote for second party. | Richard I. Hofferbert, Socioeconomic, Public Policy, and Political Data, 1890-1960. Congressional Quarterly, Guide to U.S. Elections. |
| Governor's Party Control of Legislature[a] | The degree to which the governor's party also has majority control over legislative houses at the time reorganization is attempted. | Governor's Party Control Index Coding:<br>3 = same party majority control over governorship and both houses at time of reorganization.<br>2 = same party control over governorship and one house.<br>1 = same party control of governorship only. | W. Dean Burnham, Partisan Division of American State Governments, 1834-1974. New York Times. |

REORGANIZATION
AS DIFFUSED
INNOVATION:

| | | Coding: | |
|---|---|---|---|
| Diffusion Agent Activity | The occurrence of activities which serve to diffuse innovations of executive reorganization content, structure, or strategy among states. | Absence = no diffusion agent activity in reorganization mentioned by at least three separate reorganization documents or accounts. <br><br> Presence = some diffusion agent activity present in the form of outside consultants working on study; visits from or to other states for exchange of reorganization information and ideas; emulation or incorporation of features of another government's reorganization strategies or proposals; or some other form.[b] | State reorganization study reports, official or unofficial accounts of reorganization efforts. |
| State Government Innovation Capacity | The capacity of a state government to adopt policy, service, or structural innovations. | Composite Innovation Score.[c] | Jack L. Walker, "Innovation in State Politics," in Jacob and Vines, eds., Politics in the American States, 2nd ed. (1971), p. 358. |

TABLE 5.1 (cont.)

| Variable | Theoretical Definition | Indicator | Sources for Indicator |
|---|---|---|---|
| REORGANIZATION AS ADAPTATION TO MODERNIZATION: | | | |
| Level of Modernization | A state's level in a composite of indices associated with modernization. | Rank on Industrialization Factor Score taken every tenth year, 1900-1970.d | Richard I. Hofferbert, Socioeconomic, Public Policy, and Political Data, 1890-1960. Inter-University Consortium for Political and Social Research.d |
| STRATEGY VARIABLES: | | | |
| Timing of Adoption Effort | The stage in a governor's tenure of office in which executive branch reorganization is attempted. | Coding: 1 = Early Timing = attempt to adopt is made during first one-third of governor's tenure in office. Tenure is counted in months. 2 = Middle Timing = attempt is during second one-third. | State reorganization study reports; state legislation, executive orders, constitutions; Council of State Governments' documents; consultant reports and monographs; research institute documents. Congressional Quarterly, Guide to U.S. Elections. |

3 = Late Timing = attempt is during last one-third of tenure.e

Coding:

2 = Comprehensive Tactics are pursued when all reorganization proposals are submitted as part of one all-encompassing measure.

1 = Incremental Tactics are pursued when reorganization proposals are submitted in multiple measures whether at the same time or phased over time.f

State reorganization study reports; state legislation, executive orders, constitutions; Council of State Governments' documents; consultant reports and monographs; research institute documents.

Comprehensiveness of Tactics

The degree to which reorganization adoption tactics reflect a comprehensive all-eggs-in-one-basket approach.

Coding:

1 = Executive Order or Reorganization Plan.

2 = Reorganization Statute.

3 = Statute followed by Executive Order or Reorganization Plan.

4 = Constitutional Amendment or Provision.

Same sources as for Comprehensiveness of Tactics.

Rigor of Legal Mechanism

The level of difficulty attempted in terms of legal mechanism(s) utilized to formally adopt executive branch reorganization.

TABLE 5.1 (cont.)

| Variable | Theoretical Definition | Indicator | Sources for Indicator |
|---|---|---|---|
| | | 5 = Executive Order or Reorganization Plan following Constitutional Amendment or Provision.<br><br>6 = Statute following Constitutional Provision or Amendment.<br><br>7 = Reorganization Plan or Executive Order following Constitutional Provision or Amendment and Statute (this requires three legal steps).g | |
| REORGANIZATION VARIABLES: | | | |
| Adoption Decision | The outcome of executive branch reorganization, considered as either a failure (no adoption at all) or a success (at least partial adoption). | Coding:<br>0 = No adoption at all; no facet of reorganization proposal(s) approved.<br>1 = At least one facet of reorganization was adopted. | Same sources as for Comprehensiveness of Tactics. |

| | | Coding | Source |
|---|---|---|---|
| Degree of Adoption | In cases where there is some adoption, the degree to which an executive branch reorganization plan is adopted. | Coding:<br>1 = LOW = $\geq 1\%$ $\leq 33\%$ of major recommendations or major agency proposals were adopted.<br>2 = MODERATE = $\geq 34\%$ $\leq 66\%$ adoption.<br>3 = HIGH = $\geq 67\%$ adoption.h | Same sources as for Comprehensiveness of Tactics. |
| Date of Adoption | Year(s) that an executive branch reorganization is adopted in a state. | Years that executive branch reorganizations were adopted in a state. Cut-off date for this study is 1975. Reorganizations more recent than this are frequently still taking shape. | Same sources as for Comprehensiveness of Tactics. |
| Frequency of Reorganization | The number of executive branch reorganizations in each state during the scope of this study, 1900 to 1975. | Number of executive branch reorganizations in each state from 1900 to 1975.i | Same sources as for Comprehensiveness of Tactics. |
| Degree of Reorganization Reform | The degree to which a state executive branch reorganization reflects the reform ideal of administrative orthodoxy. | Modified Bell typology of reorganizations as set forth in Chapter 3.<br>1 = Traditional Type = low degree of administrative reform. | George Bell, "Executive Reorganization and Its Effect on Budgeting." _Proceedings of the 29th Annual Meeting of the National_ |

TABLE 5.1 (cont.)

| Variable | Theoretical Definition | Indicator | Sources for Indicator |
|---|---|---|---|
| | | 2 = Secretary-Coordinator Type = moderately high degree of administrative reform.<br>3 = Cabinet Type = high degree of administrative reform.] | Association of State Budget Officers, August 1973. George Bell, "State Administrative Activities 1972-1973," Book of the States, 1974-1975 (Lexington, Ky.: Council of State Governments, 1974), p. 138. |

[a]Since it is the governor who has traditionally had more interest in pursuing executive branch reorganization, the focus here is on the number of components of state government controlled by the governor's party prior to reorganization.

[b]It is less difficult to ascertain the presence of diffusion agent activity than to make the determination that no such activity has taken place, since most documents do not flatly say there was no diffusion activity. The standard employed here to determine absence of diffusion agent activity--no mention in three separate sources--is not conclusive, but it is workable. There is a danger that this measure might be more sensitive in identifying the more visible forms of diffusion activity, such as deployment of a national consulting firm, than the less visible forms that might only be known by insiders.

[c]This measure provides a more general indication of a state government's capacity for innovativeness that is less reorganization-specific than is the Diffusion Agent Activity measure. This becomes an interesting variable to look at in determining whether states which are the most innovative on a broad range of policy measures are also the most innovative in executive branch reorganization. Jack Walker based his Composite Innovation Score on an analysis of eighty-eight different program innovations that were adopted in at least twenty-two states prior to 1965. These program innovations represented a number of functional areas: welfare, health, education, conservation, planning, administrative organization, highways, civil rights, corrections and police, labor, taxes, and professional regulation. Jack L. Walker, "Innovation in State Politics," p. 357.

[d]A state's rank on the Hofferbert Industrialization Factor Score is used as a proxy for modernization levels because it incorporates a number of indicators associated with modernization, e.g. percent population illiterate, percent population urban, personal income per capita, percentage employed in manufacturing, number of telephones per 1,000 population. Richard I. Hofferbert, "Socioeconomic Dimensions of the American States, 1890-1960," Midwest Journal of Political Science 12 (1960), 405-409 shows the indices incorporated into the Industrialization Factor for each year. The utility of this indicator is marred somewhat because the indices used are not entirely the same from year to year. A more substantial shortcoming is that the indicator reflects state ranking (a relative measure of modernization) rather than absolute levels of modernization attained. It is thus not possible to examine threshold effects with this indicator. As money and time permit, other modernization indices will be utilized in the analysis at a later date.

The Industrialization rankings are updated for 1970 by D. Morgan and W. Lyons, "Industrialization and Affluence Revisited: A Note on Socioeconomic Dimensions of American States, 1970," American Journal of Political Science (May 1975), p. 271.

TABLE 5.1 (cont.)

[e]The calculation on Timing of Adoption Effort is based on a governor's contiguous tenure rather than on each distinct term. This is done because the primary theoretical interest is on Lowi's notion that reform is more likely at the beginning of a new administration and decreases as problems and conflicts set in. A future analysis will examine the more cyclical-oriented facet of timing more related to a governor's individual term of office.

For purposes of this study, if a reorganization effort was begun Early but did not fail or get adopted until Middle or Late, these latter timings were assigned.

[f]Because of the criteria established for defining what constitutes an executive branch reorganization, the most incremental tactics—isolated, one-, two-, or three-agency reorganizations not part of a broader plan—are not analyzed in this study. A narrower range of tactics, those applying to broader reorganization efforts, is what this indicator is intended to capture. The most extreme incremental tactics are thus excluded from the scope of this study. This omission does not appear to be a serious one, however, since executive reorganizations which are part of an overall plan are rarely stretched out with only one or two agencies reorganized per year.

[g]The coding ranges from those legal mechanisms which require the concurrence of fewest numbers of people and which require the fewest legal steps to those which require the concurrence of larger numbers of people and multiple legal steps.

hThis assessment is extremely difficult without asking those involved in state reorganizations which proposals were intended to be "sacrificial lambs" and which they considered vital to the entire reform. The problem of assigning weights to specific proposals is compounded by the large numbers of recommendations (many extremely specific and minute) contained in some reorganization proposals. An attempt has been made to create a reasonable proxy for degree of adoption by comparing the ratio of major reorganization proposals recommended with those adopted by statute, reorganization plan, constitutional amendment, or other mechanism. The proponents and planners often themselves identify those recommendations they consider to be major in the reorganization study report. Where "major" recommendations are not identified, the Degree of Adoption reflects the ratio of agencies to be established by reorganization to those actually enacted. The documentation that is necessary to determine degree of adoption, particularly documentation for the earlier state reorganizations, is often unavailable.

iThis study excludes Alaska and Hawaii because they were granted statehood later and have only recently considered major executive branch reorganizations.

jImplicit in the administrative orthodoxy and in the work of The Council of State Governments is the notion that the Cabinet Type most nearly approximates the orthodox reform ideal, while the Traditional Type least approximates it. The Secretary-Coordinator Type falls in between but closer to the Cabinet Type.

## Research Hypotheses

As shown by the first four chapters of this book, social scientists and government practitioners have accumulated much knowledge about state reorganizations. A great deal of that knowledge needs to be tested systematically and updated because it has been derived from a single method of research, based on a limited sample of states or narrow time periods or based on observing reorganization dynamics that may no longer apply in the 1960s and 1970s.

In an effort to bring some order to the conceptual disarray in the study of state reorganization, I have formulated forty hypotheses to test the state of our knowledge to date. Formulating and testing hypotheses is not the only way to proceed, but it does provide a base upon which other scholars can build, and it allows other pieces of knowledge to be put into some framework. Readers may be disappointed if they expect tight, well-defined theoretical linkages between variables in these hypotheses. In many instances there is not much previous knowledge upon which to build.

Research hypotheses are used here instead of null hypotheses (which postulate no relationship between the variables being examined). Each research hypothesis will be stated in full and followed by a brief discussion of the rationale behind it. The hypotheses will be presented in the same order in which the variables were displayed in Figure 5.1 — the perspective variables' hypothesized relationship with strategy and then with reorganization variables, followed by the strategy variables' relationship with reorganization outcome variables.

### Reorganization as Political Competition

*1. The higher the level of electoral competition for governorship prior to attempted reorganization in a state, the later the timing of the reorganization adoption effort.*

This hypothesis reflects the conventional wisdom that state adoption of executive reorganization will take longer in a new administration in the face of higher political risk, as measured by the level of party competitiveness for the governorship in the most recent election prior to reorganization.

*2. The higher the level of electoral competition for governorship prior to attempted reorganization in a state, the more incremental the adoption tactics pursued.*

This hypothesis tests whether there is a tendency for state decision makers to turn to a presumed "safer" tactic in the face of strong political opposition.

*3. The higher the level of electoral competition for governorship prior to attempted reorganization in a state, the less rigorous the legal-adoption mechanism utilized.*

If the contention of Walter Dodd, John Mathews, Arthur Bromage, A. E. Buck, Leslie Lipson, John Bollens, Karl Bosworth, and Austin MacDonald is correct, statutory and other lower-difficulty mechanisms are more politically feasible and therefore more likely to be utilized when political competition is stiffer.

*4. The higher the level of electoral competition for governorship prior to attempted reorganization in a state, the lower the probability of reorganization adoption.*

The assumption tested here is that stronger second-party electoral competition for a governor attempting reorganization will also be reflected in the degree of opposition to reorganization and will therefore hurt the chances of adoption.

*5. The higher the level of electoral competition for governorship prior to attempted reorganization in a state, the lower the degree of reorganization adoption.*

Not only is it expected that stiffer political opposition will decrease likelihood of adoption; in the face of sterner opposition, the proportion of a reorganization plan that is passed is likely also to be lower. Some minor or less-controversial provisions may be adopted, but the bulk of the reorganization program will be defeated.

*6. The higher the level of electoral competition for governorship prior to attempted reorganization in a state, the earlier the date of reorganization.*

In Hypothesis 1 it is expected that higher political opposition will delay reorganization adoption within a governor's tenure in office. The expectation here is that more competitive two-party states with higher turnover in office are more likely to have earlier attempts at adoption than less competitive one-party states where the administrative status quo has never been severely challenged.

*7. The higher the level of electoral competition for governorship prior to attempted reorganization in a state, the lower the degree of reorganization reform attained.*

This hypothesis tests the assumption that higher political competition and risk are more likely to inhibit the attempt of more thoroughgoing executive reorganization and to lessen the chances for major reform if it is attempted.

*8. The higher the level of governor's party control of the legislature at the time of attempted reorganization, the earlier the timing of adoption effort.*

With legislative control more loaded in favor of the governor's party, it is expected that reorganization will be attempted early in the administration, before political conditions erode.

*9. The higher the level of governor's party control of the legislature at the time of attempted reorganization, the more comprehensive the reorganization tactics pursued.*

This hypothesis tests to see if there is a tendency for governors to use bold, single-package reorganization tactics when political control is loaded in their favor, and to use lower-risk incremental tactics in the face of stiffer opposition.

*10. The higher the level of governor's party control of the legislature at the time of attempted reorganization, the more rigorous the legal adoption mechanism utilized.*

Again, where political conditions are regarded as more propitious, we could expect an increased tendency for reorganizers to use a rigorous and permanent legal mechanism to solidify their reform.

*11. The higher the level of governor's party control of the legislature at the time of attempted reorganization, the higher the probability of adoption.*

This hypothesis tests Bosworth's contention that the circumstances for reorganization are most favorable politically when the party sponsoring reorganization has complete or substantial control over state government.

*12. The higher the level of governor's party control of the legislature at the time of attempted reorganization, the higher the degree of reorganization adoption.*

Not only is it expected that the odds for adoption should improve with greater political control; it is also anticipated that the sponsoring majority party would be able to get more of their reorganization program approved.

*13. The higher the level of governor's party control of the legislature at the time of attempted reorganization, the earlier the date of adoption.*

If party control were to be operationalized differently to reflect an index of control for all gubernatorial elections over time, the hypothesized relationship would be different. Primarily one-party states would rank higher on party control but might not have the impetus or the need to reorganize. As operationalized for this research, high party control prior to reorganization facilitates favorable adoption, and is therefore expected to increase the chances of adopting at an earlier date.

*14. The higher the level of governor's party control of the legislature at the time of attempted reorganization, the higher the degree of reorganization reform attained.*

This hypothesis tests to see if there is a tendency for reorganizers with substantial political control to try for and attain a more ambitious, higher-reform type of reorganization.

*Reorganization as Diffused Innovation*

*15. In states where reorganization diffusion-agent activity is present during an attempt to reorganize, the timing of adoption effort is earlier.*

It is expected that the presence of diffusion agents, many of whom have a preassembled reform package, would expedite the reform schedule. An alternative hypothesis that bears watching is that the reorganization schedule might be delayed while a more idealistic and less localized reorganization package brought in by an external diffusion agent was "watered down" to accommodate indigenous political interests and governmental conditions.

*16. In states where reorganization diffusion-agent activity is present during an attempt to reorganize, the adoption tactics pursued are more comprehensive.*

This hypothesis essentially tests the assumption that diffusion agents, particularly the national consulting organizations such as the Institute of Public Administration, its predecessor the New York Bureau of Municipal Research, and Griffenhagen Associates, have been less willing to have their reorganization proposals presented in piecemeal fashion. Not wanting to see parts of the total package lost, they would strongly advocate the use of comprehensive tactics by the reorganization sponsor.

*17. In states where reorganization diffusion-agent activity is present during an attempt to reorganize, a more rigorous legal-adoption mechanism will be utilized.*

Again, this hypothesis reflects the assumption that more idealistic diffusion agents will advocate the utilization of a constitutional amendment or similarly rigorous legal-adoption mechanism, so that their "reform masterpiece" will not easily be undone or replaced by opposition forces. Another factor that may reinforce this tendency is the frequent need to utilize constitutional provision to enact the thoroughgoing reorganization that diffusion agents have tended to recommend.

*18. In states where reorganization diffusion-agent activity is present during an attempt to reorganize, the probability of adoption is lower.*

This follows from the assessment that the tactics, legal mechanism, and reorganization type typically advocated by diffusion agents are judged to be more difficult politically. Because many diffusion agents, particularly in the earlier waves of state reorganization, were national consulting firms, this hypothesis indirectly tests Bosworth's contention that the work of such firms has "rarely been the means of producing directly positive legislative responses."[27]

*19. In states where reorganization diffusion-agent activity is present during an attempt to reorganize, the degree of reorganization adopted is higher.*

The assumption to be tested here is that, while the ambitious tactics, legal mechanism, and reorganization type traditionally advocated by diffusion agents are less likely to result in adoption, if there is adoption, it is likely to be substantial.

*20. In states where reorganization diffusion-agent activity is present during an attempt to reorganize, the date of adoption is earlier.*

This hypothesis reflects the thinking that orthodox-reform diffusion agents have been more active in the earlier decades of this century. A tendency that bears watching is for more recent diffusion-agent activity to be oriented more toward political feasibility and less toward administrative orthodoxy. If this is a trend, the alternative hypothesis on diffusion may be more accurate for the most recent period.

*21. In states where reorganization diffusion-agent activity is present during an attempt to reorganize, the degree of reorganization reform attained is higher.*

This hypothesis tests the assumption that more idealistic reforms will be proposed by diffusion agents and, if adopted, are more likely to approximate the orthodox-reform ideal.

*Reorganization as Adaptation to Modernization*

*22. The higher the level of modernization in a state, the earlier the timing of adoption effort.*

The underlying rationale here is that more modernized states are more likely to have adequate communications and staff support systems for faster detection of performance gaps and faster preparation of reorganization proposals.

*23. The higher the level of modernization in a state, the more incremental the reorganization adoption tactics.*

It is expected that in more modernized states there is less need for drastic adjustments in state government organization, adjustments that often require the more ambitious comprehensive tactics.

*24. The higher the level of modernization in a state, the less rigorous the adoption mechanism.*

Analogously, less drastic adjustments to state organization do not typically require the more rigorous legal-adoption mechanisms such as constitutional amendment.

*25. The higher the level of modernization in a state, the higher the probability of reorganization adoption.*

Underlying this hypothesis is an assessment that decision makers in more modernized states are more aware of the need for state executive branch reorganization to maintain or increase that state's level of modernization.

*26. The higher the level of modernization in a state, the lower the degree of reorganization adoption.*

While it is expected that the probability of reorganization adoption will be higher in more modernized states, it is also anticipated that in those states there will be a larger number of proposals competing for attention and that only a few provisions of some of those proposals will be adopted.

*27. The higher the level of modernization in a state, the earlier the date of reorganization adoption.*

Following the logic of Samuel Beer and Frederick Mosher on modernization, it is expected that more modernized states will encounter the economic, social, and political pressures for state government reorganization at an earlier time than do less modernized states. In addition, the more modernized states are expected to have the necessary support levels to carry out reorganization at an earlier date.

28.  *The higher the level of modernization in a state, the higher the degree of reorganization reform.*

This hypothesis tests the assumption that more modernized states have typically evolved further toward the orthodox reform ideal of state organization than have less developed states. If this hypothesis holds, we should expect to see New York, California, Michigan, Illinois, and other more modernized states adopting Cabinet and Secretary-Coordinator reorganizations.

*Relationships Between Strategy Variables and Reorganization Outcome Variables*

TIMING OF THE ADOPTION EFFORT

29.  *The earlier the timing of adoption effort, the higher the probability of reorganization adoption.*

This hypothesis directly tests the conventional wisdom propounded by Theodore Lowi and the National Governors' Association that the early portion of a new administration is the most propitious time to attempt reform. A rival hypothesis would reflect Gilmore's caution about not attempting reorganization too early, before adequate preparation has been made.

30.  *The earlier the timing of adoption effort, the greater the degree of reorganization adoption.*

It is expected that the honeymoon period of a new administration (before political capital is expended or competing interests or complications set in) is also the time when a greater portion of a reorganization package will get more receptive treament. A competing hypothesis would be that shorter legislative and interest-group exposure to a complex proposal is likely to result in lack of understanding about what reorganization entails, leading to less complete acceptance of such proposals.

31.  *The earlier the timing of adoption effort, the earlier the date of reorganization adoption.*

Reorganizations advanced earlier are thought to be more likely to be adopted at an earlier date.

*32. The earlier the timing of adoption effort, the higher the degree of reorganization reform attained.*

The rationale here is that state reorganizations planned and advanced early in a governor's administration are more likely to be broad and thoroughgoing, while those advanced later are more likely to be patchwork efforts. I would expect governors to lay the broad organizational foundations for their administration early, making smaller adjustments later. Going against this hypothesis are late, major reorganizations by governors who want to leave an administrative legacy or who want to entrench more party appointees.

COMPREHENSIVENESS OF TACTICS

*33. The more comprehensive the reorganization adoption tactics pursued, the lower the probability of adoption.*

This hypothesis tests to see whether advocates of comprehensive tactics (e.g., Jimmy Carter) or advocates of incremental tactics (e.g., Harvey Walker) are propounding the strategy more likely to ensure some adoption.

*34. The more comprehensive the reorganization adoption tactics pursued, the higher the degree of adoption.*

If adoption does take place, the proportion of a reorganization plan accepted is likely to be high, because comprehensive tactics are basically an "all-or-nothing" strategy.

*35. The more comprehensive the reorganization adoption tactics pursued, the earlier the date of adoption.*

This hypothesis reflects the assessment that many early administrative orthodoxy reformers tended to advocate comprehensive tactics. It would also appear logical to expect tactics to become more incremental in later waves of reorganization (in the face of increasing political competitiveness) in many states.

*36. The more comprehensive the reorganization adoption tactics pursued, the higher the degree of reorganization reform attained.*

This hypothesis is based on the assumption that comprehensive tactics have been most utilized by orthodox reformers, reformers who also advocated more thoroughgoing executive branch reorganization conforming to the reform ideal.

RIGOR OF LEGAL ADOPTION MECHANISM

*37. The more rigorous the legal-adoption mechanism utilized, the lower the probability of reorganization adoption.*

As the number of legal hurdles increases and the number of people who have to agree on reorganization expands, it is expected that the odds for adoption would drop. According to this reasoning, a simpler, more direct mechanism such as a legislative bill would stand a better chance of passing than would the more involved process of constitutional amendment. This hypothesis tests the conventional wisdom espoused by Walter Dodd, John Mathews, Arthur Bromage, A. E. Buck, Leslie Lipson, John Bollens, Karl Bosworth, and Austin MacDonald that a legislative act is superior to a constitutional amendment for attaining adoption.

*38. The more rigorous the legal-adoption mechanism utilized, the higher the degree of reorganization adoption.*

Although the more rigorous legal mechanisms are generally regarded as more difficult to adopt, a stringent mechanism (e.g., constitutional amendment) that is approved is likely to be approved in toto.

*39. The more rigorous the legal-adoption mechanism utilized, the later the date of reorganization adoption.*

This hypothesis is based on the assumption that because stringent legal mechanisms are more difficult to get accepted, often they are postponed or avoided.

*40. The more rigorous the legal-adoption mechanism utilized, the higher the degree of reorganization reform.*

It is expected that less stringent mechanisms would be used for less drastic reorganizations and that the more rigorous constitutional mechanisms would be reserved and possibly required for more wide-sweeping Cabinet and Secretary-Coordinator reorganizations.

Research findings concerning these forty hypotheses will be presented in the following chapter after a discussion of some descriptive findings.

## Notes

1. Examples of one-state reorganization case studies include Frank D. Lowden, "Reorganization in Illinois and Its Results," *The Annals* (May 1924):155-60. F. E. Horack, *Reorganization of State Government in Iowa*, Iowa Applied History Series, vol. 2, no. 2 (Iowa City: Iowa State Historical Society, 1914). J. W. Manning, "The Blue Grass State Reorganizes," *National Municipal Review* 23 (April 1934):201-04. R. L. Carleton et al., *The Reorganization and Consolidation of State Administration in Louisiana* (Baton Rouge: Louisiana State University Bureau of Governmental Research, 1937). Stuart A. MacCorkle, "Administrative Reorganization in Tennessee," *The Southwestern Social Science Quarterly* 14 (March 1934):319-32. Harvey Walker, "Ohio Appraises Its Reorganized State Government," *National Municipal Review* 18 (April 1929):249-53. Richard S. Childs, "New York State Reorganizes," *National Municipal Review* 15 (May 1926):265-69. J. M. Mathews, "Administrative Reorganization in Illinois," Supplement to *National Municipal Review*, (November 1922). See the bibliography for other examples.

2. Recent accounts of reorganization in a single state included: Afak Haydor, "Gubernatorial Leadership: An Evaluation of Executive Reorganization in Arkansas," Paper presented to the Southern Political Science Association meeting in Atlanta, Georgia, 1973. T. McN. Simpson, III, "Appraising the Carter Administration," Paper, University of Tennessee, 1975. Robert C. Casselman, "Massachusetts Revisisted: Chronology of a Failure," *Public Administration Review* 33 (March/April 1973):129-35. Samuel K. Gove, "Administrative Reorganization: The Illinois Case," Paper presented at the Symposium on Administrative Reform and Public Policy, The University of Nebraska, Lincoln, Nebraska, April 13-14, 1978.

3. Herbert Jacob and Kenneth N. Vines, eds., *Politics in the American States: A Comparative Analysis*, 2d ed. (Boston: Little, Brown & Co., 1971), pp. vii-viii.

4. George W. Downs, Jr., *Bureaucracy, Innovation, and Public Policy* (Lexington, Mass.: Lexington Books, 1976), p. 67.

5. Among those writers reporting on state reorganization efforts they participated in are: Frank Lowden (Illinois); Robert Casselman (Massachusetts); Harvey Walker (Ohio); Richard S. Childs (New York); and John M. Mathews (Illinois).

6. Joan E. Ehrlich, "State Executive Reorganizations," *The University of Virginia Newsletter* 51 (March 1975):26-27. Leslie Lipson, *The American Governor: From Figurehead to Leader* (Chicago: Greenwood Press, 1939). Frederick C. Mosher, ed., *Governmental Reorganization: Cases and Commentary* (Indianapolis: Bobbs-Merrill, 1967). A. E. Buck, *Administrative Consolidation in State Governments*, 5th ed. (New York: National Municipal League, 1930); *Reorganization of State Governments in the United States* (New York: Columbia University Press, 1938). James R. Bell and Earl L. Darrah, *State Executive Reorganization* (Berkeley: Bureau of Public Administration, University of California, 1961). These works contain capsule accounts of a number of different state reorganizations. However, there is little conscious comparison among states or among reorganizations.

7. James F. Keeley, "Comparative Case Studies and Theory Building," Unpublished Paper, Stanford University, January 1976, p. 16.

8. Mosher, ed., *Governmental Reorganization: Cases and Commentary*, p. xiv.

9. Keeley, "Comparative Case Studies and Theory Building," p. 18. A more extensive treatment of this issue is found in R. T. Holt and J. E. Turner, "The Methodology of Comparative Research," in *The Methodology of Comparative Research*, R. T. Holt and J. E. Turner, eds. (New York: Free Press, 1971), pp. 1–20.

10. More extensive discussion of the potentials as well as the limitations of the case-study method can be found in: Keeley, "Comparative Case Studies and Theory Building." Harry Eckstein, "Case Study and Theory in Political Science," in *Handbook of Political Science*, vol. 7, Fred I. Grunstein and Nelson Polsby, eds. (Reading, Mass.: Addison-Wesley Publishing Co., 1975), pp. 79–137. Morris Davis and Marvin G. Weinbaum, *Metropolitan Decision Processes: An Analysis of Case Studies* (Chicago: Rand McNally, 1969). Edwin O. Bock, ed., *Essays on the Case Method in Public Administration* (Brussels: International Institute of Administrative Services, 1962). Herbert Kaufman, "The Next Step in Case Studies," *Public Administration Review* 18 (Winter 1958):56–57. Richard E. Walton, "Advantages and Attributes of the Case Study," *Journal of Applied Behavioral Science* 8 (January 1972):76–86. B. M. Russett, "International Behavior Research: Case Studies and Cumulation," in *Approaches to the Study of Political Science*, M. Hass and H. S. Kariel, eds. (Scranton: Chandler Publishing Co., 1970), pp. 425–43.

11. Karl A. Bosworth, "The Politics of Management Improvement in the States," *American Political Science Review* 47 (March 1953):84–99.

12. Ibid., p. 93.

13. Theodore Lowi, "Toward Functionalism in Political Science: The Case of Innovation in Party Systems," *American Political Science Review* 57 (September 1963):570–83.

14. Jerald Hage, *Techniques and Problems of Theory Construction in Sociology*, (New York: John Wiley & Sons, 1972), p. 19.

15. Ibid., pp. 36–40.

16. Bosworth, "The Politics of Management Improvement in the States," p. 88.

17. The process of deriving continuous theoretical statements from the comparison of diverse case studies is discussed in Hage, *Techniques and Problems of Theory Construction in Sociology*, pp. 55–56.

18. Jack Walker, "Innovation in State Politics," in *Politics in the American States: A Comparative Analysis*, 2d ed., Herbert Jacob and Kenneth Vines, eds. (Boston: Little, Brown and Co., 1971), p. 358. Richard I. Hofferbert, *Socioeconomic, Public Policy, and Political Data, 1890–1960*. Data set from the Interuniversity Consortium for Political and Social Research.

19. Congressional Quarterly, *Guide to U.S. Elections* (Washington, D.C.: Congressional Quarterly, 1975).

20. Walter Dean Burnham, *Partisan Division of American State Governments, 1834–1974*. Data set from the Interuniversity Consortium for Political and Social Research.

21. Eugene J. Webb et al., *Unobtrusive Measures: Non-reactive Research in the Social Sciences* (Chicago: Rand McNally College Publishing Co., 1966), p. 14.

22. Ibid.

23. Richard Carlson, Director of Research, Council of State Governments, interview, April 26, 1977.

24. Norman H. Nie et al., *Statistical Package for the Social Sciences*, 2d ed., rev. (New York: McGraw-Hill, 1975).

25. See for example Hubert M. Blalock, Jr., *Social Statistics* (New York: McGraw-Hill, 1972), pp. 361, 480. Dennis J. Palumbo, *Statistics in Political and Behavioral Science* (New York: Appleton-Century-Crofts, 1969), p. 177. Herman J. Loether and Donald G. McTavish, *Descriptive and Inferential Statistics: An Introduction* (Boston: Allyn and Bacon, 1976), pp. 310–11. Nie et al., *Statistical Package for the Social Sciences*, pp. 3–6, 320.

26. Among those taking the more permissive view are Robert P. Abelson and John W. Tukey, "Efficient Conversion of Non-Metric Information into Metric Information," in *The Quantitative Analysis of Social Problems*, 2d ed., Edward R. Tufte, ed. (Reading, Mass.: Addison-Wesley Publishing Co., 1970), pp. 407–17. Sanford Labovitz, "The Assignment of Numbers to Rank Order Categories," *American Sociological Review* 35 (1970):515–24; "Statistical Usage in Sociology: Sacred Cows and Ritual," *Sociological Methods and Research* 1 (1972):13–38.

27. Bosworth, "The Politics of Management Improvement in the States," p. 93.

# 6

# Findings on Reorganization Patterns, Perspectives, Strategies, and Structures

*We must use all available weapons of attack, face our problems realistically and not retreat to the land of fashionable sterility, learn to sweat over our data with an admixture of judgment and intuitive rumination, and accept the usefulness of particular data even when the level of analysis available for them is markedly below that for other data in the empirical area.*

— Arnold Binder, "Statistical Theory"

## Patterns in State Reorganization: A Summary

Before directly addressing the hypotheses, I would like to examine some descriptive findings. This is useful in two ways. First, there is value in description itself, especially when there has been no other description of state-reorganization characteristics and patterns covering the adjacent forty-eight states over a lengthy seventy-six-year span. Second, knowing these characteristics and patterns can give the reader a better understanding of the variables and data on which interpretation of the hypotheses rests. It is particularly important, I think, to sense the flavor of the research and to get a feel for the characteristics and limitations of the data. Too often social scientists and government practitioners are confronted with correlation or regression coefficients without any exposure to the frequency distributions or other characteristics of the data that underpin these relationships.

In addition to the following description of reorganization patterns over time and by region, data on each of the 151 state reorganizations is included in Appendix A. Information on each reorganization includes year of adoption or failure to adopt; type of reorganization; timing, tactics, and legal mechanism utilized; and degree of adoption accomplished.

Appendix A shows that much of this information is not available. Bear in mind, however, that this study represents the first attempt to conduct research of this scope in an effort to make comparisons and to detect reorganization patterns. Some of these patterns emerge more clearly from a summary of findings, as can be seen in Table 6.1.

*Adoption Success*

Of the 151 state executive branch reorganizations attempted in this century, information about adoption results was obtained for 92 reorganizations. Of these, 39 (42.4 percent) resulted in no adoption at all and 53 (57.6 percent) resulted in adoption of at least some proposals. Of the 53 "successes," 18 (19.6 percent of total) had a low degree of adoption, 7 (7.6 percent) resulted in a moderate degree of adoption, and 28 (30.4 percent) were found to have a high degree of adoption. Taking into account a possible bias in the records toward adoption, it would still appear that odds ran 57 percent in favor of at least some adoption taking place.

These odds have shifted over time, increasing from the 38 percent and 33 percent adoption rates in the first two waves of reorganization to the 90 percent rate of adoption in the wave following the first Hoover Commission (1947–75). See Table 6.2 for a comparison of these organizational characteristics over the three major waves of state reorganization.

Just as receptivity to reorganization adoption has varied over time, executive branch reorganization has fared differently in different regions. There is considerable disagreement over which regional groupings capture the essential character of the various regions, how many demarcations should be delineated, whether single or multiple sets of regional classifications are more appropriate, and how border states should be handled.[1] Of the several groupings examined, I found Jack Walker's most appropriate for the purposes of my study. Walker's eight regional groupings are generally more sensitive to regional political and social differences than are broader administrative demarcations such as census regions. In addition, the use of Walker's classification facilitates comparison of state executive reorganization (a structural innovation) with other policy innovations. See Table 6.3 for a comparison based on regional groupings of states.

State reorganization adoption generally has fared better in the New England, Southeast, and Far West regions. The rate of adoption has been lowest in the Mid-Atlantic, Plains, and Southwest regions. The Southeast has been the most active region in an absolute sense — thirty-seven attempts at executive branch reorganization and thirteen partial or complete adoptions. However, when the number of states in each region is taken into account, New England has been the most receptive region for executive branch reorganization, followed by the Far West and the Southeast.

TABLE 6.1

Characteristics of State Executive
Reorganization, 1900-1975:  A Summary

| | Frequency | Percent[a] |
|---|---|---|
| **ADOPTION DECISION** | | |
| Failure to Adopt | 39 | 42.4 |
| Partial or Complete Adoption | 53 | 57.6 |
| | N= 92 | 100.0 |
| **DEGREE OF ADOPTION** | | |
| Low | 18 | 34.0 |
| Moderate | 7 | 13.2 |
| High | 28 | 52.8 |
| | N= 53 | 100.0 |
| **TYPE OF REORGANIZATION** | | |
| Traditional | 54 | 52.4 |
| Secretary-Coordinator | 7 | 6.8 |
| Cabinet | 42 | 40.8 |
| | N=103 | 100.0 |
| **TIMING** | | |
| Early | 76 | 57.1 |
| Middle | 44 | 33.1 |
| Late | 13 | 9.8 |
| | N=133 | 100.0 |
| **TACTICS** | | |
| Incremental | 51 | 44.3 |
| Comprehensive | 64 | 55.7 |
| | N=115 | 100.0 |
| **LEGAL ADOPTION MECHANISM** | | |
| Executive Order or Reorganization Plan | 2 | 1.6 |
| Statute | 88 | 72.1 |
| Statute followed by Executive Order | 1 | .8 |
| Constitutional Amendment | 11 | 9.0 |
| Constitutional Amendment followed by Reorganization Plan or Executive Order | 1 | .8 |
| Constitutional Amendment followed by Statute | 17 | 13.9 |
| Constitutional Amendment followed by Statute and Executive Order | 2 | 1.6 |
| | N=122 | 99.8 |

[a]Totals do not always sum to 100% due to rounding.

TABLE 6.2

Characteristics of State Reorganization by Wave

|  | Post-Taft Wave (1914-1936) | |
| --- | --- | --- |
|  | Frequency | Percent[a] |
| ADOPTION DECISION | | |
| Failure to Adopt | 29 | 61.7 |
| Partial or Complete Adoption | 18 | 38.3 |
|  | N = 47 | 100.0 |
| DEGREE OF ADOPTION | | |
| Low | 10 | 55.6 |
| Moderate | 1 | 5.6 |
| High | 7 | 38.9 |
|  | N = 18 | 100.1 |
| TYPE OF REORGANIZATION | | |
| Traditional | 25 | 47.2 |
| Secretary-Coordinator | 1 | 1.9 |
| Cabinet | 27 | 50.9 |
|  | N = 53 | 100.0 |
| TIMING | | |
| Early | 41 | 64.1 |
| Middle | 17 | 26.6 |
| Late | 6 | 9.4 |
|  | N = 64 | 100.1 |
| TACTICS | | |
| Incremental | 20 | 36.4 |
| Comprehensive | 35 | 63.6 |
|  | N = 55 | 100.0 |
| LEGAL ADOPTION MECHANISM | | |
| Executive Order or Reorganization Plan | 0 | |
| Statute | 45 | 77.6 |
| Statute followed by Executive Order | 0 | |
| Constitutional Amendment | 5 | 8.6 |
| Constitutional Amendment followed by Reorganization Plan or Executive Order | 0 | |
| Constitutional Amendment followed by Statute | 8 | 13.8 |
| Constitutional Amendment followed by Statute and Executive Order | 0 | |
|  | N = 58 | 100.0 |

[a]Totals do not always sum to 100% due to rounding.

| Post-Brownlow Wave (1937-1946) | | Post-First-Hoover Wave (1947-1975) | |
|---|---|---|---|
| Frequency | Percent | Frequency | Percent |
| 6 | 66.7 | 4 | 11.1 |
| 3 | 33.3 | 32 | 88.9 |
| N = 9 | 100.0 | N = 36 | 100.0 |
| 2 | 66.7 | 6 | 18.8 |
| 0 | | 6 | 18.8 |
| 1 | 33.3 | 20 | 62.5 |
| N = 3 | 100.0 | N = 32 | 100.1 |
| 9 | 81.8 | 20 | 51.3 |
| 0 | | 6 | 15.4 |
| 2 | 18.2 | 13 | 33.3 |
| N = 11 | 100.0 | N = 39 | 100.0 |
| 13 | 68.4 | 22 | 44.0 |
| 4 | 21.1 | 23 | 46.0 |
| 2 | 10.5 | 5 | 10.0 |
| N = 19 | 100.0 | N = 50 | 100.0 |
| 6 | 40.0 | 25 | 55.6 |
| 9 | 60.0 | 20 | 44.4 |
| N = 15 | 100.0 | N = 45 | 100.0 |
| 0 | | 2 | 4.1 |
| 12 | 80.0 | 31 | 63.3 |
| 0 | | 1 | 2.0 |
| 2 | 13.3 | 4 | 8.2 |
| 0 | | 1 | 2.0 |
| 1 | 6.7 | 8 | 16.3 |
| N = 15 | 100.0 | N = 49 | 4.1 |
| 0 | | 2 | 100.0 |

TABLE 6.3

Characteristics of State Reorganization by Region[a]

| | NEW ENGLAND | |
|---|---|---|
| | Frequency | Percent[b] |
| ADOPTION DECISION | | |
| Failure to Adopt | 2 | 14.3 |
| Partial or Complete Adoption | 12 | 85.7 |
| | N = 14 | 100.0 |
| DEGREE OF ADOPTION | | |
| Low | 5 | 41.7 |
| Moderate | 2 | 16.7 |
| High | 5 | 41.7 |
| | N = 12 | 100.1 |
| TYPE OF REORGANIZATION | | |
| Traditional | 5 | 35.7 |
| Secretary-Coordinator | 1 | 7.1 |
| Cabinet | 8 | 57.1 |
| | N = 14 | 99.9 |
| TIMING | | |
| Early | 7 | 43.8 |
| Middle | 8 | 50.0 |
| Late | 1 | 6.3 |
| | N = 16 | 100.1 |
| TACTICS | | |
| Incremental | 9 | 64.3 |
| Comprehensive | 5 | 35.7 |
| | N = 14 | 100.0 |
| LEGAL ADOPTION MECHANISM | | |
| Executive Order or | | |
| Reorganization Plan | 0 | |
| Statute | 14 | 93.3 |
| Statute followed by Executive Order | 1 | 6.7 |
| Constitutional Amendment | 0 | |
| Constitutional Amendment followed | | |
| by Reorganization Plan | | |
| or Executive Order | 0 | |
| Constitutional Amendment followed | | |
| by Statute | 0 | |
| Constitutional Amendment followed | | |
| by Statute and Executive Order | 0 | |
| | N = 15 | 100.0 |

| MID-ATLANTIC | | SOUTHEAST | | GREAT LAKES | |
|---|---|---|---|---|---|
| Frequency | Percent | Frequency | Percent | Frequency | Percent |
| 5 | 62.5 | 8 | 38.1 | 3 | 42.9 |
| 3 | 37.5 | 13 | 61.9 | 4 | 57.1 |
| N = 8 | 100.0 | N = 21 | 100.0 | N = 7 | 100.0 |
| 0 | | 5 | 38.5 | 1 | 25.0 |
| 0 | | 1 | 7.7 | 0 | |
| 3 | 100.0 | 7 | 53.8 | 3 | 75.0 |
| N = 3 | 100.0 | N = 13 | 100.0 | N = 4 | 100.0 |
| 5 | 41.7 | 12 | 48.0 | 5 | 62.5 |
| 0 | | 2 | 8.0 | 0 | |
| 7 | 58.3 | 11 | 44.0 | 3 | 37.5 |
| N = 12 | 100.0 | N = 25 | 100.0 | N = 8 | 100.0 |
| 10 | 76.9 | 19 | 61.3 | 10 | 76.9 |
| 2 | 15.4 | 11 | 35.5 | 2 | 15.4 |
| 1 | 7.7 | 1 | 3.2 | 1 | 7.7 |
| N = 13 | 100.0 | N = 31 | 100.0 | N = 13 | 100.0 |
| 7 | 53.8 | 12 | 40.0 | 2 | 20.0 |
| 6 | 46.2 | 18 | 60.0 | 8 | 80.0 |
| N = 13 | 100.0 | N = 30 | 100.0 | N = 10 | 100.0 |
| 0 | | 1 | 3.2 | 0 | |
| 9 | 64.3 | 21 | 67.7 | 9 | 81.8 |
| 0 | | 0 | | 0 | |
| 3 | 21.4 | 3 | 9.7 | 0 | |
| 0 | | 0 | | 0 | |
| 2 | 14.3 | 6 | 19.4 | 2 | 18.2 |
| 0 | | 0 | | 0 | |
| N = 14 | 100.0 | N = 31 | 100.0 | N = 11 | 100.0 |

TABLE 6.3 (cont.)

|  | PLAINS | |
| --- | --- | --- |
|  | Frequency | Percent |
| ADOPTION DECISION | | |
| Failure to Adopt | 7 | 53.8 |
| Partial or Complete Adoption | 6 | 46.2 |
|  | N = 13 | 100.0 |
| DEGREE OF ADOPTION | | |
| Low | 1 | 16.7 |
| Moderate | 1 | 16.7 |
| High | 4 | 66.7 |
|  | N = 6 | 100.1 |
| TYPE OF REORGANIZATION | | |
| Traditional | 6 | 50.0 |
| Secretary-Coordinator | 2 | 16.7 |
| Cabinet | 4 | 33.3 |
|  | N = 12 | 100.0 |
| TIMING | | |
| Early | 9 | 47.4 |
| Middle | 5 | 26.3 |
| Late | 5 | 26.3 |
|  | N = 19 | 100.0 |
| TACTICS | | |
| Incremental | 3 | 20.0 |
| Comprehensive | 12 | 80.0 |
|  | N = 15 | 100.0 |
| LEGAL ADOPTION MECHANISM | | |
| Executive Order or | | |
| Reorganization Plan | 0 | |
| Statute | 11 | 68.8 |
| Statute followed by Executive Order | 0 | |
| Constitutional Amendment | 2 | 12.5 |
| Constitutional Amendment followed | | |
| by Reorganization Plan | | |
| or Executive Order | 1 | 6.3 |
| Constitutional Amendment followed | | |
| by Statute | 1 | 6.3 |
| Constitutional Amendment followed | | |
| by Statute and Executive Order | 1 | 6.3 |
|  | N = 16 | 100.2 |

| SOUTHWEST | | MOUNTAINS | | FAR WEST | |
|---|---|---|---|---|---|
| Frequency | Percent | Frequency | Percent | Frequency | Percent |
| 6 | 60.0 | 3 | 50.0 | 5 | 38.5 |
| 4 | 40.0 | 3 | 50.0 | 8 | 61.5 |
| N = 10 | 100.0 | N = 6 | 100.0 | N = 13 | 100.0 |
| 3 | 75.0 | 1 | 33.3 | 2 | 25.0 |
| 1 | 25.0 | 0 | | 2 | 25.0 |
| 0 | | 2 | 66.7 | 4 | 50.0 |
| N = 4 | 100.0 | N = 3 | 100.0 | N = 8 | 100.0 |
| 6 | 75.0 | 8 | 72.7 | 7 | 53.8 |
| 0 | | 0 | | 2 | 15.4 |
| 2 | 25.0 | 3 | 27.3 | 4 | 30.8 |
| N = 8 | 100.0 | N = 11 | 100.0 | N = 13 | 100.0 |
| 4 | 40.0 | 8 | 61.5 | 9 | 50.0 |
| 5 | 50.0 | 4 | 30.8 | 7 | 38.9 |
| 1 | 10.0 | 1 | 7.7 | 2 | 11.1 |
| N = 10 | 100.0 | N = 13 | 100.0 | N = 18 | 100.0 |
| 4 | 42.9 | 4 | 44.4 | 11 | 64.7 |
| 3 | 57.1 | 5 | 55.6 | 6 | 35.3 |
| N = 7 | 100.0 | N = 9 | 100.0 | N = 17 | 100.0 |
| 0 | | 0 | | 1 | 6.3 |
| 7 | 77.8 | 6 | 60.0 | 11 | 68.8 |
| 0 | | 0 | | 1 | 6.3 |
| 2 | 22.2 | 0 | | 1 | 6.3 |
| 0 | | 0 | | 0 | |
| 0 | | 4 | 40.0 | 1 | 6.3 |
| 0 | | 0 | | 1 | 6.3 |
| N = 9 | 100.0 | N = 10 | 100.0 | N = 16 | 100.3 |

TABLE 6.3 (cont.)

---

[a]The delineations for region are those devised by
Jack L. Walker, "Innovation in State Politics," in
Herbert Jacob and Kenneth Vines, eds., Politics in
the American States (1971), pp. 372-373. These
regions are:

NEW ENGLAND: Connecticut, Maine, Massachusetts,
Rhode Island, New Hampshire, Vermont
(6 states);

MID-ATLANTIC: Delaware, Maryland, New Jersey, New York,
Pennsylvania (5 states);

SOUTHEAST: Alabama, Arkansas, Florida, Georgia,
Kentucky, Louisiana, Mississippi, North
Carolina, South Carolina, Tennessee,
Virginia, West Virginia (12 states);

GREAT LAKES: Illinois, Indiana, Michigan, Ohio,
Wisconsin (5 states);

PLAINS: Iowa, Kansas, Minnesota, Missouri,
Nebraska, North Dakota, South Dakota
(7 states);

SOUTHWEST: Arizona, New Mexico, Oklahoma, Texas
(4 states);

MOUNTAINS: Colorado, Idaho, Montana, Utah, Wyoming
(5 states);

FAR WEST: California, Nevada, Oregon, Washington
(4 states).

[b]Totals do not always sum to 100% due to rounding.

The most recent period had the highest ratio of adoptions to attempts, and also had the highest proportion of reorganizations attaining a high degree of adoption (62.5 percent compared to 33.3 percent for the post-Brownlow period and 38.9 percent for the post-Taft wave). On a regional basis, the Mid-Atlantic (100 percent), Great Lakes (75 percent), Plains (67 percent), and Mountains (67 percent) have had the greatest percentage of high degree of adoption. The generally lower rate of reorganization activity in these regions makes the "N" relatively smaller, possibly exaggerating the importance of each high adoption.

Regions where a low degree of adoption has been most common are the Southwest (75 percent), New England (41.7 percent), and the Southeast (38.5 percent). Executive branch reorganization has faced the strongest resistance in the Southwest, where 60 percent of attempts have been defeated and 75 percent of the "successes" have been at low degree of adoption. In New England and the Southeast very partial passage of reorganization proposals has helped account for the relatively high rate of adoption.

## Type of Reorganization

As might be expected, the less ambitious Traditional type of reorganization was applied more frequently (fifty-four times, 52.4 percent) than the more reform-minded Secretary-Coordinator (seven times, 6.8 percent) and Cabinet (forty-two times, 40.8 percent) models. However, application of the more rigorous Cabinet type, patterned after the federal executive branch model, has been applied more than expected in light of the greater political and legal efforts usually needed for thoroughgoing reform.

Most of this application of the Cabinet type occurred in the first wave. The period 1914–36 accounted for twenty-seven (64 percent) of the forty-two Cabinet reorganizations that have been attempted. The Secretary-Coordinator type has been used almost exclusively in the most recent period. One of the hallmarks of the recent and most successful wave has been a more even balance among the types of reorganization attempted.

There are distinct regional patterns involving reorganization type. Use of the Cabinet model has been higher in the three easternmost regions: New England (57.1 percent), the Mid-Atlantic (58.3 percent), and the Southeast (44 percent). In fact, twenty-six (62 percent) of all state Cabinet-type reorganization attempts have been in these three regions. The regions that have used the Cabinet model least have been those farthest west: the Southwest (25 percent), Mountains (27.3 percent), and the Far West (30.8 percent). These regions have accounted for only 16.7 percent of all Cabinet reorganization efforts. States closer to Washington, D.C., have tended to emulate the federal model to a greater degree than those more geographically removed. Again, balance among types appears to be important, with three of the four regions having the most even balance also holding the highest adoption rates: New England, the Far West, and the Southeast.

## Timing of Reorganization Effort

As expected, the majority of reorganization attempts have been undertaken in the early stage (first third) of a governor's administration. Seventy-six (57.1 percent) of reorganization efforts for which there is information on timing were attempted in the early phase, forty-four (33.1 percent) in the middle portion, and thirteen (9.8 percent) late in a governor's tenure in office. Reorganization sponsors seem to have taken seriously the advice to attempt reorganization earlier rather than later.

As with the other reorganization characteristics, timing shows patterns by wave and region. The distribution of timing strategies was virtually the same for the post-Taft and post-Brownlow waves. A considerable shift in timing strategy took place in the third (post-first-Hoover) wave, in which there was practically the same application of early (twenty-two times, 44 percent) and middle (twenty-three times, 46 percent) timing strategies. The considerably lower incidence (10 percent) of late timing is consistent with findings for the earlier two periods.

In terms of regional differences, early timing has had the highest relative use in the Great Lakes (76.9 percent) and Mid-Atlantic (76.9 percent) regions and the lowest use in the Southwest region (40 percent). By far the highest absolute (five times) and relative (26 percent) use of late timing has occurred in the Plains states. It is interesting to note that this relatively high occurrence of reorganization efforts late in a governor's tenure was evenly distributed among the Plains states and was not the result of the practices of one or two states.

## Adoption Tactics

The greater overall use of the comprehensive adoption tactic (sixty-four times, 55.7 percent) over the presumably less risky incremental strategy (fifty-one times, 44.3 percent) is surprising. Some light is shed on this finding by observing that comprehensive tactics were pursued at a far higher rate during the post-Taft (63.6 percent) and post-Brownlow (60 percent) waves than during the post-first-Hoover period (44.4 percent). In fact, the greater probability of adoption in the post-first-Hoover period and the better record in terms of degree of adoption can both be partly explained by this shift in tactics. This finding will be pursued further in the discussion of hypotheses tests.

On a regional basis, comprehensive "all-eggs-in-one-basket" tactics have predominated in the Great Lakes (eight times, 80 percent) and Plains (twelve times, 80 percent) regions. This tendency is, in part, the result of the powerful influence the orthodox reformers had in these two regions. Results reported in the hypotheses tests show a relatively strong association between presence of diffusion-agent activity and application of more comprehensive tactics. The regions where incremental tactics have received relatively higher use (Far West, 64.7 percent; New England, 64.3 percent) have also been two of the three regions with the highest rate of adoption. In the Southeast region a 61.9 percent rate of adoption was achieved even though comprehensive tactics were pursued 60 percent of the time.

*Legal-Adoption Mechanism*

Legislative statute has been the predominant legal strategy used by state reorganizers. Statutes were used eighty-eight times (72.1 percent) during the period covered by this study. This finding is consistent with the writings discussed earlier that touted the superiority of the statutory device over the constitutional mechanism. The constitutional amendment strategy was utilized eleven times or in 9 percent of the cases where information on legal device was available. The combination of constitutional amendment followed by statute was utilized in seventeen reorganization attempts (13.9 percent of the time). Reliance on the statutory mechanism was considerably higher for the post-Taft (77.6 percent) and post-Brownlow (80 percent) waves than for the post-first-Hoover (63.3 percent) wave. Indeed the most recent wave was notable because of the wide range of legal-adoption strategies applied during that wave. My research shows that seven basic legal strategies were used in the post-first-Hoover wave — as compared with three for the earlier two waves. The greater legal flexibility that goes with the wider range of legal options has been part of the better adoption rate of the third wave. Even though some of these newer devices, such as reorganization plans and executive orders, have rarely been applied even in states where they are available, the imaginative use of these mechanisms in conjunction with other legal devices has made a difference in adoption rates.

The analysis by region shows a good example of creative legal strategy. The Mountains region shows a far higher utilization rate (40 percent) of constitutional amendment followed by statute than any other region. This finding can be explained partly by the deliberate process of diffusion. South Dakota officials sought a legal strategy for adopting executive reorganization in the early 1970s. In 1972 South Dakota emulated neighboring Montana's 1970 strategy of forcing action by first passing a constitutional amendment that mandated reorganization into no more than twenty departments by a specified date. Bills passed later implemented in specific terms the general outlines established by constitutional amendment. A consultant familiar with the Montana process and strategy was brought in to assist with South Dakota's effort, thereby serving as diffusion agent. Idaho, another neighbor of Montana's, approved a similar constitutional amendment in 1972.[2]

Of the three regions in which state reorganization has had the highest rate of adoption, both the Far West and the Southeast show a diversity of legal strategies, while states in New England have been preoccupied with the statutory mechanism. The two regions in which there have been the lowest adoption rates (Mid-Atlantic, 37.5 percent; Southwest, 40 percent) have also been those with the highest relative utilization of the constitutional amendment device (21 and 22 percent, respectively).

Having surveyed some of the patterns concerning state reorganization outcomes, types, and strategies, let us now turn to examining results relevant to the hypotheses posed earlier.

### Hypotheses Tests

This section summarizes the findings for each of the forty hypotheses presented in Chapter 5. Included are measure of association, significance level, an "N" used to calculate that measure. I use significance levels even though this study covers what there is reason to believe is the entire population of state executive branch reorganizations from 1900 to 1975.

There are several reasons for using significance levels. One, the N of state reorganizations may be a population, but the N's for each hypothesis vary because of missing data. Significance is a useful means of judging importance of relationship because it reflects variations in these N's. Two, the results of my study give a comprehensive historical description of state reorganization from 1900 to 1975. But reorganization is an ongoing phenomenon. Significance levels are needed to make inferences beyond the time period covered here. Governors and other state reorganizers should consider significance in order to know how much confidence to place in the action guidelines presented in Chapter 7. Three, the use of significance levels in hypothesis testing is widely practiced and understood.[3]

The statistical measure used is M. G. Kendall's tau-b. I have used this measure for a number of reasons. Tau-b is suitable for analysis of the primarily ordinal-level data used in this study as well as for higher-level data.[4] This Kendall measure is also appropriate for the kinds of hypotheses I have formulated. "These measures [of ordinal association] can be interpreted as being based on predictions that are operational statements of 'the more the X, the more the Y,' or, alternatively, 'Y increases with X.'"[5] Another reason for using this measure lies in its interpretation in terms of proportionate reduction in error (PRE). PRE measures are "ratios of the amount of error made in predicting under two situations: first, where there is no more information than simply the distribution of the dependent variable itself, and second, where there is additional knowledge about an independent variable and the way the dependent variable is distributed within the categories of that independent variable."[6] In basic form,

$$\text{PRE} = \frac{\text{Reduction in Errors Knowing the Independent Variable}}{\text{Original Amount of Error}}$$

For ordinal variables the primary interest has been in predicting rank order of pairs on the dependent variable based on ordering of the independent variable. This kind of prediction capability is generally consistent with the information capabilities of state decision makers who often know they want more or less of something but are not able to state in quantifiable terms exactly how much more or less. In the words of David Hildebrand, James Laing, and Howard Rosenthal, "Recent research in human cognition . . . suggests that it is useful to assume that people have limited information processing, hence quantifying capability."[7] Thus, it is typical for state decision makers to think in such terms as: "If comprehensive tactics are used rather than incremental tactics, is this likely to increase or decrease the degree of reorganization adoption obtained?" The logic behind the statistical measure used is thus consistent with the information needs of reorganization decision makers.

There is not complete agreement about the interpretation of tau-b as a PRE measure. In 1971 Jae-On Kim concluded that, "For the moment, tau-b does not have a simple PRE interpretation and therefore lacks a *simple* probabilistic interpretation of its intermediate values."[8] According to Loether and McTavish,

> The more complicated the denominator the more difficult it becomes to express a clear operational definition in a PRE sense, and this is true of tau-b. It is, however, one of the more useful of the ordinal, symmetrical measures, and it is superior to tau-a because it does take account of the non-trivial ties in expressing the relationship between two variables.[9]

More recently, Hildebrand, Laing, and Rosenthal, and also Eric Uslaner, have affirmed the PRE interpretability of tau-b.[10] For this study I used a PRE interpretation of tau-b consistent with this newer interpretation. Observing that values of symmetric Somer's d, clearly interpretable in PRE terms, are almost always extremely close to those of tau-b in this study, lends further credence to tau-b as a PRE measure.

Another reason for utilizing Kendall's tau-b stems from the conservative nature of its values. With the data in this study the values of Kendall's tau statistics tend to be lower than the corresponding values of other common measures of ordinal association, such as Goodman and Kruskal's gamma or Spearman's rho. In research of an exploratory nature, such as this study, caution and understatement would appear a better policy.

Finally, Kendall's tau-b is used for associations involving rectangular as well as square matrices. Unlike tau-b, tau-c has been normalized so that tau-c can reach a value of 1.0 (perfect ordering of ranks) when the matrix is not square. Correspondingly, values of tau-c are generally higher than those of tau-b for rectangular matrices.[11] However, this correction factor also increases the difficulty of interpreting tau-c as a predictive or PRE statistic.[12] This added difficulty in interpretation weighs against slightly higher values tau-c would generally attain under special conditions.

Findings for each of the forty hypotheses are summarized in Table 6.4. A low or nonexistent association can be interpreted as indicating little or no reduction in predictive error. Strictly speaking, in this study no association means no *monotonic* association. "By using a PRE measure of association . . . we are actually evaluating the hypothesis that the data will exhibit a given type of association. . . . Consequently, an indication of no association given by a specific index does not necessarily imply lack of another type of association."[13] A sign in the opposite direction indicates that the opposite guessing rule, in this case the opposite hypothesis, generally would be more appropriate. For example, findings for hypothesis 3 indicate that "the higher the degree of electoral competition, the greater the rigor of legal mechanism" would be a more appropriate prediction rule than the hypothesis initially formulated.

*Reorganization as Political Competition:*
*Major Findings*

*Degree of Electoral Competition for Governorship.* The most surprising findings relating to political competition concern the positive impact of electoral competition on Adoption Decision (.14) and Degree of Reorganization Adoption (.15). It was anticipated that more intense political competition, as evidenced by higher second-party competition at the gubernatorial election before reorganization, would decrease both the likelihood and degree of adoption. One interpretation of these findings is that a closer election spurs the narrowly elected governor and governor's party on to increased efforts to reorganize in an effort to solidify or enhance their electoral position. After elections that are not as hotly contested, the urge to entrench through reorganization may not be as strong.

A time period comparison shows that the hypothesized negative relationship does hold for reorganization in the most recent, post-first-Hoover wave (tau-b = −.26) even though the overall association is positive. See

Appendix B for time-period and regional comparisons on reorganization outcomes.

In terms of Adoption Decision, only three of the eight regions show the hypothesized negative relationship (Mountains, Southeast, and Mid-Atlantic), and in the latter two there is virtually no association. The other regions show a positive relationship, although New England shows almost no relationship.

Only two regions (Plains and Far West) showed the hypothesized negative relationship between Degree of Electoral Competition for Governorship and Degree of Reorganization Adoption. Of these two, only the association for the Far West (tau-b = −.52) is substantial. A regional analysis likewise shows results counter to the hypothesized direction. Only the first wave shows a negative relationship. The explanation offered before with respect to Adoption Decision would also appear to hold with Degree of Reorganization Adoption. Governors who win by thinner margins may feel greater need to reorganize and put more effort into that cause. The slimness of electoral victory is not a major obstacle to reorganization. After the election, there is often some reconciliation. Political opponents may rally around the newly elected governor because they need to curry his favor. Other opponents may not actively support the new governor's actions but may adopt a wait-and-see attitude, at least during the honeymoon period, when most reorganizations are attempted.

*Governor's Party Control of Legislature.* My expectation was that Governor's Party Control of legislative houses before reorganization would have more impact on adoption than does electoral competition. Governor's Party Control of the Legislature is a more direct measure of a governor's ability to garner the votes necessary to adopt reorganization. This expectation did not hold. The magnitudes of the associations with Adoption Decision (−.10) and Degree of Adoption (−.01) are lower than the corresponding association with Degree of Electoral Competition, although only the latter is noticeably lower.

More fundamentally, the expected positive relationship between Governor's Party Control and Adoption Decision and Degree of Adoption did not hold overall. Four explanations come to mind: First, the legislative control index utilized in this study took into account majority control in a legislative house but did not account for size of majority. A 51 percent majority, for example, was given the same weight as a 75 percent of 100 percent party control of seats. While a small working majority is sufficient for many purposes, it may not prevail on a sensitive issue such as administrative reorganization, where committee jurisdictions and legislative influence on the bureaucracies are at stake.

Another explanation involves the phenomenon of party factionalism. In

TABLE 6.4

Hypotheses, Variables, Levels of Measurement, and Findings

| NO.[a] | INDEPENDENT VARIABLE | DEPENDENT VARIABLE | +,−[b] | FINDING | NOTES[c] |
|---|---|---|---|---|---|
| (1) | Degree of Electoral Competition for Governorship (INTERVAL) | Timing of Adoption Effort (ORDINAL) | + | tau-b = .08<br>sig. = .15<br>N = 133 | not significant (at the .05 level) |
| (2) | Degree of Electoral Competition for Governorship (INTERVAL) | Comprehensiveness of Tactics (ORDINAL) | − | tau-b = .01<br>sig. = .47<br>N = 115 | not significant |
| (3) | Degree of Electoral Competition for Governorship (INTERVAL) | Rigor of Legal Mechanism (ORDINAL) | − | tau-b = .16<br>sig. = .03<br>N = 122 | significant; not in hypothesized direction |
| (4) | Degree of Electoral Competition for Governorship (INTERVAL) | Adoption Decision (ORDINAL) | − | tau-b = .14<br>sig. = .09<br>N = 92 | not significant |
| (5) | Degree of Electoral Competition for Governorship (INTERVAL) | Degree of Adoption (ORDINAL) | − | tau-b = .15<br>sig. = .12<br>N = 53 | not significant |

| | Independent Variable | Dependent Variable | | Statistics | Result |
|---|---|---|---|---|---|
| (6) | Degree of Electoral Competition for Governorship (INTERVAL) | Date of Adoption (INTERVAL) | − | tau-b = .12 <br> sig. = .05 <br> N = 151 | significant; not in hypothesized direction |
| (7) | Degree of Electoral Competition for Governorship (INTERVAL) | Degree of Reorganization Reform<sup>d</sup> (ORDINAL) | − | tau-b = −.10 <br> sig. = .17 <br> N = 82 | not significant |
| (8) | Governor's Party Control of Legislature (ORDINAL) | Timing of Adoption Effort (ORDINAL) | − | tau-b = −.22 <br> sig. = .004 <br> N = 125 | significant; in hypothesized direction |
| (9) | Governor's Party Control of Legislature (ORDINAL) | Comprehensiveness of Tactics (ORDINAL) | + | tau-b = .09 <br> sig. = .17 <br> N = 108 | not significant |
| (10) | Governor's Party Control of Legislature (ORDINAL) | Rigor of Legal Mechanism (ORDINAL) | + | tau-b = −.10 <br> sig. = .12 <br> N = 115 | not significant |
| (11) | Governor's Party Control of Legislature (ORDINAL) | Adoption Decision (ORDINAL) | + | tau-b = −.10 <br> sig. = .17 <br> N = 89 | not significant |

TABLE 6.4 (cont.)

| NO. | INDEPENDENT VARIABLE | DEPENDENT VARIABLE | +,- | FINDING | NOTES |
|---|---|---|---|---|---|
| (12) | Governor's Party Control of Legislature (ORDINAL) | Degree of Adoption (ORDINAL) | + | tau-b = -.01 sig. = .48 N = 51 | not significant |
| (13) | Governor's Party Control of Legislature (ORDINAL) | Date of Adoption (INTERVAL) | - | tau-b = -.23 sig. = .002 N = 141 | significant; in hypothesized direction |
| (14) | Governor's Party Control of Legislature (ORDINAL) | Degree of Reorganization Reform$^d$ (ORDINAL) | + | tau-b = -.07 sig. = .27 N = 76 | not significant |
| (15) | Diffusion Agent Activity (ORDINAL) | Timing of Adoption Effort (ORDINAL) | - | tau-b = .04 sig. = .40 N = 45 | not significant |
| (16) | Diffusion Agent Activity (ORDINAL) | Comprehensiveness of Tactics (ORDINAL) | + | tau-b = .33 sig. = .02 N = 45 | significant; in hypothesized direction |

| | | | | Statistics | |
|---|---|---|---|---|---|
| (17) | Diffusion Agent Activity (ORDINAL) | Rigor of Legal Mechanism (ORDINAL) | + | tau-b = .24<br>sig. = .04<br>N = 48 | significant; in hypothesized direction |
| (18) | Diffusion Agent Activity (ORDINAL) | Adoption Decision (ORDINAL) | – | tau-b = -.13<br>sig. = .21<br>N = 42 | not significant |
| (19) | Diffusion Agent Activity (ORDINAL) | Degree of Adoption (ORDINAL) | + | tau-b = -.17<br>sig. = .17<br>N = 29 | not significant |
| (20) | Diffusion Agent Activity (ORDINAL) | Date of Adoption (INTERVAL) | – | tau-b = -.23<br>sig. = .04<br>N = 58 | significant; in hypothesized direction |
| (21) | Diffusion Agent Activity (ORDINAL) | Degree of Reorganization Reform d (ORDINAL) | + | tau-b = -.03<br>sig. = .45<br>N = 31 | not significant |
| (22) | Level of Modernization (ORDINAL) | Timing of Adoption Effort (ORDINAL) | – | tau-b = -.08<br>sig. = .16<br>N = 130 | not significant |

TABLE 6.4 (cont.)

| NO. | INDEPENDENT VARIABLE | DEPENDENT VARIABLE | +,- | FINDING | NOTES |
|---|---|---|---|---|---|
| (23) | Level of Modernization (ORDINAL) | Comprehensiveness of Tactics (ORDINAL) | - | tau-b = -.12 sig. = .09 N = 111 | not significant |
| (24) | Level of Modernization (ORDINAL) | Rigor of Legal Mechanism (ORDINAL) | - | tau-b = .02 sig. = .40 N = 118 | not significant |
| (25) | Level of Modernization (ORDINAL) | Adoption Decision (ORDINAL) | + | tau-b = .08 sig. = .20 N = 91 | not significant |
| (26) | Level of Modernization (ORDINAL) | Degree of Adoption (ORDINAL) | - | tau-b = .26 sig. = .02 N = 52 | significant; not in hypothesized direction |
| (27) | Level of Modernization (ORDINAL) | Date of Adoption (INTERVAL) | - | tau-b = -.10 sig. = .09 N = 147 | not significant |

| | Independent Variable | Dependent Variable | | Statistics | |
|---|---|---|---|---|---|
| (28) | Level of Modernization (ORDINAL) | Degree of Reorganization Reform[d] (ORDINAL) | + | tau-b = .06<br>sig. = .28<br>N = 80 | not significant |
| (29) | Timing of Adoption Effort (ORDINAL) | Adoption Decision (ORDINAL) | − | tau-b = −.07<br>sig. = .26<br>N = 81 | not significant |
| (30) | Timing of Adoption Effort (ORDINAL) | Degree of Adoption (ORDINAL) | − | tau-b = −.13<br>sig. = .17<br>N = 49 | not significant |
| (31) | Timing of Adoption Effort (ORDINAL) | Date of Adoption (INTERVAL) | + | tau-b = .15<br>sig. = .03<br>N = 133 | significant; in hypothesized direction |
| (32) | Timing of Adoption Effort (ORDINAL) | Degree of Reorganization Reform[d] (ORDINAL) | − | tau-b = .09<br>sig. = .20<br>N = 82 | not significant |
| (33) | Comprehensiveness of Tactics (ORDINAL) | Adoption Decision (ORDINAL) | − | tau-b = −.38<br>sig. = .001<br>N = 72 | significant; in hypothesized direction |

TABLE 6.4 (cont.)

| NO. | INDEPENDENT VARIABLE | DEPENDENT VARIABLE | + | − | FINDING | NOTES |
|---|---|---|---|---|---|---|
| (34) | Comprehensiveness of Tactics (ORDINAL) | Degree of Adoption (ORDINAL) | + | | tau-b = .37 <br> sig. = .004 <br> N = 46 | significant; in hypothesized direction |
| (35) | Comprehensiveness of Tactics (ORDINAL) | Date of Adoption (INTERVAL) | | − | tau-b = −.17 <br> sig. = .03 <br> N = 115 | significant; in hypothesized direction |
| (36) | Comprehensiveness of Tactics (ORDINAL) | Degree of Reorganization Reform[d] (ORDINAL) | + | | tau-b = −.15 <br> sig. = .12 <br> N = 68 | not significant |
| (37) | Rigor of Legal Mechanism (ORDINAL) | Adoption Decision (ORDINAL) | | − | tau-b = −.07 <br> sig. = .26 <br> N = 76 | not significant |
| (38) | Rigor of Legal Mechanism (ORDINAL) | Degree of Adoption (ORDINAL) | + | | tau-b = 0 <br> sig. = .50 <br> N = 48 | not significant |

| (39) | Rigor of Legal Mechanism (ORDINAL) | Date of Adoption (INTERVAL) | − | tau-b = .11 sig. = .10 N = 122 | not significant |
| (40) | Rigor of Legal Mechanism (ORDINAL) | Degree of Reorganization Reform$^d$ (ORDINAL) | + | tau-b = .05 sig. = .33 N = 70 | not significant |

[a]The hypothesis numbers correspond to those found in Chapter 5.

[b]It was initially hypothesized that the variables would be associated in this direction. If tau-b has the opposite sign, then the finding is not in the hypothesized direction.

[c]The conventional .05 level is the standard used for assessing significance.

[d]The results reported here were derived from Degree of Reorganization Reform being operationalized in terms of low and high degree of reform by combining Secretary-Coordinator and Cabinet types into one (high reform) group. This can be justified theoretically because these two types are much closer to each other on an ordinal scale than to the Traditional (low reform) type.

some legislatures, intraparty factionalism may negate what appears to be majority control. This may be particularly relevant if a legislative leader views the governor's reorganization effort as jeopardizing that leader's political ambitions. Legislative leaders may be political competitors of the governor and may even counter with their own reorganization plan.

Third, the often crucial role of bureaucratic politics and interest-group politics may well minimize or even overwhelm the impact of formal party control. Bureaucratic or interest-group actors, whose agency control may be jeopardized, typically have a more direct stake in reorganization than do legislators. The influence these actors can exert is considerable.[14]

The above three factors are important, but, with the possible exception of legislative majorities, they are extremely difficult to operationalize on the scale of this study. These alternative explanations are the subject of further research.

A fourth explanation has been provided by Joseph Schlesinger. Schlesinger has contended that a one-party stranglehold on political control is not always conducive to administrative reorganization. According to Schlesinger's formulation, governors of industrialized, urbanized states with large populations are in greater need of formal hierarchical powers and controls to cope with increased complexity. Governors of rural states rely more heavily on informal powers and controls such as the capability of dispensing patronage and contracts.

> A New York governor . . . needs the order which formal hierarchical controls help provide. However, should the rural state governor obtain these controls he might well have an excess of power. Perhaps this explains the resistance of rural, particularly one-party rural, states to the arguments for administrative reform.[15]

Findings in this study tend to support Schlesinger's explanation. The only regions showing a negative association between Governor's Party Control and Degree of Reorganization Adoption are the Southeast, Plains, and Mountains regions. These are regions that have a relatively higher share of one-party and rural states.

Even though the hypothesized positive direction between Governor's Party Control and Tactics was found, the tau-b of .09 was still below that anticipated. The positive relationship held (.22) for the earliest wave but not for the latter two, which showed very weak associations ( – .06 for post-Brownlow and – .05 for post-first-Hoover waves). This finding reflects the increased emphasis on incremental tactics, particularly in the third wave, regardless of Governor's Party Control of Legislature.

The PRE value of Governor's Party Control of Legislature is strongest for the two time-related variables, Timing of Adoption Effort and Date of

Adoption. The overall association with Timing of Adoption Effort is – .22. The hypothesized direction holds: where Governor's Party Control of one or both houses exists, reorganization is attempted and adopted at an earlier stage.

The negative overall association ( – .23) between Governor's Party Control and Date of Adoption can be interpreted this way: there has been a greater tendency for stacked party control preceding reorganization in the earlier time periods, particularly in the post-Taft wave, than in the later periods. In fact, the only region where a greater degree of Governor's Party Control is evident in the later waves is the Mid-Atlantic (tau-b = .30).

*Reorganization as Diffused Innovation: Major Findings*

Diffusion Agent Activity fares no better than does Degree of Electoral Competition in enabling a proportionate reduction in error in predicting Adoption Decision (13 percent PRE) and Degree of Adoption (17 percent PRE if reverse is hypothesized). Diffusion Agent Activity does enable more improved prediction than does Governor's Party Control, particularly in predicting order of Degree of Adoption.

While the hypothesized negative relationship with Adoption Decision was found, the hypothesized positive relationship between Diffusion Agent Activity and Degree of Adoption was not. It would appear that the presence of diffusion activity does not generally help get more of a reorganization plan approved. This tendency appears to be particularly strong in the New England ( – .71) and Southwest ( – 1.00) regions.[16] The negative influence of reorganization diffusion in New England is expressed by one Maine official: "The modern framework for [Maine] state government is the result of a 'do-it-yourself' effort . . . with very little outside help and at minimal cost."[17]

A similar suspicion of external diffusion agents in the Southwest was identified by Robert Riggs when he tried to account for Arizona's poor record in executive reorganization before 1964.

> An additional political liability is incurred if the program for reorganization is openly and notoriously formulated by out-of-state experts, however good their personal qualifications and however meritorious their plan. Many Arizonans still have enough provincialism to resent the implication that out-of-state (especially eastern, professional) talent is needed to tell the natives how to run their government. "Griffenhagenism" after 1950 became a hiss and a byword among opponents of reorganization, as well as an effective political catchword. However regrettable, this sentiment is also a political fact of life. Future proposals will have a better chance of success if they are advertised as home-grown products.[18]

The problem of finding sufficient data to identify presence or absence of diffusion activity in a number of reorganizations prevents a more detailed regional or time comparison. A number of associations between Diffusion Agent Activity and Degree of Adoption could not be computed. The largest proportionate reduction in prediction error (33 percent) in knowing the order of Diffusion Agent Activity comes in predicting the order of Tactics. The expected preference of diffusion agents for comprehensive tactics is supported by the findings. The PRE value of Diffusion Agent Activity in predicting Tactics is even higher (55 percent) for the most recent, post-first-Hoover wave. In similar fashion, the 24 percent reduction in error in predicting the order of Legal Adoption Mechanism when knowing Diffusion Agent Activity rises to 42 percent for the most recent wave of reorganizations.

Based on the limited data available, the − .23 association between Diffusion Agent Activity and Date of Adoption indicates that diffusion activity has been more prevalent during the earlier waves. This finding may indeed be a reflection of the operationalization itself. It is generally easier to detect diffusion-agent activity if a consulting firm is utilized. Because many of the research bureau teams were most active in the earlier periods, the result may be somewhat biased against the later periods, when diffusion activity has been more diverse and perhaps more subtle. Certainly the data base on Diffusion Agent Activity needs improvement, an effort that will require considerable time and money.

In an innovation-related finding, as association of tau-b = .30 was found between State Government Innovation Capacity (operationalized as Jack Walker's Composite Innovation Score) and a variable that reflects the frequency with which states adopt executive reorganization. In other words, there is an association of .30 between state rank on general policy innovation and state rank based on frequency of reorganization. An almost one-third reduction in prediction error is generally considered useful. An even higher association (tau-b = .36) was found between State Government Innovation Capacity and the total number of reorganization attempts for a state. There is thus a moderate tendency for those states that attempt more reorganization innovations to innovate in a broader range of policy areas.

*Reorganization as Adaptation to Modernization: Major Findings*

By far the most notable modernization result is the .26 association between a state's Level of Modernization prior to reorganization and the Degree of Reorganization Adoption. I anticipated that a state's Level of Modernization, while important as a macro, underlying force, might be too broad and too remote for associations of respectable magnitude to be found. But the comparable associations for the two time periods for which there is sufficient data show that the overall finding is no fluke. The corresponding tau-b's for the post-Taft and post-first-Hoover waves are .38

and .34 respectively. Although the – .50 association for the post-Brownlow period is unstable because of the small subpopulation size, it does pull down the overall magnitude.

Another consideration about this principal finding arises because the relationship ran counter to the hypothesized direction. Not only is the relationship between Level of Modernization and Degree of Adoption positive, it is considerably greater in magnitude than the positive association expected for Adoption Decision (tau-b = .08). It would appear that the more modernized states are more likely to adopt a larger proportion of a reorganization plan than are less modernized states. This pattern holds for the Southeast, Far West, and New England regions. It does not appear to hold for the Great Lakes and Plains states, although the small subpopulations in the data make these associations unstable and certainly less than conclusive. Apparently the greater emphasis on "progress" and on state government reform that will allow continued progress does affect California, Michigan, Connecticut, and other states that periodically update their executive branch structures. That such states have the resource base which goes with modernization and industrialization would seem to augment their capability to reform.

The hypothesized positive relationship between Level of Modernization and Adoption Decision holds for all three time periods and is stronger in the latter two. The tau-b of .17 for the most recent wave approaches more closely the association Level of Modernization has with Degree of Adoption.

In general the associations between Level of Modernization and the three strategy variables are weak ( – .08 with Timing, – .12 with Tactics, and .02 with Legal Adoption Mechanism). Of the three, the relationship with Tactics is most respectable. The hypothesized negative direction was found for both the post-Taft ( – .22) and post-first-Hoover ( – .15) waves. It is surprising that the strongest of these associations is found for the earliest wave. The application of comprehensive tactics was higher in the post-Taft wave, yet there is a moderate tendency for the more modernized states to use incremental tactics during this wave. This finding can be explained in part by the preference of the New England and Mid-Atlantic States (particularly the New England states) for incremental tactics. Many of the states in these two regions also ranked among those with the highest Level of Modernization during that earlier period.[19]

The generally low effect that Level of Modernization has on the reorganization strategy variables is not surprising. It appears that a broad, macro variable such as modernization may have too remote an effect on particular reorganization strategies.

Because of its particular relevance, key findings concerning Degree of Reorganization Reform will be considered separately.

*Degree of Reorganization Reform: Major Findings*

Results show that the political, innovation, and modernization perspective variables generally have about the same strength of relationship with Reorganization Reform as they do with the other two reorganization outcomes—Adoption Decision and Degree of Adoption. This structural variable is important, because Degree of Reorganization Reform could be assumed to have a more direct bearing on state government performance than do Adoption Decision or Degree of Adoption. These other outcome variables are directly concerned, not with the quality of reorganization, but only with whether a reorganization proposal is adopted and how much of it gets approved.

The overall associations between Degree of Reorganization Reform and Degree of Electoral Competition for Governorship ( $-.13$ ), Governor's Party Control of Legislature ( $-.11$ ), Diffusion Agent Activity ( $-.12$ ), and Level of Modernization ( $.10$ ) do not allow much gain in proportionate reduction of prediction error. But two of these associations are considerably stronger for the most recent wave of state reorganizations. For this period, the association of Degree of Reorganization Reform with Degree of Electoral Competition for Governorship is $-.26$, and with Modernization Level is $.31$. Both of these findings are in the direction hypothesized. As expected, when gubernatorial competition is low, there is a tendency for the more ambitious reform type to be more feasible. Under conditions of moderate electoral competition, both reform types show a tendency to be about equally feasible. If electoral competition has been intense, the lower risk Traditional type is preferred by a ratio of two to one.

For this most recent wave, there has been a strong tendency for low-modernization states to adopt Traditional reorganizations. (See Table 6.5.) Some of these low-modernization states had not before gone through broad-scale executive branch reorganization and were tending toward the least idealistic type of reform. Florida's Traditional reorganization in 1969 is an example. Other low-modernization states had reorganized before but were changing to another variable of Traditional type. Such is the case of North Dakota in 1967.

There is also a strong pattern among states ranked moderate in Modernization Level to "upgrade" during this period to a Cabinet or Secretary-Coordinator reform.[20] Missouri's 1974 Cabinet reorganization is a case in point, the previous Traditional reorganization having occurred nineteen years earlier.

There is a tendency for those states ranked highest in Modernization Level to turn to either high or low reform. To illustrate, while New York (1960) and Massachusetts (1969) were adjusting their already highly reformed structures, Michigan was turning to a Traditional reform (1965).[21]

TABLE 6.5

Cross Classification of Level of State
Modernization and Degree of Reorganization
Reform, Post-First-Hoover Wave, 1947-1975

| | | MODERNIZATION LEVEL | | | Row Total |
| --- | --- | --- | --- | --- | --- |
| | | LOW | MODERATE | HIGH | |
| DEGREE OF REORGANIZATION REFORM | LOW Traditional Type | 11 (57.9%) (84.6%) | 3 (15.8%) (21.4%) | 5 (26.3%) (50.0%) | 19 (51.4%) |
| | HIGH Secretary-Coordinator and Cabinet Types | 2 (11.1%) (15.4%) | 11 (61.1%) (78.6%) | 5 (27.8%) (50.0%) | 18 (48.6%) |
| | Column Total | 13 (35.1%) | 14 (37.8%) | 10 (27.0%) | 37 (100%) |

Of the strategy variables, Timing of Adoption Effort has the strongest association (tau-b = - .27) with Degree of Reorganization Reform. There is a tendency for more idealistic, larger-scale reorganizations to be undertaken earlier in a governor's administration. This finding adds support to the contention of Lowi that new departures in policy are more likely to occur in the initial stages of a new administration.

Even though reorganization strategies other than Timing have not had much association with Degree of Reorganization Reform, the strategy variables have shown considerable prediction value in terms of other reorganization outcomes. Attention is now focused on these strategy variables.

*Reorganization Strategies: Major Findings*

Possibly because they are more proximate to a specific reorganization attempt than are the perspective variables, the strategy variables show some of the stronger associations with Adoption Decision and Degree of Adoption.

*Comprehensiveness of Tactics.* Of the variables used in this study, Comprehensiveness of Tactics is the best predictor in PRE terms of both Adoption Decision (PRE of 38 percent) and Degree of Adoption (PRE of 37 percent). As hypothesized, these relationships are in opposite directions. The comprehensive reorganization adoption strategy is less likely to result in adoption. But if adoption does take place, it is more likely to be a higher proportion of the total reorganization package. Because comprehensive tactics were operationalized in terms of a one-shot, all-or-nothing approach, this second result is not surprising. This is essentially the argument joined by Lipson, Harvey Walker, and Jimmy Carter: Is the greater potential payoff worth the greater risk? An examination of cross-classification tables for these associations can help answer that question. (See Table 6.6.)

For the data available, the odds of failing completely are higher using comprehensive tactics (52.5 percent) than using incremental tactics (15.6 percent). Conversely, the odds of getting at least some of the reorganization passed is far higher (84.4 percent) when incremental tactics are applied than when comprehensive tactics, with a 41.3 percent chance of adoption, are pursued. The superiority of incremental tactics as the low-risk alternative was expected. The degree of "payoff" is compared in Table 6.7.

If some adoption does take place, the odds for a high degree of adoption are higher using comprehensive tactics (78.9 percent) than when incremental tactics are utilized (44.4 percent). The probability of adopting a minor portion of the reorganization package is far greater when incrementalism is applied. These results again are as expected. A more complete picture of risks and payoffs can be gained by combining both kinds of reorganization outcome. (See Table 6.8.)

TABLE 6.6

Cross Classification of Tactics
and Adoption Decision

| | | TACTICS | | Row Total |
|---|---|---|---|---|
| | | INCREMENTAL | COMPREHENSIVE | |
| ADOPTION DECISION | NO ADOPTION | 5 (19.2%) (15.6%) | 21 (80.8%) (52.5%) | 26 (36.1%) |
| | SOME ADOPTION | 27 (58.7%) (84.4%) | 19 (41.3%) (47.5%) | 46 (63.9%) |
| Column Total | | 32 (44.4%) | 40 (55.6%) | 72 (100%) |

It can now be observed that, if there is no assurance of some adoption, incremental tactics afford less risk of no adoption (15.6 to 52.5 percent for comprehensive tactics) and have the same likelihood (37.5 percent) of resulting in high degree of adoption.

The relative advantages of one tactic over the other vary slightly by period and region. In the recent post-first-Hoover wave, which has been the most receptive to state reorganization, the strategic superiority of incremental tactics is not as clear-cut. According to data for this wave, both tac-

TABLE 6.7

Cross Classification of Tactics
and Degree of Adoption

|  |  | TACTICS | | Row Total |
|  |  | INCREMENTAL | COMPREHENSIVE | Row Total |
|---|---|---|---|---|
| DEGREE OF ADOPTION | LOW | 11 (91.7%) (40.7%) | 1 (8.3%) (5.3%) | 12 (26.1%) |
| DEGREE OF ADOPTION | MODERATE | 4 (57.1%) (14.8%) | 3 (42.9%) (15.8%) | 7 (15.2%) |
| DEGREE OF ADOPTION | HIGH | 12 (44.4%) (44.4%) | 15 (55.6%) (78.9%) | 27 (58.7%) |
| Column Total | | 27 (58.7%) | 19 (41.3%) | 46 (100%) |

Note: Comprehensive Tactics can result in
partial adoption if, for example,
a single reorganization bill is amended.

TABLE 6.8

Cross Classification of Tactics
and Combined Reorganization Outcomes

| | | TACTICS | | |
|---|---|---|---|---|
| | | INCREMENTAL | COMPREHENSIVE | Row Total |
| REORGANIZATION OUTCOMES | NO ADOPTION | 5 (19.2%) (15.6%) | 21 (80.8%) (52.5%) | 26 (36.1%) |
| | LOW ADOPTION | 11 (91.7%) (34.4%) | 1 (8.3%) (2.5%) | 12 (16.7%) |
| | MODERATE ADOPTION | 4 (57.1%) (12.5%) | 3 (42.9%) (7.5%) | ᶜ7 (9.7%) |
| | HIGH ADOPTION | 12 (44.4%) (37.5%) | 15 (55.6%) (37.5%) | 27 (37.5%) |
| | Column Total | 32 (44.4%) | 40 (55.6%) | 72 (100%) |

tics are "good bets." Incremental tactics are again the low-risk strategy. In fact, for the reorganizations on which there was information, incrementalism was 100 percent successful in leading to some adoption. Comprehensive tactics led to some adoption 78.6 percent of the time. Comprehensive tactics were slightly more likely to result in high adoption (64.3 to 55.6 percent).

The general relationships between Comprehensiveness of Tactics and Adoption Decision and Degree of Adoption hold for most regions. (See Appendix B.) The receptivity to certain tactics varies among regions, however. The Plains region has shown a greater tendency for a positive adoption decision if comprehensive tactics are used. New England's penchant for incrementalism is demonstrated by the greater relative success in attaining a higher Degree of Adoption when incremental tactics are applied.

*Timing of Adoption Effort.* Timing does not appear to be as critical a strategy choice as tactics, but proper timing has become more important in the most recent wave of reorganizations. The association between Timing of Adoption Effort and Adoption Decision during the post-first-Hoover wave is − .30. This is considerably higher than the − .07 association for all time periods. For this last wave, this means a 30 percent reduction in error predicting the rank of Adoption Decision when rank on Timing of Adoption Effort is known. For the most recent wave, earlier timing strategies have become more likely to result in adoption.

Timing also shows more influence in some regions than others. Early timing has been more successful among states in the Plains region. According to the data, all five early attempts resulted in adoption, but only one of seven attempts made in the middle and late stages of a governor's tenure achieved partial adoption. At the other extreme are states in the New England region where later timing is more likely to result in adoption. (See Appendix B.)

The relationship between Timing of Adoption Effort and Degree of Adoption (tau-b = − .26) for the third wave is also higher in magnitude than the overall association (− .13). Regional patterns are not as pronounced on this association, but there is a tendency for earlier attempts to get more receptive treatment in the Far West and Plains regions.

*Rigor of Legal-Adoption Mechanism.* As with Timing, the overall associations between Rigor of Legal Mechanism and Adoption Decision (− .07) and Degree of Adoption (0) do not totally reflect the influence of the legal strategy variable. The association between Rigor of Legal Mechanism and Adoption Decision is − .32 for the most recent wave of reorganizations. Table 6.9 shows this relationship.

It can be seen that there is a strong, indeed perfect, association between

TABLE 6.9

Cross Classification of Rigor of Legal
Mechanism and Adoption Decision

| | | RIGOR OF LEGAL MECHANISM | | | Row Total |
|---|---|---|---|---|---|
| | | LOW[a] | MODERATE[b] | HIGH[c] | |
| ADOPTION DECISION | NO ADOPTION | 0 (0%) (0%) | 3 (100%) (100%) | 0 (0%) (0%) | 3 (9.1%) |
| | SOME ADOPTION | 23 (76.7%) (100%) | 0 (0%) (0%) | 7 (23.3%) (100%) | 30 (90.9%) |
| Column Total | | 23 (69.7%) | 3 (9.1%) | 7 (21.2%) | 33 (100%) |

Notes: [a]Legal mechanisms in this class consist
of non-constitutional devices including
statute, executive order, and reorganization
plan.

[b]This class consists of constitutional
amendment when not used in conjunction with
other legal instruments.

[c]This class is comprised of multiple-stage
legal processes which include constitutional
amendment along with other legal hurdles.

particular legal strategies and reorganization-adoption success or failure.[22] Even if more complete data on legal strategies could be obtained for the post-first-Hoover wave, the extra data points are not likely to change this pattern drastically.

These findings confirm the superiority of nonconstitutional, primarily statutory, legal strategies for state reorganization over the constitutional-amendment strategy. Also in evidence is the considerable effectiveness of the legal-strategy innovation discussed earlier in this chapter, whereby constitutional amendment is used as a part of a multiple-phase legal process.

Even though no overall association between Rigor of Legal Adoption Mechanism and Degree of Adoption is found (tau-b = 0), the corresponding association for the most recent wave is .23. This provides a considerable proportionate reduction of error in prediction. The more rigorous legal strategies appear to be particularly resisted in the Southeast and Mid-Atlantic regions and have been most favorably received in the Plains and Mountains states. (See Appendix B.)

I have devoted much attention to the three strategy variables because these are more at the command of state reorganization decision makers and can be more readily manipulated to achieve a desired reorganization outcome. Further application of these findings on strategies will be made in the concluding chapter in the form of action guidelines for state decision makers.

## Notes

1. For a discussion of methodological issues about regionalism, see Ira Sharkansky, *Regionalism in American Politics* (Indianapolis: Bobbs-Merrill, 1970) and Daniel J. Elazar, *American Federalism: A View From the States* (New York: Thomas Crowell, 1966).

2. James L. Martin, interview with James L. Garnett, February 16, 1977.

3. See for example Ramon E. Henkel, *Tests of Significance* (Beverly Hills, Calif.: Sage Publications, 1976), pp. 7–9. Herman J. Loether and Donald G. McTavish, *Descriptive and Inferential Statistics: An Introduction* (Boston: Allyn and Bacon, 1974), p. 470.

4. Hubert M. Blalock, Jr., *Social Statistics,* (New York: McGraw-Hill, 1972) pp. 415–26. Loether and McTavish, *Descriptive and Inferential Statistics,* pp. 221–30.

5. David K. Hildebrand, James D. Laing, and Howard Rosenthal, *Analysis of Ordinal Data* (Beverly Hills, Calif.: Sage Publications, 1977), p. 14.

6. Loether and McTavish, *Descriptive and Inferential Statistics,* p. 212.

7. Hildebrand, Laing, and Rosenthal, *Analysis of Ordinal Data,* p. 16.

8. Thomas P. Wilson, "A Proportional-Reduction-in-Error Interpretation for Kendall's Tau-b," *Social Forces* 47 (December 1968):340–42. Jae-On Kim, "Predictive Measures of Ordinal Association," *American Journal of Sociology* 76 (March 1971): 891–907.

9. Loether and McTavish, *Descriptive and Inferential Statistics,* p. 230.

10. Hildebrand, Laing, and Rosenthal, *Analysis of Ordinal Data,* p. 52. Eric M. Uslaner, interview with James L. Garnett, January 16, 1978.

11. Blalock, *Social Statistics,* p. 423. Loether and McTavish, *Descriptive and Inferential Statistics,* p. 230.

12. Hildebrand, Laing, and Rosenthal, *Analysis of Ordinal Data,* p. 52. Blalock, *Social Statistics,* p. 423.

13. Kim, "Predictive Measures of Ordinal Association," p. 893.

14. For illustrative cases of bureaucratic and interest-group influence on state reorganization, see Frederick C. Mosher, ed., *Governmental Reorganization: Cases and Commentary* (Indianapolis: Bobbs-Merrill, 1967).

15. Joseph A. Schlesinger, "The Politics of the Executive," in *Politics in the American States: A Comparative Analysis,* 2d ed., Herbert Jacob and Kenneth Vines, eds. (Boston: Little, Brown and Co., 1971), p. 234.

16. Even though the subpopulations are small for both of these associations, the magnitudes are sufficient to indicate a clearly negative relationship.

17. Philip M. Savage, *State of Maine Governmental Reorganization: A Summary of New Departments and Agencies Approved by the 105th Legislature,* State Planning Office, Executive Department, June 30, 1971–July 7, 1971.

18. Robert E. Riggs, *The Movement for Administrative Reorganization in Arizona* (Tucson: University of Arizona Press, 1964), p. 67.

19. For example, the ten states with the highest levels of modernization (operationalized as Hofferbert's Industrialization Rank) in 1920 were: (1) Rhode Island, (2) Massachusetts, (3) Connecticut, (4) New Jersey, (5) New York, (6) Michigan, (7) Pennsylvania, (8) New Hampshire, (9) Ohio, (10) Illinois. Seven of the ten are from the New England and Mid-Atlantic regions.

20. It should be repeated that the assumption of superiority identified with the Cabinet and Secretary-Coordinator types is an assumption of others. This assumption has yet to be tested in research.

21. The fact that Republican Governor Romney faced two houses of the legislature controlled by Democrats may have had some part in the decision.

22. Table 6.9 shows a good example of what was discussed earlier regarding the interpretation of association. The Kendall's tau-b for this particular association ( – .32) is as low as it is because it tests the accuracy of the specific hypothesized relationship (in this case monotonic decreasing) between the rigorousness of the legal mechanism and the likelihood of adoption. What in fact is present is a polytonic relationship, first monotonic decreasing, then monotonic increasing for different values of Legal Mechanism.

**7**

# Conclusions, Action Guidelines, and Directions for Further Research

---

*Most of the rationalizers of state reorganization . . . appear to proceed blithely on the assumption that God looks after fools, drunkards and the liberties of the people.*
—Charles S. Hyneman, "Administrative Reorganization: An Adventure into Science and Theology"

This research has focused on three fundamental issues concerning state executive branch reorganizations: why they occur, what structural forms they take, and what strategies can be utilized and with what effect. The purpose of this research has been to survey the state of our knowledge about these issues, to sort and systematize this knowledge for further reference, and, for the first time, to analyze these issues using statistical tools.

This chapter presents conclusions drawn from the preceding analysis, followed by a discussion of practical applications of the findings in the form of action guidelines. And finally, since one aim of this study was to identify what we know about state reorganization, it is fitting to end with a discussion of what we do not know and how this gap might be closed.

### What Has Been Learned? Assessing the Hypotheses

Most of the hypotheses set forth in Chapter 5 were based on information categorized in Chapters 2, 3, and 4. Some hypotheses were based on previous research; others reflected "conventional wisdom." My results indicate that much of our current information cannot be conclusively confirmed. Of the forty hypotheses, results for twenty-eight (70 percent) were not significant at the .05 level, three (7.5 percent) were significant but ran counter to the hypothesized direction, and nine (22.5 percent) were significant and in the hypothesized direction. Even though these results were not stronger, they still have value. Our fragmented knowledge is furthered by the discovery that some of the expectations stemming from conventional wisdom or common sense logic did not, in fact, hold true. Our knowledge is now more realistic and perhaps more sobering.

The hypotheses for the strategy variables generally fared better than those posited for the perspective variables. Hypotheses relating to the Reorganization as Political Competition perspective particularly "missed the mark." The explanation for this failure appears to lie partly in the complexity of political phenomena. Because so many factors are interacting, a single variable may not have as straightforward a relationship as hypothesized. The impact of Governor's Party Control of the Legislature is a case in point. The literature indicates that party control should be one of those conditions most crucial to adoption success. As discussed in Chapter 6, however, other factors apparently negate or override the effect of party control.

I have pondered why the results of this study were not more spectacular and have come to the following conclusions:

1. Kendall's tau-b, the measure used, tends to produce lower values than Spearman's rho, Somer's d, Goodman and Kruskal's gamma, and other measures that I might have applied. I spurned advice to use another measure to jack up the magnitudes of these associations so my results would appear stronger. In exploratory research of this kind I believe caution is the wiser course.

2. Some of the variables and indicators I used turned out to be inadequate. Limitations and problems with Governor's Party Control, Level of Modernization, and Diffusion Agent Activity have already been pointed out. Better operationalizations need to be made and other variables added to the analysis.

3. When dealing with broad administrative reform, relationships among variables appear to be too complex to capture adequately with the simpler, more straightforward explanations found in the literature on reorganization. I mentioned this before with regard to the political competition variables. But complexity is not confined to political relationships. Innovation, modernization, and reorganization-strategy issues are likewise highly complex.

4. The behavioral revolution in social science has nearly passed by the longstanding issue of state reorganization. For this reason, our knowledge about state reorganization is not as solid as our knowledge of state electoral behavior and other topics that have received lengthy and widespread research attention. We have some catching up to do on state reorganization and state administrative issues in general.

## Fundamental Research Questions

*Why Do State Executive Branch Reorganizations Occur?*

State executive branch reorganizations occur as a result of a variety of forces acting at different times under different conditions. Even based on this preliminary and incomplete research, it appears clear that no single, dominant perspective is the best PRE-predictor of Adoption Decision for all time periods and all regions. Diffusion Agent Activity and Governor's Party Control of Legislature had the strongest effect during the post-Taft wave, State Modernization Level tended to be a better predictor during the post-Brownlow wave, and Electoral Competition for the Governorship had the strongest association with Adoption Decision in the post-first-Hoover wave. (See Table 7.1.)

The political perspective variables have the strongest association with reorganization adoption in the Far West and Great Lakes regions. Diffusion Agent Activity is most strongly associated with reorganization adoption in the Southeast and the Mid-Atlantic. Both political and diffusion influences are important to reorganization adoption in states of the Southwest. Electoral Competition for the Governorship and Modernization Level are strongest in the Plains region. With the exception of Electoral Competition for the Governorship, variables of all three perspectives are about equally strong in predicting reorganization adoption in New England states. Political variables are important in the Mountains states, but insufficient data prevent a comparison with other perspectives.

These findings are only a beginning. Further research is needed (1) to enrich these perspectives by adding other variables and (2) to implement other perspectives on reorganizations. One factor in particular that needs further exploration is the role of federal agencies and policies in stimulating or inhibiting state executive reorganization. Single-agency requirements, grant inducements, and other federal stimuli for state reorganization have had a stronger effect on triggering single-agency reorganizations than broader-scale executive branch reorganizations. (This is why federal requirements and policies have not been more prominent in my research.) The chief federal stimulus to state executive branch reorganization has been through example. Many states have been stimulated by the Taft, Brownlow, Hoover, and other federal efforts to reorganize. The way in which this federal diffusion–state emulation process works needs to be more clearly understood.

*What Forms Do Reorganized Executive Branches Take?*
*How Do These Structures Differ? What Kinds of States*
*Tend to Adopt What Types of Reorganization?*

The modified Bell typology of reorganization has been found useful for describing some key structural properties of reorganized executive branches. Of the three types, the Traditional form of reorganization generally has the following characteristics: the lowest concentration of administrative

TABLE 7.1

Best and Worst PRE Predictors of Adoption Decision by Time Period and Region

| | BEST[a] | WORST[a] |
|---|---|---|
| **TIME PERIOD** | | |
| Post-Taft Wave (1914-1936) | (.19) Diffusion Agent Activity<br>(.16) Governor's Party Control | (.04) Modernization Level<br>(.06) Electoral Competition |
| Post-Brownlow Wave (1937-1946) | (.51) Modernization Level<br>(-.29) Governor's Party Control | (.09) Electoral Competition |
| Post-First-Hoover Wave (1947-1975) | (-.26) Electoral Competition | (-.10) Governor's Party Control |
| **REGION** | | |
| New England | (-.35) Diffusion Agent Activity<br>(-.29) Governor's Party Control<br>(-.26) Modernization Level | (.03) Electoral Competition |

| Region | Best Predictors | Worst Predictors |
|---|---|---|
| Mid-Atlantic | (-1.00) Diffusion Agent Activity<br>(.29) Governor's Party Control | (-.07) Electoral Competition |
| Southeast | (.53) Diffusion Agent Activity<br>(-.25) Governor's Party Control | (0.00) Modernization Level<br>(-.03) Electoral Competition |
| Great Lakes | (.92) Electoral Competition<br>(.47) Governor's Party Control | (-.35) Modernization Level |
| Plains | (.41) Modernization Level<br>(.36) Electoral Competition | (-.15) Governor's Party Control |
| Southwest | (-.32) Diffusion Agent Activity<br>(.29) Electoral Competition | (-.10) Governor's Party Control |
| Mountains | (-.33) Electoral Competition | (.20) Governor's Party Control |
| Far West | (.45) Electoral Competition<br>(-.44) Governor's Party Control | (-.19) Modernization Level |

[a]Associations reported are Kendall's tau-b. For the very best predictors the values would be 1.00 (perfect association) or -1.00 (perfect negative association) between variables). For the very worst predictors the values would be 0.00 (no association).

authority in the hands of the governor, the greatest number of agencies remaining after reorganization, the lowest degree of functional consolidation, the lowest gubernatorial appointive power, the highest proportion of agencies with plural executives, and the highest degree of management authority retained by transplanted agencies. On all these dimensions except the last, the Secretary-Coordinator type ranks as the most reform oriented, with the Cabinet model ranking in between. However, because the Cabinet type adheres most closely to the orthodox reform ideal regarding centralization-decentralization of managerial authority, it is judged by the Council of State Governments and others to represent the highest degree of reform.

Most state reorganizations have been the least politically and administratively ambitious Traditional type. This has been particularly true of the last two waves of reorganization. The Traditional type has predominated in the Great Lakes region and west of the Mississippi River. The Cabinet type, patterned after the federal model, has been largely an eastern phenomenon. Sixty-two percent of all Cabinet reorganizations have occurred in the three easternmost regions—New England, the Mid-Atlantic, and the Southeast. The Secretary-Coordinator model is a phenomenon of the last wave and is geographically dispersed. Traditional reorganizations are more prevalent among states ranking low in modernization level. Over the last thirty years, the more modernized states have tended to adopt Cabinet or Secretary-Coordinator forms of reorganization. Nevertheless, there has been a pattern of states moving toward more orthodox reform types. Thus, some states that adopted Cabinet reorganizations in the first wave have followed with Traditional reorganizations in the third wave.

*How Are State Executive Reorganizations Conducted?*
*What Strategies Are Applied with Regard to*
*Adoption and Implementation?*

A broad range of reorganization strategies has been identified. This range covers the reorganization process from the inception of the research effort through the implementation phase. Many strategy options for the adoption process have analogs in the implementation phase. Examples are tactics, timing, and role of governor.

Even though present data limitations prevented empirical analysis of implementation strategies, there is evidence that: (1) The strategies most effective in the adoption phase (e.g., incremental tactics) may not be the most effective for implementation. (2) Adoption and implementation strategies need to be considered interdependently because strategy choices for one phase influence the outcome of the other phase.

Because strategies can be manipulated by state decision makers, the following discussion of action guidelines focuses on the choice of reorganization strategy to influence adoption outcome. The generalizations upon which the action guidelines are based constitute the overall conclusions about the three strategy variables utilized in this research.

## Action Guidelines for State Reorganizers

It is not enough to arrive at research findings on reorganization; they can only be useful if we also devote some thought to their practical import. Unless state decision makers can see the utility of findings like the ones presented here, such research is not likely to influence reorganization practices in constructive ways. In order to get our findings into the right hands and to minimize inevitable misinterpretations of results, it is advisable to develop guidelines for translating research into policy action.[1]

This study will follow the established precedent of drawing generalizations based on empirical findings and then translating these generalizations into action guidelines.[2] The generalizations drawn from the present research are selected on the basis of two criteria: (1) They must center on variables that can be manipulated by state decision makers. (2) They must generalize findings sufficiently strong that action can be taken with some degree of confidence. But it is the state decision makers and other users who must determine how much confidence to place in these results. Some governors, for example, may not regard the relationship between timing and adoption (tau-b = − .30) sufficiently strong to risk resources, political capital, and their reputation on an early timing strategy. Other governors might be willing to take this calculated risk.

For the purpose of devising action guidelines, additional computer runs were made, taking certain contingencies into account. Associations between the strategy variables and reorganization outcome variables were calculated under conditions of low, moderate, and high Electoral Competition for the Governorship; low, moderate, and high Level of State Modernization; and under conditions where the governor's party controlled no legislative houses, one house, and two houses.[3] These results are reported in Appendix D. It is important to consider the N's and significance levels in deciding how much faith to put in these guidelines.

### Generalization 1

There is an overall tendency for incremental tactics (proposals phased over time or multiple proposals at one time) to result in reorganization adoption. (The association between Comprehensiveness of Tactics and Adoption Decision is − .38.) This pattern holds for all three time periods and for all regions except the Plains states. Under conditions where the governor's party does not control either legislative house, the choice between tactical options is about even (tau-b = − .04). Under conditions where the governor's party controls one house, incremental tactics tend to be more closely related to adoption (tau-b = − .75). Incremental tactics also appear to be particulary effective when a state is ranked high (tau-b = − .62) or low (tau-b = − .61) in modernization level. The advantage of incremental tactics is not as clear when a state has a moderate level of modernization (tau-b = − .06).

*Action Guidelines.* If the objective is to minimize the risk of having a state executive reorganization defeated, incremental tactics are superior to comprehensive tactics except in the Plains states and where the governor's party does not control either house of the legislature[4] or where a state has a moderate level of modernization.

## Generalization 2

Two sets of legal strategies are related to higher chances for reorganization adoption in the most recent post-Hoover wave of state reorganizations. Either the strategy of reorganization by statute or through multiple stages including constitutional amendment is decidedly superior to the use of constitutional amendment by itself (tau-b = − .32). Geographically, this basic pattern holds fairly well except for the Great Lakes and Plains regions and, to a lesser extent, New England. Where the governor's party does not have control over either legislative house, the association is reversed (tau-b = − .29), implying that more rigorous legal strategies, which reduce the importance of legislative action, are more effective. This same tendency, less pronounced (.21), is indicated where only one house is controlled by the governor's party. Balanced use of legal strategies has led to greater adoption success both by region and time period.

*Action Guidelines.* To minimize the risk of having a state executive reorganization defeated, use the legal strategies of legislative statute or, as an alternative, multiple-stage strategies incorporating the use of constitutional amendment with other legal devices. Where the governor's party controls one house or no house, more drastic, nonstatutory strategies are indicated. The more rigorous legal strategies are generally to be preferred in the Great Lakes and Plains states; a multiple-stage strategy is effective in the Mountains states. Supporters of state reorganization should be advised to work toward getting sanction for a range of legal mechanisms that could be applied in their state. Legal flexibility is identified with adoption success.

## Generalization 3

Findings for the most recent wave of state reorganizations (1947–75) show that reorganizations attempted in the first one-third of a governor's administration are more likely to be adopted in whole or in part than are later attempts. (The association between Timing of Adoption Effort and Adoption Decision is − .30 for this period.) This pattern holds particularly strongly in the Plains region (tau-b = − .80). There is a tendency in this direction in Great Lakes states (tau-b = − .35), but later timing strategies tend to be more successful in New England (tau-b = .39) and in the Mountains states (tau-b = .40). In the other regions there is not as clear a pattern showing the advantage of a particular timing strategy. Early timing tends to be more effective after a governor has had a low degree of electoral competition at the preceding election than after a hotly contested election. (The respective associations are − .43 under conditions of low electoral competition and .05 when there has been high electoral competition at the election prior to reorganization.) Early timing tends to be more successful if a state has a moderate level of modernization (tau-b with Adoption Decision is − .28) and less successful under conditions of low or high levels of modernization.

*Action Guidelines.* In general, reorganization sponsors are advised to attempt executive branch reorganizations early in a governor's administration to minimize risk that a reorganization will be defeated. Unless particular state experience has been to the contrary, reorganizers in New England and Mountains states are advised to consider later timing strategies. A deemphasis of early timing strategy is also advised in states where the previous party competition for the governorship has been high and in states with a high (upper third) or low (lower third) modernization rank.

State decision makers should take into account particular constraints, patterns, and customs in their state before selecting a strategy based on the above action guidelines. These guidelines offer direction concerning reorganization *adoption* only. *Implementation* feasibility must also be taken into account before selecting an adoption strategy. We have learned that those strategies most effective in accomplishing reorganization adoption may well jeopardize the implementation process.

## Directions for Further Research:
## Much Is Left to Learn

The focus of this study was kept broad to facilitate an overview and to map the terrain for further exploration. A number of research directions remain to be pursued. They include:

### Upgrading and Expanding the Data Base

This research has attempted to pull together information on reorganization in forty-eight states that has never before been brought together. Such a consolidation is necessary if we are to learn more than just what happened regarding Massachusetts's reorganization in 1969 or Idaho's reorganization of 1974. The intent has been to develop a data base that will serve as a foundation upon which others can build. In the current data base there are gaps to be filled and pieces of information to be verified.

As discussed earlier, data on state reorganization failures particularly need developing. Much of the current information comes from sponsors or supporters of reorganization. State government officials are often reluctant to supply information about failures. Professional and research organizations that serve state government constituents have shown reluctance to study reorganizations unfavorable to these constituents. Unless information on reorganization failures is collected and analyzed, our ability to learn from past mistakes and to improve future performance will be limited.

It is important that other variables be utilized to "flesh out" the political, innovation, and modernization perspectives. Political variables that warrant pursuit include extent of intraparty factionalism, rate and time of party turnover, degree of interest-group support, and degree of support among bureaucratic actors. Likewise, variables that reflect a state's absolute level of modernization would supplement the present relative measure. Such variables include population density, percent urban population, and rate of illiteracy. Additional bureaucratic variables should be considered as part of the innovation perspective or as part of yet another approach. Among such variables which appear to hold promise are occupational training of governor, interstate mobility of administrators, and activity of associations of state officials.

### In-Depth Case Studies of State Reorganization as Part of an Iterative Research Process

Another logical "next step" is an in-depth case-study exploration of selected state reorganizations in order to test in a more detailed context the relationships discovered in this study. These case studies could in turn spawn additional issues and variables for investigation, as well as help modify or confirm the present findings. If this continuous, iterative research process is to be effective, the comparative case study method must be used to its full potential, as discussed in Chapter 5. If the precautions discussed there are not properly observed, the result will be another generation of case studies with limited theoretical and applied utility.

### Broad-Based Investigation of Additional Adoption Strategies

Other strategies may turn out to be as crucial as, or more critical than, those examined in this study. Strategy variables that merit intensive exploration include: type and size of reorganization study commission, primary composition of study team (consultants, in-house staff, blue-ribbon citizen panel, combination), scope and character of reorganization study, size of research budget, variety and type of promotional strategies utilized, size of promotion budget, and role of key groups and leaders in adoption campaign.

What is in fact needed is an in-depth study on the scale of the U.S. Advisory Commission on Intergovernmental Relations' study on "Factors Affecting Voter Reaction to Governmental Reorganization in Metropolitan Areas." That particular research explored the impact of a series of variables on voter reaction to government reorganization in eighteen metropolitan areas. Variables investigated were: scope of proposals, background of proposals, issues involved in reorganization, role of various community elements, and types of promotional methods and media used in promotion. A study analogous to this, but dealing with the research and promotion of state reorganization, could produce important new knowledge about how these phases of the reorganization process work.

### In-Depth Attention to Implementation of Reorganization

State reorganization *implementation* is badly in need of thorough investigation. Only two theoretical and research perspectives examined in Chapter 2 (the Administrative Orthodoxy and Political Competition perspectives) devote attention to the crucial implementation phase. The obstacles to high-caliber research on implementation are formidable. But the reward appears to be worth the extra effort. To close this gap in our knowledge of the reorganization process would bring us one step closer to the actual performance consequences of state reorganization.

### Evaluation of Reorganization's Impact on State Government Performance

As stated earlier, the performance issue is probably the most fundamental, and most difficult, question concerning reorganization. Determining the performance of a public organizational arrangement is normally an extremely complex task because operational goals are not always stated, impacts are delayed, and the causes of performance outcomes are hard to trace, verify, or untangle from one another.[5]

The dearth of such evaluations is testimony that state executive reorganization is difficult, and perhaps even undesirable, to evalute. In 1976 Anita Gottlieb contended,

> Not one example exists of a real effort to evaluate the costs and benefits of the executive reorganizations of the past decade. With the exception of a state-

ment in Kentucky's response to the request for information on evaluation . . .
little mention is made of measuring the level of service delivery following
reorganization.[6]

Until we have a more realistic concept of what effects reorganization has
and does not have on performance, cynicism such as that expressed by
Charles Hyneman will remain.

My intent has not been to shirk the crucial issue of performance. Rather,
the intent has been to tackle some other fundamental issues first, in order to
build a knowledge base that can aid in dealing with the performance question. Without better knowledge than we have now, we are not in the position to determine what difference reorganization makes.

*Researching the Link between State Executive Reorganization
and Management-Improvement Efforts*

Reorganization is often criticized as being superficial "box-shuffling,"
which does not affect the actual management of public organizations.
There has been a pattern for state governments to undertake wide-
sweeping management improvement efforts after undergoing executive
branch reorganization. For example, Oregon's Project Seventies Task
Force presented reorganization proposals that were acted on by the 1969
legislature. This effort, primarily oriented toward structural change, was
immediately followed by the Management Seventies Task Force, which
focused primarily on improving management practices and developing
management capabilities.[7] A similar pattern occurred in Colorado, where
the Commission for Reorganization of the Executive Branch was followed
(after the 1968 reorganization) by the Commission on Efficiency and
Economy. Identifying and tracing similar patterns in other states raised
some interesting research questions: What are the legal, political, administrative, and funding relationships between a state's executive
reorganization and later management-improvement drives? Is the gap between policy formulators and policy implementors more or less evident
under this arrangement? Framed in Waldo's terms, does the distinction
between *structural* and *procedural* administrative reforms warrant, even
necessitate, two separate but related efforts? Which has proven most effective, to emphasize both structural and procedural changes at the same time
or to follow emphasis on major structural reorganization with attention to
detailed management practices? The present research, with its focus on
structural reorganization, needs to be supplemented with an in-depth exploration of management practices in state government. A perceived
heightened interest at the present time in public management makes this
kind of research even more opportune.

*In-Depth Research Focused at the*
*Organizational Level of Analysis*

The level of analysis for this study has been an entire executive branch. Focus on such a macro level can help discern overall patterns, but it does little to clarify behavior at the state operating level — the agency. Research focused at the organizational level is needed if we are to learn more about the dynamics of reorganization within agencies and among agencies.

One way of exploring these dynamics during an executive reorganization would be to "track" organizational units and subunits in order to detect changes internal to the units and changes in interorganizational relations.

## An Integrative Orientation for Future Research

These and other future research tasks on state executive reorganization must be undertaken with the view toward integrating these pieces into a meaningful whole. There has been a strong tendency for researchers to concentrate on viewing reorganization through one conceptual lens without taking advantage of the insights contributed by other perspectives or without adequately understanding how that particular approach fits within the total conceptual scheme. Most political scientists studying state reorganization tend to look through a Political Competition lens, some dwell on the Administrative Orthodoxy approach, and very few apply a Socioeconomic Determinants perspective. Scholars of public administration tend to confine their interest to the Administrative Orthodoxy and Political Competition perspectives. Economists and sociologists have yet to bring their research orientations and tools to bear on this issue in a significant way. While more demanding than the prevalent piecemeal approach, an integrated research approach appears to hold greater promise than does continued preoccupation with any single perspective. To attain the integration necessary for substantially increasing our knowledge of state reorganization, researchers must attempt to span boundaries between perspectives, both those theoretical perspectives examined in this study and other relevant approaches. An alternative research strategy to this perspective-spanning approach is to concentrate on more organized, cooperative research projects. This would involve specialists, each looking at particular pieces of the reorganization "puzzle" with the view toward fitting those pieces together.

As with the individual theoretical perspectives, both of these research strategies have strengths and limitations. The perspective-spanning approach affords greater coordination of effort and higher likelihood of ultimate synthesis of knowledge. The organized, team-project strategy has the virtue of bringing greater expertise to bear on any single facet of reorganization research. In view of our limited knowledge about state reorganization, both learning strategies are needed.

### Notes

1. For example, the Coleman Report on American educational policy has been criticized for providing "no clear guidance for translating the statistical findings into policy action." Glen G. Cain and Harold W. Watts, "Problems in Making Policy Inferences from the Coleman Report," *American Sociological Review* 35 (April 1970):229. For further treatment of the problems and potentials involved in translating research into action, see Craig G. Heatwole, Lawrence F. Keller, and Gary L. Wamsley, "Action Research and Public Policy Analysis: Sharpening the Political Perspectives of Public Policy Research," Paper prepared for delivery at the 1975 annual meeting of the American Political Science Association, September 2-5, 1975. R. Scott Brooks et al., "Perils of Policy Analysis: Action Research in a Cruel World," Paper prepared for delivery at the 1975 annual meeting of the Southern Political Science Association, November 6-8, 1975.

2. A series of such efforts have been undertaken by Rothman and others. Perhaps the most notable of these works is Jack Rothman, *Planning and Organizing for Social Change: Action Principles from Social Science* (New York: Columbia University Press, 1974). Another effort along this track is: Fred M. Cox, John L. Ehrlich, Jack Rothman, and John E. Tropman, eds., *Strategies of Community Organization: A Book of Readings,* 2d ed. (Itasca, Ill.: F. E. Peacock Publishers, 1974).

3. For a presentation of reorganization strategies using odds cast in percentages, see James L. Garnett, "Strategies for Governors Who Want to Reorganize," *State Government* 52 (Summer 1979):135-43.

4. It appears that under conditions of solid legislative opposition, there is some merit to Jimmy Carter's espoused strategy of presenting one major proposal and putting pressure on the legislature to accept it.

5. For an extensive discussion of the difficulties involved in operationalizing the goals of administrative reform, see Robert Backoff, "Operationalizing Administrative Reform for Improved Governmental Performance," *Administration and Society* 6 (May 1974):73-106. Robert C. Fried, *Performance in American Bureaucracy* (Boston: Little, Brown and Co., 1976), pp. 62-79, 411-26. Useful treatments of the effects of time in evaluating performance can be found in: Yehezkel Dror, *Public Policymaking Re-examined* (San Francisco: Chandler, 1968). Lester M. Salamon, "Followups, Letdowns, and Sleepers: The Time Dimension in Policy Evaluation," in *Public Policy Making in a Federal System*, Charles O. Jones and Robert D. Thomas eds. (Beverly Hills: Sage, 1976). James A. Caporaso and Leslie L. Roos, Jr., eds., *Quasi-Experimental Approaches: Testing Theory and Evaluating Policy* (Evanston, Ill.: Northwestern University Press, 1973). One effort to evaluate the budget and personnel impacts of state reorganization is Kenneth J. Meier, "Government Reorganization for Economy and Efficiency: Some Lessons from State Government," Paper de-

livered at the 1979 annual meeting of the Midwest Political Science Association, April 19–21, 1979.

6. Anita F. Gottlieb, "State Executive Reorganization: A Study of Hallucination, Supposition, and Hypothesis" (Ph.D. dissertation, George Washington University, 1976), p. 140.

7. Management Seventies Task Force, *Summary of Recommendations and Status of Implementation as of October 1, 1970* (Salem: State of Oregon Executive Department, 1970).

# State by State Data on Executive Branch Reorganizations, 1914–75

TABLE A.1

State by State Data on Executive Branch Reorganizations, 1914-1975[a]

| YEAR | | TYPE[b,c] | STRATEGY[b] | | | DEGREE OF ADOPTION[b,f] | NOTES[g] |
| Fail | Adopt | | TIMING[d] | TACTICS[e] | MECHANISM | | |
|---|---|---|---|---|---|---|---|
| ALABAMA | | | | | | | |
| | 1932 | Traditional[c] (see notes) | Middle | M.D. | M.D. | Low | (1) |
| | 1939 | Traditional[c] | Early | Incremental | Statute | M.D. | |
| ARIZONA | | | | | | | |
| 1921 | | Cabinet[c] (proposed) | Middle | M.D. | Statute | None | |
| 1933 | | M.D. | Early | M.D. | M.D. | None | |
| | 1949 | Cabinet[c] | Middle | M.D. | M.D. | Low | |
| | 1968 | Traditional[c] | Early | M.D. | Statute | M.D. | |
| | 1971-74 | Traditional | Middle | Incremental | Statute | Moderate | (2) |

| | Year | Type | Timing | Approach | Method | Level |
|---|---|---|---|---|---|---|
| ARKANSAS | 1921 | Cabinet[c] (proposed) | Early | M.D. | Statute | None |
| | 1929 | Cabinet[c] | Early | Incremental | Statute | Low |
| | 1968 | Cabinet[c] | Early | M.D. | M.D. | M.D. |
| | 1971 | Cabinet | Early | Comprehensive | Statute | M.D. |
| CALIFORNIA | 1919 | Traditional[c] | Middle | M.D. | M.D. | None |
| | 1921 | Traditional[c] | Late | Incremental | Statute | High |
| | 1927 | Traditional[c] | Early | Incremental | Statute | M.D. |
| | 1929 | Traditional[c] | Middle | Incremental | M.D. | M.D. |
| | 1961 | Secretary-Coordinator | Early | Incremental | Statute and Executive Order | High |
| | 1963 | Traditional[c] | Middle | Incremental | Reorganization Plan | Moderate |
| | 1968 | Secretary-Coordinator | Early | Comprehensive | Reorganization Plan following Constitutional Amendment and Statute | High |

TABLE A.1 (cont.)

| | YEAR | | TYPE | STRATEGY | | | DEGREE OF ADOPTION | NOTES |
|---|---|---|---|---|---|---|---|---|
| | Fail | Adopt | | TIMING | TACTICS | MECHANISM | | |
| COLORADO | 1923 | | Cabinet[c] | Early | Comprehensive | Statute | None | |
| | | 1933 | Traditional[c] | Early | Incremental | Constitutional Amendment and Statute | M.D. | |
| | | 1941 | Traditional[c] | Middle | Comprehensive | Statute | M.D. | |
| | | 1968 | Traditional | Middle | Comprehensive | Statute | High | |
| CONNECTICUT | 1921 | | Cabinet[c] | Early | Comprehensive | Statute | None | |
| | | 1937 | Traditional[c] | Late | Incremental | Statute | Low | |
| | | 1950 | M.D. | M.D. | Incremental | Statute | Low | |
| | | 1967 | Traditional[c] | Middle | Incremental | Statute | High | (3) |
| DELAWARE | 1919 | | Cabinet[c] | M.D. | M.D. | M.D. | None | |
| | | 1950 | Traditional[c] | M.D. | M.D. | M.D. | M.D. | |
| | | 1969-70 | Cabinet | Early | Incremental | Statute | High | |

| | Year | | | | Statute following Constitutional Amendment | |
|---|---|---|---|---|---|---|
| **FLORIDA** | 1969 | Traditional | Middle | Comprehensive | Statute following Constitutional Amendment | Moderate |
| **GEORGIA** | 1929 | M.D. | Middle | Comprehensive | Statute | None |
| | 1931 | Traditional[c] | Early | Comprehensive | Statute | High |
| | 1972 | Traditional | Early | Comprehensive | Statute | High |
| **IDAHO** | 1919 | Cabinet[c] | Early | Comprehensive | Statute | M.D. (4) |
| | 1967 | Traditional[c] | Early | Incremental | Statute | Low |
| | 1974 | Traditional | Late | Incremental | "Legislative Proposals" following Constitutional Amendment | High |
| **ILLINOIS** | 1915 | Cabinet[c] | M.D. | M.D. | M.D. | None |
| | 1917 | Cabinet[c] | Early | Comprehensive | Statute | M.D. (5) |
| | 1969 | M.D. | Early | M.D. | Statute | High |

TABLE A.1 (cont.)

| | YEAR | | TYPE | STRATEGY | | | DEGREE OF ADOPTION | NOTES |
|---|---|---|---|---|---|---|---|---|
| | Fail | Adopt | | TIMING | TACTICS | MECHANISM | | |
| INDIANA | | 1933 | Traditional[c] | Early | Comprehensive | Statute | M.D. | |
| IOWA | 1915 | | Secretary-Coordinator[c] | M.D. | M.D. | M.D. | None | |
| IOWA | | 1967 | M.D. | Late | M.D. | Statute | M.D. | |
| KANSAS | | 1970-75 | Traditional | Late | Incremental | Statute and Executive Order following Constitutional Amendment | M.D. | |

| State | | | | | | | |
|---|---|---|---|---|---|---|---|
| | | | | | | | (6) |
| KENTUCKY | 1924 | Cabinet^c | Early | Comprehensive | Constitutional Amendment (see notes) | None | |
| | 1934 | Traditional^c | Early | Comprehensive | Statute | M.D. | |
| | 1936 | Traditional^c | Early | Comprehensive | Statute | M.D. | |
| | 1952 | M.D. | Middle | Comprehensive | Constitutional Amendment | None | |
| | 1956 | M.D. | M.D. | Comprehensive | Statute | M.D. | |
| | 1972-73 | Secretary-Coordinator | Middle | Incremental | Executive Order | High | |
| | | | | | | | (7) |
| LOUISIANA | 1940 (see notes) | Cabinet^c | Early | Incremental | Constitutional Amendment and Statute | Low | |
| | | | | | | | (8) |
| | 1942 | M.D. | Middle | Incremental | Statute | M.D. | |
| | 1975 | M.D. | Late | Comprehensive | Statute following new constitution | High | |

TABLE A.1 (cont.)

| | YEAR | | TYPE | STRATEGY | | | DEGREE OF ADOPTION | NOTES |
|---|---|---|---|---|---|---|---|---|
| | Fail | Adopt | | TIMING | TACTICS | MECHANISM | | |
| **MAINE** | | 1931 | Cabinet[c] | Middle | Comprehensive | Statute | Low | |
| | | 1957 | Cabinet[c] | Middle | M.D. | M.D. | Low | |
| | | 1971 | Cabinet | Middle | Incremental | Statute | High | |
| **MARYLAND** | | 1922 | Traditional[c] | Early | Comprehensive | Statute | Low | |
| | | 1941 | Traditional[c] | M.D. | Comprehensive | Statute | M.D. | |
| | | 1969–70 | Cabinet | Early | Incremental | Statute | High | (9) |
| **MASSACHUSETTS** | | 1919 | Traditional[c] | Early | Comprehensive | Statute following Constitutional Amendment limiting agencies to 20 or less | Moderate | |
| | | 1921 | Cabinet[c] | Early | M.D. | Statute | Low | |
| | | 1969 | Secretary-Coordinator | Early | Incremental (see notes) | Statute | High | (10) |

| State | Year | Type | | | | |
|---|---|---|---|---|---|---|
| MICHIGAN | 1921 | Traditional[c] | Early | Incremental | Statute | M.D. |
| | 1935 | M.D. | Early | Incremental | Constitutional Amendment and Statute | Low |
| | 1937 | M.D. | Early | M.D. | M.D. | M.D. |
| | 1965 | Traditional[c] | Middle | Comprehensive | Statute following Constitutional Amendment limiting agencies to 25 or less | M.D. |
| MINNESOTA | 1914 | M.D. | Late | M.D. | M.D. | None |
| | 1925 | M.D. | Early | Comprehensive | Statute | High |
| | 1939 | M.D. | Early | Comprehensive | Statute | M.D. |
| | 1969 | Cabinet[c] | Middle | Comprehensive | Statute | Moderate |
| MISSISSIPPI | 1932 | Cabinet[c] | Early | M.D. | M.D. | Low | (11) |

TABLE A.1 (cont.)

| | YEAR | | TYPE | STRATEGY | | | DEGREE OF ADOPTION | NOTES |
|---|---|---|---|---|---|---|---|---|
| | Fail | Adopt | | TIMING | TACTICS | MECHANISM | | |
| MISSOURI | 1921 | | M.D. | Early | Incremental | Statute | Low | (12) |
| | 1924 | | M.D. | Late | Comprehensive | Constitutional Amendment | None | |
| | 1927 | | Cabinet[c] | Middle | Comprehensive | Statute | None | |
| | | 1945 | Traditional´ | Early | Comprehensive | Constitutional Provision | High | (13) |
| | | 1974 | Cabinet | Early | Comprehensive | Statute following Constitutional Amendment limiting number of departments to 14 or less | High | |
| MONTANA | 1943 | | M.D. | Early | M.D. | M.D. | None | |
| | | 1971 | Traditional | Middle | Comprehensive | Statute following Constitutional Amendment limiting number of departments to 20 or less | M.D. | |

| State | Year | | | | | | |
|---|---|---|---|---|---|---|---|
| NEBRASKA | 1919 | Traditional[c] | Early | Comprehensive | Statute | M.D. | |
| | 1920 | Traditional[c] | M.D. | Comprehensive | Constitutional Amendment | M.D. | |
| | 1933 | Traditional[c] | Middle | M.D. | M.D. | M.D. | |
| | 1935 | Traditional[c] | Early | M.D. | M.D. | M.D. | |
| NEVADA | 1925 | Cabinet[c] | Middle | Incremental | Statute | Low | (14) |
| | 1963 | M.D. | Middle | Comprehensive | Statute | M.D. | |
| NEW HAMPSHIRE | 1933 | Traditional[c] | M.D. | M.D. | M.D. | None | |
| | 1950 | Traditional[c] | Middle | Comprehensive | Statute | High | |
| | 1961 | M.D. | Middle | M.D. | M.D. | M.D. | |

TABLE A.1 (cont.)

| YEAR | | TYPE | STRATEGY | | | DEGREE OF ADOPTION | NOTES |
| Fail | Adopt | | TIMING | TACTICS | MECHANISM | | |
|---|---|---|---|---|---|---|---|
| | 1915 | Traditional^c | Middle | Incremental | Statute | M.D. | |
| 1926 | | M.D. | Early | Incremental | Statute | None | |
| | 1931 | Cabinet | Late | Incremental | Statute | M.D. | |
| 1944 | | M.D. | Early | Comprehensive | Constitutional Provision | None | |
| | 1948 | M.D. | Early | M.D. | Statute after Constitutional Amendment to limit number of departments to 20 or less | M.D. | |

NEW JERSEY

| | 1952 | Traditional | M.D. | M.D. | M.D. | M.D. | |
| 1968-69 | | M.D. | Middle | Incremental | Statute | Low | |

NEW MEXICO

| Year | Type | Period | Approach | Legal Basis | Notes |
|---|---|---|---|---|---|
| 1915 | Cabinet[C] | Early | Comprehensive | Constitutional Provision | None |
| 1921 | M.D. | Early | Incremental | Constitutional Amendment | None |
| 1926 | Cabinet[C] | Middle | Incremental | Statutes following Constitutional Amendment limiting number of departments to 22 or less | M.D. |
| 1960 | Cabinet[C] | Early | Incremental | Statute | High |
| 1923 | Traditional | Middle | Comprehensive | Statute | None |
| 1931 | Cabinet[C] | Middle | Incremental | Statute | M.D. |
| 1971-75 | Traditional | (see notes) | Incremental | Statutes following Constitutional Amendment limiting number of departments to 25 or less | M.D. (15) |

NEW YORK

NORTH CAROLINA

TABLE A.1 (cont.)

| | YEAR | | TYPE | STRATEGY | | | DEGREE OF ADOPTION | NOTES |
| | Fail | Adopt | | TIMING | TACTICS | MECHANISM | | |
|---|---|---|---|---|---|---|---|---|
| NORTH DAKOTA | 1943 | | M.D. | Late | Incremental | Statute | None | |
| | | 1967 | Traditional[c] | Middle | M.D. | M.D. | None | |
| OHIO | 1921 | | Cabinet | Early | Comprehensive | Statute | High | |
| | | 1929 | M.D. (see notes) | Early | M.D. | M.D. | M.D. | (16) |
| OKLAHOMA | 1936 | | Traditional[c] | M.D. | M.D. | M.D. | Low | |
| | 1974 | | Traditional[c] | Late | Comprehensive | Constitutional Amendment | None | (17) |
| | | 1975 | M.D. (see notes) | Early | Incremental | Constitutional Amendment | M.D. | (18) |

| State | Year | Form | Timing | Type | Method | Degree |
|---|---|---|---|---|---|---|
| | 1919 | M.D. | Early | Incremental | Statute and Constitutional Amendment were required by plan but reorganization did not reach that stage | None |
| OREGON | 1927 | Cabinet[c] | Early | Incremental | Statute | None |
| | 1930 | Cabinet[c] | Late | Comprehensive | Constitutional Amendment | None |
| | 1935 | Cabinet[c] | Early | Comprehensive | Statute | None |
| | 1969 | Traditional[c] | Early | Incremental | Statute | Moderate |
| PENN-SYLVANIA | 1923 | Traditional[c] | Early | Comprehensive | Statute | M.D. |
| RHODE ISLAND | 1935 | Cabinet[c] | Middle | Incremental | Statute | High |
| | 1939 | M.D. | Early | Comprehensive | Statute | M.D. |
| SOUTH CAROLINA | 1945 | Traditional[c] | Early | M.D. | M.D. | None |

TABLE A.1 (cont.)

| YEAR | | TYPE | STRATEGY | | | DEGREE OF ADOPTION | NOTES |
| Fail | Adopt | | TIMING | TACTICS | MECHANISM | | |
|---|---|---|---|---|---|---|---|
| **SOUTH DAKOTA** | | | | | | | |
| 1923 | | M.D. | Middle | Comprehensive | Statute | None | (19) |
| | 1925 | M.D. | Early | Comprehensive | Statute | M.D. | |
| | 1973 | Cabinet | Early | Comprehensive | Executive Order following Constitutional Amendment limiting number of departments to 20 or less | High | |
| **TENNESSEE** | | | | | | | |
| | 1923 | Cabinet[c] | Early | Comprehensive | Statute | High | |
| | 1937 | Cabinet[c] | Early | Comprehensive | Statute | M.D. | |
| | 1945 | M.D. | Early | M.D. | M.D. | M.D. | |
| | 1955 | M.D. (see notes) | Middle | Incremental | Statute | M.D. | (20) |
| | 1959 | Cabinet[c] | Early | Comprehensive | Statute | M.D. | |

| State | Year | | | | | | |
|---|---|---|---|---|---|---|---|
| TEXAS | 1933 | Traditional[c] | M.D. | Comprehensive | Statute | None | (21) |
| | 1935 | M.D. | Early | Comprehensive | Statute | None | (21) |
| | 1937 | M.D. | Middle | Comprehensive | Statute | None | (21) |
| UTAH | 1937 | Traditional[c] | Middle | M.D. | M.D. | None | |
| | 1941 | Traditional[c] | Early | M.D. | M.D. | M.D. | |
| | 1967 | M.D. | Early | Incremental | Statute | M.D. | |
| VERMONT | 1923 | Cabinet | Early | Incremental | Statute | M.D. | |
| | 1947 | M.D. | Early | Incremental | Statute | M.D. | |
| | 1970-71 | Cabinet | Middle | Incremental | Statute | Moderate | |

TABLE A.1 (cont.)

| | YEAR | | TYPE | STRATEGY | | | DEGREE OF ADOPTION | NOTES |
|---|---|---|---|---|---|---|---|---|
| | Fail | Adopt | | TIMING | TACTICS | MECHANISM | | |
| VIRGINIA | 1924 | | M.D. | M.D. | Incremental | Statute and Constitutional Amendment proposed but not utilized | None | |
| | | 1927 | Traditional[c] | Early | Comprehensive | Statute | High | |
| | | 1942 | M.D. | Early | Incremental | Statute | M.D. | |
| | | 1948 | M.D. | Middle | M.D. | M.D. | M.D. | |
| | | 1972 | Secretary-Coordinator | M.D. | Comprehensive | Statute | High | |
| WASHINGTON | | 1921 | Traditional[c] | Middle | Comprehensive | Statute | M.D. | |
| | | 1935 | M.D. | Early | Comprehensive | Statute | M.D. | |
| | | 1967 | M.D. | Early | Incremental | Statute | High | |
| | | 1969 | M.D. | Middle | Incremental | Statute | Low | |

| | Year | | | | | | |
|---|---|---|---|---|---|---|---|
| **WEST VIRGINIA** | 1933 | M.D. (see notes) | M.D. | Incremental | Constitutional Amendment and Statute | Low | (22) |
| | 1961 | Traditional[C] | Early | Incremental | Statute | M.D. | |
| | 1963 | M.D. | M.D. | Comprehensive | Constitutional Amendment restricting number of departments to 20 or less | None | |
| **WISCONSIN** | 1925 | M.D. | Late | Comprehensive | Statute | None | |
| | 1927 | M.D. | Early | Comprehensive | Statute | None | |
| | 1929 | M.D. | Early | M.D. | M.D. | M.D. | |
| | 1937 | Traditional[C] | M.D. | Comprehensive | Statute | M.D. | |
| | 1967 | Traditional | Middle | Comprehensive | Statute | High | (23) |
| **WYOMING** | 1934 | Cabinet[C] | Early | M.D. | Statute applied, Constitutional Amendment necessary to adopt Griffenhagen Plan | M.D. | (24) |

TABLE A.1 (cont.)

[a]The research extended back to 1900, but no state executive branch reorganizations were found for the years 1900-1913.

[b]M.D. indicates Missing Data.

[c]For the reorganizations indicated, information concerning all five dimensions is not known. In these cases typification is based on at least three dimensions.

[d]As defined for this study,
Early Timing is adoption or attempt at adoption during first one-third of governor's uninterrupted term.
Middle Timing is adoption or attempt at adoption during second one-third.
Late Timing is adoption or attempt at adoption during third one-third.

[e]As defined in this study,
Comprehensive Tactics are pursued when all reorganization proposals are submitted as part of one all-encompassing reorganization measure be it statute, constitutional amendment, executive order, or other mechanism. The characteristic element of this tactic is its all-eggs-in-one-basket approach.
Incremental Tactics are pursued when reorganization proposals are submitted in multiple reorganization measures, whether at the same time or phased over time.

[f]As defined for this study,
High Degree of Adoption means that 67% or more of the major recommendations or major agency proposals were adopted.
Moderate indicates 34% through 66% adoption.
Low indicates 33% or less, but with at least some small part adopted.

$^g$Notes on individual reorganizations:

(1) Traditional Type failed. Some budget reorganization passed.

(2) Phased reorganization over several years part of overall reorganization plan.

(3) Proposals in governor's message.

(4) Study commission not utilized.

(5) 1915 study proposals modified substantially and resubmitted.

(6) Griffenhagen & Associates long-term proposal did not reach the required Constitutional Amendment stage.

(7) Constitutional Amendment approved by voters in 1940 nullified as unconstitutional by State Supreme Court. Some reorganization provisions unaffected.

(8) 1942 Statutes reinstated part of reorganization nullified in 1940.

(9) Executive Reorganization Committee appointed by Governor Agnew in 1968, giving Governor Mandel advanced start on planning.

(10) Even though only one act was utilized, tactics are considered Incremental since proposal called for two-phase reorganization process.

(11) Cabinet Type attempted. Only one major functional area--higher education--was reorganized.

(12) A number of proposals adopted by legislature were submitted to referendum and defeated.

(13) New constitution including reorganization features was adopted in toto.

(14) Orthodox reorganization model proposed by New York Bureau of Municipal Research.

(15) Adoptions occurred in more than one phase of governor's term.

TABLE A.1 (cont.)

(16) Not enough dimensions known to type this reorganization, but it was Traditional in orientation, proposing replacement of single executive with boards.

(17) Constitutional Amendment to restrict departments to 20 or less was defeated by voters.

(18) Reduction in number of statewide elected officers is Cabinet in orientation.

(19) Governor withheld 1922 report done by New York Bureau of Municipal Research. A legislature-initiated bill was not acted upon.

(20) Not enough dimensions known to type 1955 reorganization, but it appears to have been Traditional-oriented.

(21) Joint Legislative Committee on Organization and Economy hired Griffenhagen & Associates to conduct study. A bill to enact Griffenhagen Plan was killed in 1933, 1935, and 1937.

(22) Not enough dimensions known to type accurately, but 1933 reorganization was Cabinet in tone, though most not adopted.

(23) There were many amendments to reorganization bill, but most major proposals were adopted. 1967 Legislature adopted other reorganization statutes that were not part of Kellett Commission Plan and which later had to be fitted into new state reorganization.

(24) Precise data on degree of adoption missing, but it is probably low (see Buck, Reorganization of State Governments in the United States, p. 260).

# Reorganization Outcomes: Tables Showing Time Period and Regional Comparisons

TABLE B.1

Associations Between Adoption Decision
and the Set of Independent Variables by Wave

| Wave | Electoral Competition | Governor's Party Control | Diffusion Agent Activity | Modernization Level | Timing of Adoption Effort | Comprehensiveness of Tactics | Rigor of Legal Mechanism |
|---|---|---|---|---|---|---|---|
| Post-Taft (1914-1936) | .06 sig.=.32 N=47 | .16 sig.=.14 N=45 | .19 sig.=.19 N=23 | .04 sig.=.38 N=47 | -.14 sig.=.18 N=39 | -.32 sig.=.03 N=34 | -.07 sig.=.31 N=37 |
| Post-Brownlow (1937-1946) | .09 sig.= N=9 | -.29 sig.= N=9 | NC | .51 sig.= N=9 | -.05 sig.=.51 N=9 | -.33 sig.= N=6 | .40 sig.= N=6 |
| Post-First-Hoover (1947-1975) | -.26 sig.=.06 N=36 | -.10 sig.=.27 N=35 | NC | .17 sig.=.15 N=35 | -.30 sig.=.04 N=33 | -.36 sig.=.02 N=32 | -.32 sig.=.03 N=33 |
| Overall Association | .14 sig.=.09 N=92 | -.10 sig.=.17 N=89 | -.13 sig.=.21 N=42 | .08 sig.=.20 N=91 | -.07 sig.=.26 N=81 | -.38 sig.=.001 N=72 | -.07 sig.=.26 N=76 |
| Hypothesized Direction | - | + | - | + | - | - | - |

Statistic reported is Kendall's tau-b.

NC indicates that association could not be computed.

TABLE B.2

Associations Between Degree of Reorganization Adoption
and the Set of Independent Variables by Wave

| Wave | Electoral Competition | Governor's Party Control | Diffusion Agent Activity | Modern-ization Level | Timing of Adoption Effort | Comprehen-siveness of Tactics | Rigor of Legal Mechanism |
|---|---|---|---|---|---|---|---|
| Post-Taft (1914-1936) | -.06 sig.=.39 N=18 | .29 sig.=.11 N=17 | NC | .38 sig.=.05 N=18 | -.04 sig.=.43 N=16 | .50 sig.=.03 N=14 | -.34 sig.=.10 N=15 |
| Post-Brownlow (1937-1946) | .81 sig.= N=3 | -.81 sig.= N=3 | NC | -.50 sig.= N=3 | -.50 sig.= N=3 | 1.00 sig.= N=3 | 0 sig.= N=3 |
| Post-First-Hoover (1947-1975) | .12 sig.=.24 N=32 | .08 sig.=.31 N=31 | -.12 sig.=.31 N=16 | .34 sig.=.02 N=31 | -.26 sig.=.07 N=30 | .29 sig.=.05 N=29 | .23 sig.=.10 N=30 |
| Overall Association | .15 sig.=.12 N=53 | -.01 sig.=.48 N=51 | -.17 sig.=.17 N=29 | .26 sig.=.02 N=52 | -.13 sig.=.17 N=49 | .37 sig.=.004 N=46 | 0 sig.=.50 N=48 |
| Hypothesized Direction | - | + | + | - | - | + | + |

Statistic reported is Kendall's tau-b.

NC indicates that association could not be computed.

TABLE B.3

Associations Between Degree of Reorganization Reform
and the Set of Independent Variables by Wave

| Wave | Electoral Competition | Governor's Party Control | Diffusion Agent Activity | Modern- ization Level | Timing of Adoption Effort | Comprehen- siveness of Tactics | Rigor of Legal Mechanism |
|---|---|---|---|---|---|---|---|
| Post- Taft (1914–1936) | .02 sig. = .43 N = 53 | -.29 sig. = .02 N = 50 | .09 sig. = .32 N = 26 | -.09 sig. = .25 N = 53 | -.05 sig. = .36 N = 46 | -.09 sig. = .29 N = 39 | .11 sig. = .24 N = 42 |
| Post- Brownlow (1937–1946) | -.46 sig. = .06 N = 11 | .33 sig. = .14 N = 11 | NC | 0 sig. = .50 N = 11 | -.36 sig. = N = 9 | -.15 sig. = N = 8 | .40 sig. = N = 8 |
| Post-First- Hoover (1947–1975) | -.26 sig. = .05 N = 39 | -.11 sig. = .24 N = 36 | -.18 sig. = .23 N = 17 | .31 sig. = .03 N = 37 | -.30 sig. = .03 N = 35 | -.06 sig. = .36 N = 32 | -.02 sig. = .45 N = 33 |
| Overall Association | -.13 sig. = .18 N=103 | -.11 Sig. = .23 N = 97 | -.12 sig. = .28 N = 48 | -.10 sig. = .24 N=101 | -.27 sig. = .04 N = 90 | -.13 sig. = .22 N = 79 | .02 sig. = .45 N = 83 |
| Hypothesized Direction | - | + | + | + | - | + | + |

Statistic reported is Kendall's tau-b.

NC indicates that association could not be computed.

TABLE B.4

Associations Between Adoption Decision
and the Set of Independent Variables by Region

| Region | Electoral Competition | Governor's Party Control | Diffusion Agent Activity | Modernization Level | Timing of Adoption Effort | Comprehensiveness of Tactics | Rigor of Legal Mechanism |
|---|---|---|---|---|---|---|---|
| New England | .03<br>sig. = .46<br>N = 14 | -.29<br>sig. = .14<br>N = 14 | -.35<br>sig. =<br>N = 7 | -.26<br>sig. = .18<br>N = 14 | .39<br>sig. = .09<br>N = 12 | -.42<br>sig. = .09<br>N = 11 | .09<br>sig. = .38<br>N = 12 |
| Mid-Atlantic | -.07<br>sig. =<br>N = 8 | .29<br>sig. =<br>N = 8 | -1.00<br>sig. =<br>N = 4 | NC | NC | -.75<br>sig. =<br>N = 7 | -.75<br>sig. =<br>N = 7 |
| Southeast | -.03<br>sig. = .44<br>N = 21 | -.25<br>sig. = .13<br>N = 21 | .53<br>sig. = .03<br>N = 13 | 0<br>sig. = .50<br>N = 20 | -.08<br>sig. = .36<br>N = 17 | -.21<br>sig. = .20<br>N = 17 | -.05<br>sig. = .42<br>N = 18 |
| Great Lakes | .92<br>sig. =<br>N = 7 | .47<br>sig. =<br>N = 7 | NC | -.35<br>sig. =<br>N = 7 | -.35<br>sig. =<br>N = 6 | -.41<br>sig. =<br>N = 5 | .32<br>sig. =<br>N = 6 |

TABLE B.4 (cont.)

| Region | Electoral Competition | Governor's Party Control | Diffusion Agent Activity | Modernization Level | Timing of Adoption Effort | Comprehensiveness of Tactics | Rigor of Legal Mechanism |
|---|---|---|---|---|---|---|---|
| Plains | .36 sig. = .09 N = 13 | -.15 sig. = N = 10 | NC | .41 sig. = .08 N = 13 | -.80 sig.=.002 N = 12 | .10 sig. = N = 10 | .31 sig. = N = 10 |
| Southwest | .29 sig. = N = 10 | -.10 sig. = N = 10 | -.32 sig. = N = 6 | NC | .19 sig. = N = 8 | -1.00 sig. = N = 6 | -.26 sig. = N = 7 |
| Mountains | -.33 sig. = N = 6 | .20 sig. = N = 6 | NC | NC | .40 sig. = N = 6 | -.58 sig. = N = 4 | .33 sig. = N = 4 |
| Far West | .45 sig. = .06 N = 13 | -.44 sig. = .05 N = 13 | NC | -.19 sig. = .24 N = 13 | .04 sig. = .43 N = 13 | -.41 sig. = .09 N = 12 | -.18 sig. = .27 N = 12 |
| Overall Association | .14 sig. = .09 N = 92 | -.10 sig. = .17 N = 89 | -.13 sig. = .21 N = 42 | .08 sig. = .20 N = 91 | -.07 sig. = .26 N = 81 | -.38 sig.=.001 N = 72 | -.07 sig. = .26 N = 76 |
| Hypothesized Direction | - | + | - | + | - | - | - |

Statistic reported is Kendall's tau-b.

NC indicates that association could not be computed.

TABLE B.5

Associations Between Degree of Reorganization Adoption
and the Set of Independent Variables by Region

| Region | Electoral Competition | Governor's Party Control | Diffusion Agent Activity | Modernization Level | Timing of Adoption Effort | Comprehensiveness of Tactics | Rigor of Legal Mechanism |
|---|---|---|---|---|---|---|---|
| New England | .51 sig.=.03 N=12 | .07 sig.=.40 N=12 | -.71 sig.= N=6 | .18 sig.=.26 N=12 | -.09 sig.=.38 N=11 | -.16 sig.= N=10 | -.05 sig.=.43 N=11 |
| Mid-Atlantic | NC | NC | NC | NC | NC | NC | NC |
| Southeast | .18 sig.=.25 N=13 | -.12 sig.=.33 N=13 | NC | .45 sig.=.06 N=12 | .09 sig.=.38 N=11 | .68 sig.=.01 N=11 | -.54 sig.=.04 N=11 |
| Great Lakes | NC | NC | NC | -.33 sig.= N=4 | .33 sig.= N=4 | 1.00 sig.= N=3 | -1.00 sig.= N=4 |

TABLE B.5 (cont.)

| Region | Electoral Competition | Governor's Party Control | Diffusion Agent Activity | Modern-ization Level | Timing of Adoption Effort | Comprehen-siveness of Tactics | Rigor of Legal Mechanism |
|---|---|---|---|---|---|---|---|
| Plains | -.12 sig. = N = 6 | -.57 sig. = N = 4 | NC | -.30 sig. = N = 6 | -.45 sig. = N = 6 | .75 sig. = N = 6 | .60 sig. = N = 6 |
| Southwest | .58 sig. = N = 4 | .33 sig. = N = 4 | -1.00 sig. = N = 4 | NC | .82 sig. = N = 3 | NC | NC |
| Mountains | .50 sig. = N = 3 | -.50 sig. = N = 3 | NC | NC | .82 sig. = N = 3 | .50 sig. = N = 3 | .50 sig. = N = 3 |
| Far West | -.52 sig. = N = 8 | .15 sig. = N = 8 | NC | .46 sig. = N = 8 | -.36 sig. = N = 8 | .34 sig. = N = 8 | .52 sig. = N = 8 |
| Overall Association | .15 sig. = .12 N = 53 | -.01 sig. = .48 N = 51 | -.17 sig. = .17 N = 29 | .26 sig. = .02 N = 52 | -.13 sig. = .17 N = 49 | .37 sig.=.004 N = 46 | 0 sig. = .50 N = 48 |
| Hypothesized Direction | - | + | + | - | - | + | + |

Statistic reported is Kendall's tau-b.

NC indicates that association could not be computed.

# Relationships Between Strategy Variables and Reorganization Outcomes Under Political and Socioeconomic Contingencies

*Note*: Diffusion Agent Activity, which is treated here as a strategy variable, can also be regarded as a command variable that state decision makers can manipulate in order to influence reorganization outcomes. In these tables, the Types of Reorganization Attempted were defined as Traditional (low reform) type and Cabinet/Secretary-Coordinator (high reform) type.

TABLE D.1

Associations Between Adoption Decision and a Set of Strategy Variables
Under Varying Conditions of Governor's Party Control of Legislature

| Under Conditions of | Diffusion Agent Activity | Type of Reorganization Attempted | Timing of Adoption Effort | Comprehensiveness of Tactics | Rigor of Legal Mechanism |
|---|---|---|---|---|---|
| Governor's Party Control of 0 Houses | -.20 sig. = .25 N = 12 | .03 sig. = .46 N = 13 | -.21 sig. = .19 N = 17 | -.04 sig. = .44 N = 15 | .29 sig. = .12 N = 16 |
| Governor's Party Control of 1 House | NC | -.71 sig. = N = 6 | .13 sig. = N = 8 | -.75 sig. = N = 8 | .22 sig. = N = 8 |
| Governor's Party Control of 2 Houses | -.08 sig. = .35 N = 25 | -.02 sig. = .46 N = 44 | -.03 sig. = .40 N = 53 | -.45 sig. = .001 N = 47 | -.19 sig. = .08 N = 50 |
| Overall Association | -.13 sig. = .21 N = 42 | -.06 sig. = .32 N = 64 | -.07 sig. = .26 N = 81 | -.38 sig. = .001 N = 72 | -.07 sig. = .26 N = 76 |
| Hypothesized Direction | — | Not Hypothesized | — | — | — |

Statistic reported is Kendall's tau-b.

NC indicates that association could not be computed.

TABLE B.6

Associations Between Degree of Reorganization Reform
and the Set of Independent Variables by Region

| Region | Electoral Competition | Governor's Party Control | Diffusion Agent Activity | Modernization Level | Timing of Adoption Effort | Comprehensiveness of Tactics | Rigor of Legal Mechanism |
|---|---|---|---|---|---|---|---|
| New England | -.53<br>sig. = .02<br>N = 14 | -.20<br>sig. = .22<br>N = 14 | -.40<br>sig. =<br>N = 7 | -.56<br>sig. = .02<br>N = 14 | -.29<br>sig. = .15<br>N = 13 | -.21<br>sig. = .25<br>N = 11 | -.43<br>sig. = .08<br>N = 12 |
| Mid-Atlantic | .03<br>sig. = .46<br>N = 12 | .11<br>sig. = .35<br>N = 12 | -.32<br>sig. =<br>N = 6 | NC | .05<br>sig. =<br>N = 9 | -.58<br>sig. =<br>N = 10 | .40<br>sig. =<br>N = 10 |
| Southeast | -.09<br>sig. = .32<br>N = 25 | -.09<br>sig. = .32<br>N = 24 | -.20<br>sig. = .22<br>N = 16 | -.14<br>sig. = .24<br>N = 24 | -.22<br>sig. = .15<br>N = 23 | -.10<br>sig. = .32<br>N = 20 | -.05<br>sig. = .42<br>N = 21 |
| Great Lakes | .11<br>sig. =<br>N = 8 | .19<br>sig. =<br>N = 8 | .50<br>sig. =<br>N = 3 | .29<br>sig. =<br>N = 8 | -.50<br>sig. =<br>N = 6 | .26<br>sig. =<br>N = 7 | -.26<br>sig. =<br>N = 7 |

TABLE B.6 (cont.)

| Region | Electoral Competition | Governor's Party Control | Diffusion Agent Activity | Modernization Level | Timing of Adoption Effort | Comprehensiveness of Tactics | Rigor of Legal Mechanism |
|---|---|---|---|---|---|---|---|
| Plains | -.12 sig. = .33 N = 12 | .22 sig. = N = 7 | NC | .45 sig. = .08 N = 11 | .26 sig. = N = 10 | -.29 sig. = N = 8 | .41 sig. = N = 8 |
| Southwest | -.15 sig. = N = 8 | -.40 sig. = N = 8 | .41 sig. = N = 5 | NC | 0 sig. = N = 5 | NC | -.25 sig. = N = 5 |
| Mountains | .39 sig. = .11 N = 11 | -.04 sig. = .45 N = 11 | NC | -.19 sig. = .27 N = 11 | -.53 sig. = .04 N = 11 | .45 sig. = N = 8 | -.16 sig. = N = 9 |
| Far West | .22 sig. = .21 N = 13 | -.41 sig. = .07 N = 13 | NC | -.43 sig. = .06 N = 13 | -.28 sig. = .16 N = 13 | .35 sig. = .12 N = 12 | .54 sig. = .04 N = 11 |
| Overall Association | -.13 sig. = .18 N=103 | -.11 sig. = .23 N = 97 | -.12 sig. = .28 N = 48 | -.10 sig. = .24 N=101 | -.27 sig. = .04 N = 90 | -.13 sig. = .22 N = 79 | .02 sig. = .45 N = 83 |
| Hypothesized Direction | - | + | + | + | - | + | + |

Statistic reported is Kendall's tau-b.

NC indicates that association could not be computed.

# State Track Records on Reorganization Adoption: A Comparison, 1900–75

TABLE C.1

State Track Records on Reorganization Adoption:
A Comparison, 1900-1975

| State | A | F | R | State | A | F | R |
|-------|---|---|---|-------|---|---|---|
| California | 6 | 1 | 86% | Ohio | 2 | 0 | 100% |
| Tennessee | 5 | 0 | 100% | Rhode Island | 2 | 0 | 100% |
| Michigan | 4 | 0 | 100% | Delaware | 2 | 1 | 67% |
| Nebraska | 4 | 0 | 100% | Georgia | 2 | 1 | 67% |
| Washington | 4 | 0 | 100% | Illinois | 2 | 1 | 67% |
| Virginia | 4 | 1 | 80% | New Hampshire | 2 | 1 | 67% |
| Kentucky | 4 | 2 | 67% | North Carolina | 2 | 1 | 67% |
| Idaho | 3 | 0 | 100% | Oklahoma | 2 | 1 | 67% |
| Louisiana | 3 | 0 | 100% | South Dakota | 2 | 1 | 67% |
| Maine | 3 | 0 | 100% | Utah | 2 | 1 | 67% |
| Maryland | 3 | 0 | 100% | West Virginia | 2 | 1 | 67% |
| Massachusetts | 3 | 0 | 100% | New York | 2 | 2 | 50% |
| Vermont | 3 | 0 | 100% | Florida | 1 | 0 | 100% |
| Arkansas | 3 | 1 | 75% | Indiana | 1 | 0 | 100% |
| Colorado | 3 | 1 | 75% | Kansas | 1 | 0 | 100% |
| Connecticut | 3 | 1 | 75% | Mississippi | 1 | 0 | 100% |
| Minnesota | 3 | 1 | 75% | Pennsylvania | 1 | 0 | 100% |
| Arizona | 3 | 2 | 60% | Wyoming | 1 | 0 | 100% |
| Missouri | 3 | 2 | 60% | Iowa | 1 | 1 | 50% |
| New Jersey | 3 | 2 | 60% | Montana | 1 | 1 | 50% |
| Wisconsin | 3 | 2 | 60% | Oregon | 1 | 4 | 20% |
| Alabama | 2 | 0 | 100% | South Carolina | 0 | 1 | 0% |
| Nevada | 2 | 0 | 100% | North Dakota | 0 | 2 | 0% |
| New Mexico | 2 | 0 | 100% | Texas | 0 | 3 | 0% |
|  |  |  |  | All States | 112 | 39 | 74% |

A = Number of Adoptions

F = Number of Failures

R = Adoption Rate

TABLE D.4

Associations Between Degree of Reorganization Adoption and a Set of Strategy Variables
Under Varying Conditions of Governor's Party Control of Legislature

| Under Conditions of | Diffusion Agent Activity | Type of Reorganization Attempted | Timing of Adoption Effort | Comprehensiveness of Tactics | Rigor of Legal Mechanism |
|---|---|---|---|---|---|
| Governor's Party Control of 0 Houses | -.38<br>sig. =<br>N = 10 | -.05<br>sig. =<br>N = 10 | -.49<br>sig. = .05<br>N = 11 | .21<br>sig. = .24<br>N = 11 | .17<br>sig. = .29<br>N = 11 |
| Governor's Party Control of 1 House | .52<br>sig. =<br>N = 4 | .81<br>sig. =<br>N = 3 | -.57<br>sig. =<br>N = 5 | .75<br>sig. =<br>N = 6 | .75<br>sig. =<br>N = 6 |
| Governor's Party Control of 2 Houses | -.25<br>sig. = .18<br>N = 14 | -.10<br>sig. = .29<br>N = 29 | .09<br>sig. = .31<br>N = 31 | .31<br>sig. = .05<br>N = 27 | -.31<br>sig. = .04<br>N = 29 |
| Overall Association | -.17<br>sig. = .17<br>N = 29 | -.01<br>sig. = .47<br>N = 43 | -.13<br>sig. = .17<br>N = 49 | .37<br>sig. = .004<br>N = 46 | 0<br>sig. = .50<br>N = 48 |
| Hypothesized Direction | + | Not Hypothesized | - | + | + |

Statistic reported is Kendall's tau-b.

TABLE D.5

Associations Between Degree of Reorganization Adoption and a Set of Strategy Variables Under Varying Conditions of Electoral Competition for Governorship

| Under Conditions of | Diffusion Agent Activity | Type of Reorganization Attempted | Timing of Adoption Effort | Comprehensiveness of Tactics | Rigor of Legal Mechanism |
|---|---|---|---|---|---|
| Low Electoral Competition for the Governorship | .32<br>sig. =<br>N = 6 | -1.00<br>sig. =<br>N = 6 | NC | 1.00<br>sig. =<br>N = 5 | -.32<br>sig. =<br>N = 6 |
| Moderate Electoral Competition for the Governorship | -.29<br>sig. = .14<br>N = 14 | .28<br>sig. = .08<br>N = 24 | -.29<br>sig. = .05<br>N = 28 | .21<br>sig. = .14<br>N = 25 | .21<br>sig. = .14<br>N = 25 |
| High Electoral Competition for the Governorship | -.24<br>sig. =<br>N = 9 | .02<br>sig. = .47<br>N = 13 | -.09<br>sig. = .35<br>N = 15 | .45<br>sig. = .03<br>N = 16 | -.24<br>sig. = .15<br>N = 17 |
| Overall Association | -.17<br>sig. = .17<br>N = 29 | -.01<br>sig. = .47<br>N = 43 | -.13<br>sig. = .17<br>N = 49 | .37<br>sig. = .004<br>N = 46 | 0<br>sig. = .50<br>N = 48 |
| Hypothesized Direction | + | Not Hypothesized | - | + | + |

Statistic reported is Kendall's tau-b.

NC indicates that association could not be computed.

TABLE D.6

Associations Between Degree of Reorganization Adoption and a Set of Strategy Variables
Under Varying Conditions of State Modernization Level

| Under Conditions of | Diffusion Agent Activity | Type of Reorganization Attempted | Timing of Adoption Effort | Comprehensiveness of Tactics | Rigor of Legal Mechanism |
|---|---|---|---|---|---|
| Low Level of State Modernization | -.21<br>sig. = .24<br>N = 11 | .38<br>sig. = .09<br>N = 12 | .07<br>sig. = .39<br>N = 14 | .48<br>sig. = .05<br>N = 12 | .48<br>sig. = .05<br>N = 12 |
| Moderate Level of State Modernization | -.21<br>sig. = .22<br>N = 13 | -.24<br>sig. = .16<br>N = 17 | -.36<br>sig. = .06<br>N = 18 | .50<br>sig. = .02<br>N = 18 | -.16<br>sig. = .24<br>N = 18 |
| High Level of State Modernization | -.17<br>sig. =<br>N = 5 | .35<br>sig. = .10<br>N = 14 | -.06<br>sig. = .40<br>N = 16 | .07<br>sig. = .40<br>N = 15 | -.25<br>sig. = .15<br>N = 17 |
| Overall Association | -.17<br>sig. = .17<br>N = 29 | -.01<br>sig. = .47<br>N = 43 | -.13<br>sig. = .17<br>N = 49 | .37<br>sig. = .004<br>N = 46 | 0<br>sig. = .50<br>N = 48 |
| Hypothesized Direction | + | Not Hypothesized | - | + | + |

Statistic reported is Kendall's tau-b.

# Selected Bibliography

## Books and Monographs

Abernathy, Byron R. *Some Persisting Questions Concerning the Constitutional State Executive*. Lawrence: University of Kansas Governmental Research Center, 1960.

Allison, Graham T. *Essence of Decision: Explaining the Cuban Missile Crisis*. Boston: Little, Brown & Co., 1971.

Anderson, William; Penniman, Clara; and Weidner, Edward. *Government in the Fifty States*. New York: Holt, Rinehart and Winston, 1960.

Argyris, Chris, and Schön, Donald A. *Theory in Practice: Increasing Professional Effectiveness*. San Francisco: Jossey-Bass, 1974.

Avery, Mary W. *Government of Washington State*. Seattle: University of Washington Press, 1966.

Bell, James R., and Darrah, Earl L. *State Executive Reorganization*. Berkeley: Bureau of Public Administration, University of California, 1961.

Beyle, Thad L., and Williams, J. Oliver. *The American Governor in Behavioral Perspective*. New York: Harper and Row, 1972.

Bollens, John C. *Administrative Reorganization in the States Since 1939*. Berkeley: University of California Bureau of Public Administration, 1947.

Brooks, Glenn E. *When Governors Convene: The Governors' Conference and National Politics*. Baltimore: Johns Hopkins University Press, 1961.

Buck, A. E. *Administrative Consolidation in State Governments*. 5th ed. New York: National Municipal League, 1930.

————. *Reorganization of State Governments in the United States*. New York: Columbia University Press, 1938.

Cleveland, Frederick A., and Buck, A. E. *The Budget and Responsible Government*. New York: Macmillan Co., 1920.

Congressional Quarterly. *Guide to U.S. Elections, 1789–1974*. Washington, D.C.: Congressional Quarterly, 1975.

Conover, W. J. *Practical Nonparametric Statistics*. New York: John Wiley and Sons, 1971.

Cornwell, Elmer E., Jr.; Goodman, Jay S.; and Swanson, Wayne R. *State Constitutional Conventions: The Politics of the Revision Process in Seven States*. New York: Praeger, 1975.

Council of State Governments. *Examples of Organization of the Governor's Office*. Chicago: Council of State Governments, 1962.

————. *Modernizing State Constitutions, 1966-1972.* Lexington, Ky.: Council of State Governments, 1973.

————. *Reorganization in the States.* Lexington, Ky.: Council of State Governments, 1972.

————. *Reorganizing State Government.* Chicago: Council of State Governments, 1957.

————. *Reorganizing State Government: A Report on Administrative Management in the States and a Review of Recent Trends in Reorganization.* Chicago: Council of State Governments, 1950.

————. *State Executive Reorganization, 1967-69.* Lexington, Ky.: Council of State Governments, 1969.

————. *State Reorganization in 1950.* Chicago: The Council of State Governments, 1950.

Darrah, Earl, and Poland, Orville. *The Fifty State Governments: A Compilation of State Executive Organization Charts.* Berkeley: Bureau of Public Administration, University of California, 1961.

Downs, George W., Jr. *Bureaucracy, Innovation, and Public Policy.* Lexington, Mass.: Lexington Books, 1976.

Elazar, Daniel J. *American Federalism: A View From the States.* New York: Thomas Crowell, 1966.

Eley, Lynn W. *The Executive Reorganization Plan: A Survey of State Experience.* Berkeley: Institute of Governmental Studies, University of California, 1967.

Emmerich, Herbert. *Federal Organization and Administrative Management.* University, Ala.: University of Alabama Press, 1971.

Fesler, James W., ed. *The Fifty States and Their Local Governments.* New York: Alfred A. Knopf, 1967.

Fried, Robert C. *Performance in American Bureaucracy.* Boston: Little, Brown and Co., 1976.

Graves, W. Brooke. *Reorganization of the Executive Branch of the United States: A Compilation of Basic Information and Significant Documents, 1912-48.* Washington, D.C.: Library of Congress, 1949.

Hage, Jerald. *Techniques and Problems of Theory Construction in Sociology.* New York: John Wiley & Sons, 1972.

Hage, Jerald, and Aiken, Michael. *Social Change in Complex Organizations.* New York: Random House, 1970.

Hargrove, Erwin C. *The Missing Link: The Study of Implementation of Social Policy.* Washington, D.C.: Urban Institute, 1975.

Hessler, Iola O. *The Politics of Reorganization.* Cincinnati: University of Cincinnati Institute of Governmental Research, 1972.

Highsaw, Robert. *Reorganizing State Government.* University, Ala.: Bureau of Public Administration, University of Alabama, 1969.

Jacob, Herbert, and Vines, Kenneth N., eds. *Politics in the American States: A Comparative Analysis.* 2d ed. Boston: Little, Brown & Co., 1971.

Karl, Barry D. *Executive Reorganization and Reform in the New Deal: The Genesis of Administrative Management, 1900-1939.* Cambridge: Harvard University Press, 1963.

Kaufman, Herbert. *Administrative Feedback.* Washington, D.C.: Brookings Institution, 1973.

_____. *Are Government Organizations Immortal?* Washington, D.C.: Brookings Institution, 1976.

_____. *The Limits of Organizational Change.* University, Ala.: University of Alabama Press, 1971.

_____. *Politics and Policies in State and Local Governments.* Englewood Cliffs, N.J.: Prentice-Hall, 1963.

Legislative Drafting Fund of Columbia University. *Index Digest of State Constitutions.* New York: Oceana Press, 1959.

Lipson, Leslie. *The American Governor: From Figurehead to Leader.* Chicago: Greenwood Press, 1939.

MacDonald, Austin F. *American State Government and Administration.* New York: Thomas Y. Crowell, 1955.

Mathews, John M. *American State Government.* New York: D. Appleton and Co., 1926.

_____. *Principles of American Public Administration.* New York: D. Appleton and Co., 1922.

Mosher, Frederick C., ed. *Governmental Reorganization: Cases and Commentary.* Indianapolis: Bobbs-Merrill, 1967.

National Governors' Conference. (Now National Governors' Association.) *Innovations in State Government: Messages from the Governors.* Washington, D.C.: National Governors' Conference, 1974.

_____. *Articles of Organization of the National Governors' Conference.* As amended and adopted at the Annual Meeting, New Orleans, Louisiana, June 11, 1975.

_____. *The Critical Hundred Days: A Handbook for the New Governor.* Washington, D.C.: National Governors' Conference, 1975.

National Municipal League. *Model State Constitution.* 6th ed. New York: National Municipal League, 1963.

New York Bureau of Municipal Research. *New York State Constitution and Government: An Appraisal.* New York: New York Bureau of Municipal Research, 1915.

Nie, Norman H., et al. *Statistical Package for the Social Sciences.* 2d ed. rev. New York: McGraw-Hill, 1975.

Porter, Kirk H. *State Administration.* New York: Crofts, 1939.

Price, James L. *Handbook of Organizational Measurement.* Lexington, Mass.: Heath, 1972.

Ransone, Coleman B., Jr. *The Office of Governor in the United States.* University, Ala.: University of Alabama Press, 1956.

*Report to National Governors' Conference by the Study Committee on Constitutional Revision and Governmental Reorganization.* National Governors' Conference, 1967.

Riggs, Robert E. *The Movement for Administrative Reorganization in Arizona.* Tucson: University of Arizona Press, 1964.

Robbins, Patricia V. *How Are State Government Reorganization Studies Organized?* Madison: Wisconsin Legislative Reference Library, 1961.

Rogers, Everett M. *Diffusion of Innovations.* New York: Free Press, 1962.

Rogers, Everett M., and Shoemaker, Floyd. *Communication of Innovations: A Cross-Cultural Approach.* New York: Free Press, 1971.

Rothman, Jack. *Planning and Organizing for Social Change: Action Principles from Social Science.* New York: Columbia University Press, 1974.

Scace, Homer. *The Organization of the Executive Office of the Governor.* New York: Institute of Public Administration, 1950.

Seidman, Harold. *Politics, Position, and Power: The Dynamics of Federal Organization.* 2d ed. New York: Oxford University Press, 1975.

Sharkansky, Ira. *Regionalism in American Politics.* Indianapolis: Bobbs-Merrill, 1970.

Siegel, Sidney. *Nonparametric Statistics for the Behavioral Sciences.* New York: McGraw-Hill, 1956.

Simon, Herbert A. *Administrative Behavior: A Study of the Decision-Making Processes in Administrative Organization.* New York: Free Press, Macmillan, 1947.

Simpson, T. McN., III. *President To Be: Jimmy Carter as Governor of Georgia.* Knoxville: University of Tennessee Press, forthcoming.

Solomon, Samuel R. *The Governors of the States, 1900–1974.* Lexington, Kentucky: Council of State Governments, 1974.

Thomas, Jack E. *Administrative Reorganization of State Government.* Berkeley: University of California Bureau of Public Administration, 1939.

University of Georgia Institute of Government. *An Examination of State Implementation Strategies for Executive Reorganization.* Athens: The Institute, 1971.

————. *Functional Categories Proposed in Other States for Organization of the Executive Branch.* Athens: The Institute, 1971.

————. *Standardized Titles for State Agencies.* Athens: The Institute, 1971.

Waldo, Dwight. *The Administrative State: A Study of the Political Theory of American Public Administration.* New York: Ronald Press Co., 1948.

Walker, Harvey. *Public Administration in the United States.* New York: Farrar and Rinehart, 1937.

Webb, Eugene J., et al. *Unobtrusive Measures: Nonreactive Research in the Social Sciences.* Chicago: Rand McNally College Publishing Co., 1966.

Williams, Walter. *Social Policy Research and Analysis: The Experience in the Federal Social Agencies.* New York: Elsevier, 1971.

Zaltman, Gerald; Duncan, Robert; and Holbek, Jonny. *Innovations and Organizations.* New York: John Wiley & Sons, 1973.

## Articles, Papers, and Lectures

Allison, Graham T. "Conceptual Models and the Cuban Missile Crisis." *American Political Science Review* 63 (September 1969):689–718.

Arnold, Peri E. "Executive Reorganization and Administrative Theory: The Origin of the Managerial Presidency." Paper delivered at the Annual Meeting of the American Political Science Association, September 2–5, 1976.

Backoff, Robert. "Operationalizing Administrative Reform for Improved Governmental Performance." *Administration and Society* 6 (May 1974):73–106.

Barnett, J. D. "Reorganization of State Government in Oregon." *American Political Science Review* 9 (May 1915):287–93.

Beard, Charles A. "Reconstructing State Government." *New Republic* 4 (August 1915):1–16.

Beer, Samuel H. "The Modernization of American Federalism." *Publius* 3 (Fall 1973):50–95.

Bell, George. "Executive Reorganization and Its Effect on Budgeting." In *Summary of the Twenty-Ninth Annual Meeting of the National Association of State Budget Officers*, pp. 90–91. Lexington, Ky.: Council of State Governments, 1973.

_____. "State Administrative Organization Activities, 1972–1973." *The Book of the States, 1974–75*, pp. 137–42. Lexington, Ky.: Council of State Governments, 1974.

Bell, George A. "State Administrative Organization Activities, 1974–75." *The Book of the States, 1976–77*, pp. 105–10. Lexington, Ky.: Council of State Governments, 1976.

Bell, James R. "State Government Reorganization in California." *State Government* 35 (Spring 1962):130–35.

Berkley, George E. "Reorganizing Administration in Massachusetts." In *The Craft of Public Administration*, pp. 62–72. Boston: Allyn and Bacon, 1975.

Binder, Arnold. "Statistical Theory." *Annual Review of Psychology* 15 (1964):277–310.

Bingham, David A. "State Government Reorganization in West Virginia." *West Virginia Public Affairs Reporter* 2 (Fall 1977).

Bosworth, Karl A. "The Politics of Management Improvement in the States." *American Political Science Review* 47 (March 1953):84–99.

Botner, Stanley B. "Modernization of State Administration: Missouri's 'Little Hoover' Commissions." *University of Missouri Business and Review* 11 (January/February 1970):11–20.

Cain, Glen G., and Watts, Harold W. "Problems in Making Policy Inferences from the Coleman Report." *American Sociological Review* 35 (April 1970): 228–42.

Caldwell, Lynton K. "Perfecting State Administration, 1940–46." *Public Administration Review* 7 (Winter 1947):25–36.

Campbell, Alan K. "States at the Crossroads." *National Civil Review* 55 (November 1966):554–60.

Casselman, Robert C. "An Old State Takes a New Look at Public Management." *Public Administration Review* 31 (July/August 1971):427–34.

_____. "Massachusetts Revisited: Chronology of a Failure." *Public Administration Review* 33 (March/April 1973):129–35.

Childs, Richard S. "New York State Reorganizes." *National Municipal Review* (May 1926).

Coker, Francis W. "Dogmas of Administrative Reform as Exemplified in the Recent Reorganization of Ohio." *American Political Science Review* 16 (August 1922):388–411.

Collier, David, and Messick, Richard. "Prerequisites versus Diffusion: Testing Alternative Explanations of Social Security Adoption." *American Political Science Review* 69 (1975):1299–1315.

"Constitutional Revision and Governmental Reorganization." *State Government* 41 (Winter 1968):20-22.

The Council of State Governments. "State Administrative Reorganization, 1945-47." In *The Book of States, 1948-1949*, pp. 167-70. Lexington, Ky.: Council of State Governments, 1948.

————. "State Administrative Reorganization, 1947-1949." In *The Book of States, 1950-1951*, pp. 157-61. Chicago: Council of State Governments, 1950.

————. "State Administrative Reorganization, 1950-1951." In *The Book of States, 1952-1953*, pp. 147-57. Chicago: Council of State Governments, 1952.

————. "State Administrative Reorganization, 1952-1953." In *The Book of States, 1954-1955*, pp. 155-62. Chicago: Council of State Governments, 1954.

————. "State Administrative Organization, 1954-1955." In *The Book of States, 1956-1957*, pp. 149-55. Chicago: Council of State Governments, 1956.

————. "State Administrative Organization, 1956-1957." In *The Book of States, 1958-1959*, pp. 111-17. Chicago: Council of State Governments, 1958.

————. "State Administrative Organization, 1958-1959." In *The Book of States, 1960-1961*, pp. 115-29. Chicago: Council of State Governments, 1960.

————. "State Administrative Organization, 1960-1961." In *The Book of States, 1962-1963*, pp. 135-46. Chicago: Council of State Governments, 1962.

————. "State Administrative Organization, 1962-1963." In *The Book of States, 1964-1965*, pp. 137-52. Chicago: Council of State Governments, 1964.

————. "State Administrative Organization and Management, 1964-1965." In *The Book of States, 1966-1967*, pp. 127-54. Chicago: Council of State Governments, 1966.

————. "State Administrative Organization Activities, 1968-1969." In *The Book of States, 1970-1971*, pp. 135-65. Lexington, Ky.: Council of State Governments, 1970.

————. "State Administrative Organization Activities, 1972-1973." In *The Book of States, 1974-1975*, pp. 137-70. Lexington, Ky.: Council of State Governments, 1974.

————. "State Administrative Organization Activities, 1974-1975." In *The Book of States, 1976-1977*, pp. 105-9. Lexington, Ky.: Council of State Governments, 1976.

Crawford, F. G. "New York State Reorganization." *American Political Science Review* 20 (February 1926):76-79.

Eckstein, Harry. "Case Study and Theory in Political Science." In *Handbook of Political Science*, edited by Fred I. Greenstein and Nelson Polsby, vol. 7, pp. 79-137. Reading, Mass.: Addison-Wesley Publishing Co., 1975.

Edwards, William H. "A Factual Summary of State Administrative Reorganization. *Southwestern Social Science Quarterly* 11 (June 1938):53-67.

————. "The State Reorganization Movement." *Dakota Law Review* 1, no. 1 (1927): 13-30; 1, no. 2 (1927):15-41; and 2, no. 1 (1928):17-67; and 2, no. 2 (1928):103-9.

Ehrlich, Joan E. "State Executive Reorganizations." *The University of Virginia Newsletter* 51 (March 1975):26-27.

Ford, H. J. "The Reorganization of State Government." *Proceedings of the Academy of Political Science* 3 (1912-13):78-84.

Gallagher, Hubert R., "State Reorganization Surveys." *Public Administration Review* 9 (Autumn 1949):252–56.

Garnett, James L. "Different Conceptual Lenses for Viewing Executive Branch Reorganization: Variations on a Recurring Theme." Lecture at the Maxwell School of Citizenship and Public Affairs, Syracuse University, April 13, 1977.

———. "Strategies for Governors Who Want to Reorganize," *State Government* 52 (Summer 1979):135–43.

———. "The State of the Art in State Executive Branch Reorganization: A Review and Some Projections," *International Journal of Public Administration* 2, no. 1 (January 1980):51–80.

———. "Why State Executive Reorganizations Occur: Competing and Complementary Theoretical Perspectives." Paper delivered at the 1978 Symposium on Administrative Reform, The University of Nebraska, Lincoln, Nebraska, April 13–14, 1978.

Garnett, James L., and Levine, Charles H. "State Executive Branch Reorganization: Patterns and Performance." *Administration and Society* 12 (November 1980).

Gove, Samuel K. "Administrative Reorganization: The Illinois Case." Paper presented at the Symposium on Administrative Reform and Public Policy, University of Nebraska, Lincoln, Nebraska, April 13–14, 1978.

Graves, W. Brooke. "Some New Approaches to State Administrative Reorganization." *Western Political Quarterly* 9 (September 1956):743–54.

Gregg, Phillip M. "Units and Levels of Analysis: A Problem of Policy Analysis in Federal System." *Publius* 4 (Fall 1974):59–86.

Gulick, Luther. "Governmental Reorganization." *Tax Digest* (Fourth Quarter 1968): 26–29.

Hofferbert, Richard I. "Socioeconomic Dimensions of the American States, 1890–1960." *Midwest Journal of Political Science* 12 (1968):401–18.

———. "State and Community Policy Studies: A Review of Comparative Input-Output Analysis." *Political Science Annual* 3 (1972):3–72.

Hyneman, Charles S. "Administrative Reorganization: An Adventure into Science and Theology." *Journal of Politics* 1 (1939):62–75.

Jacob, Herbert, and Lipsky, Michael. "Outputs, Structure, and Power: An Assessment of Changes in the Study of State and Local Politics." *Journal of Politics* 30 (1968):510–38.

Jacobson, J. Mark. "Evaluating State Administrative Structure: The Fallacy of the Statistical Approach." *American Political Science Review* 22 (November 1929):928–35.

Kaufman, Herbert. "Emerging Conflicts in the Doctrines of Public Administration." *American Political Science Review* 50 (December 1956):1057–73.

Kaufman, Herbert, and Seidman, David. "The Morphology of Organizations." *Administrative Science Quarterly* 15 (December 1970):439–51.

Keeley, James F. "Comparative Case Studies and Theory Building." Unpublished paper. Stanford University, January 1976.

Lazarsfeld, Paul F. "Some Remarks on Typological Procedure in Social Research." *Zeitschrift für Sozial Forschung* 6 (1937):119–39.

Lederle, John, and Strauss, Dorothee E. "The Little Hoover Commissions." *Michigan Governmental Digest No. 4.* University of Michigan: Bureau of Government, 1949.

Levine, Charles H., et al. "Organizational Design: A Post Minnowbrook Perspective for the 'New' Public Administration." *Public Administration Review* 35 (July/August 1975):425–35.

Levy, Marion J. "Social Patterns (Structures) and Problems of Modernization." In *Readings on Social Change,* edited by Wilbert E. Moore, pp. 189–208. Englewood Cliffs, N.J.: Prentice-Hall, 1967.

Lowden, Frank D. "Reorganization in Illinois and Its Results." *The Annals* (May 1924):155–60.

Lowi, Theodore. "Toward Functionalism in Political Science: The Case of Innovation in Party Systems." *American Political Science Review* 57 (September 1963): 570–83.

Martin, Roscoe. "Alabama's Administrative Reorganization of 1939." *Journal of Politics.* 2 (November 1946):436–47.

Mathews, J. M. "State Administrative Reorganization." *American Political Science Review* 16 (August 1922):387–98.

_____. "Administrative Reorganization in Illinois." Supplement to *National Municipal Review.* November 1922.

McKinney, John C. "The Process of Typification." In *Theoretical Sociology,* edited by John C. McKinney and Edward A. Tiryakian. New York: Appleton, Century, Crofts, 1966.

Miles, Rufus E., Jr. "Considerations for a President Bent on Reorganization." *Public Administration Review* 37 (March/April 1977):155–62.

Mileur, Jerome. "The Politics of State Administrative Studies." *University of Massachusetts Bureau of Governmental Research Bulletin* 1 (1967):1–4.

Millspaugh, A. C. "Democracy and Administrative Organization." In *Essays in Political Science, in Honor of Westel Woodbury Willoughby,* edited by John M. Mathews and James Hart, pp. 64–73. Baltimore: Johns Hopkins University Press, 1937.

Morgan, D., and Lyons, W. "Industrialization and Affluence Revisited: A Note on Socioeconomic Dimensions of American States, 1970." *American Journal of Political Science* 19 (May 1975):263–76.

Noell, James J. "On the Administrative Sector of Social Systems: An Analysis of the Size and Complexity of Government Bureaucracies in the American States." *Social Forces* 52 (June 1974):549–58.

Peirce, Neal R. "Structural Reform of Bureaucracy Grows Rapidly." *National Journal* 7 (April 1975):502–8.

Perkins, John A. "Reflections on State Reorganizations." *American Political Science Review* 45 (June 1951):507–11.

"Piecemeal Revision Approach Succeeds in South Dakota." *National Civic Review* 62 (February 1973):85.

"Recent Trends in State Executive Reorganization in the Midwest." *Midwest Review of Public Administration* 7 (January 1973):25–55.

"Reorganization Proposals Made in Three More States (Montana, Oregon, Utah)."

*National Civic Review* 50 (March 1961):144–45.

Rose, Douglas D. "National and Local Forces in State Politics: The Implications of Multi-Level Policy Analysis." *American Political Science Review* 67 (December 1973):1162–73.

Rosenbaum, Walter A., and Henderson, Thomas A. "Explaining Comprehensive Governmental Consolidation: Toward a Preliminary Theory." *The Journal of Politics* 34 (1972):428–57.

Rourke, Francis E. "The Politics of Administrative Organization: A Case History." *The Journal of Politics* 19 (1957):461–78.

Salamon, Lester M. "Follow-ups, Letdowns, and Sleepers: The Time Dimension in Policy Evaluation." In *Public Policy Making in a Federal System,* edited by Charles O. Jones and Robert D. Thomas. Beverly Hills, Calif.: Sage, 1976.

Schlesinger, Joseph A. "The Politics of the Executive." In *Politics in the American States: A Comparative Analysis,* edited by Herbert Jacobs and Kenneth N. Vines, pp. 210–37. Boston: Little, Brown and Co., 1971.

Seidman, Harold. "The Politics and Strategies of Reorganization." Lecture given at the Maxwell School of Citizenship and Public Affairs, Syracuse University, March 3, 1977.

Sharkansky, Ira. "Environment, Policy, Output, and Impact: Problems of Theory and Method in the Analysis of Public Policy." In *Policy Analysis in Political Science,* edited by Ira Sharkansky and Richard I. Hofferbert. Chicago: Markham, 1970.

Sherman, Harvey M. "State Reorganization." *The Book of the States, 1941–42,* pp. 62–70. Chicago: Council of State Governments, 1942.

Sigelman, Lee. "The Quality of Administration: An Exploration in the American States." *Administration and Society* 8 (May 1976):107–44.

Simmons, Robert H. "American State Executive Studies: A Suggested Departure." *Western Political Quarterly* 17 (1964):777–83.

Simpson, T. McN., III. "Appraising the Carter Administration." Paper. University of Tennessee, 1975.

Stanley, David T. "Sam, You Made the Frame Too Long." *Public Administration Review* 23 (July/August 1972):349.

"State Reorganization Studies." *State Government* 23 (September 1950):200–4.

"States Reorganize for Environment." *National Civic Review* 65 (December 1976): 563.

"Streamlining the Structure of State Government." In *The State of the States in 1974,* pp. 19–24. Washington, D.C.: National Governors' Conference, 1974.

Thompson, Victor A. "Bureaucracy and Innovation." *Administrative Science Quarterly* 10 (June 1965):1–20.

Tiryakian, Edward A. "Typological Classification." *International Encyclopedia of the Social Sciences,* pp. 177–86. New York: Macmillan, 1968.

Van Meter, Donald S., and Van Horn, Carl E. "The Policy Implementation Process." *Administration and Society* 6 (February 1975):445–88.

Vaughan, Donald S. "Administration Reorganization Procedures." *Public Administration Survey* 18 (January 1971):1–4.

Waldo, Dwight. "Organizational Analysis: Some Notes on Methods and Criteria."

*Public Administration Review* 7 (Autumn 1947):236-44.

———. "Organization Theory: An Elephantine Problem." *Public Administration Review* 21 (Autumn 1961):210-25.

Walker, Harvey. "Ohio Appraises Its Reorganized State Government." *National Municipal Review* 15 (April 1929):249-53.

———. "Theory and Practice in State Administrative Organization." *National Municipal Review* 19 (1930):249-54.

Walker, Jack L. "Innovation in State Politics." In *Politics in the American States: A Comparative Analysis.* 2d ed., edited by Herbert Jacob and Kenneth Vines, pp. 354-87. Boston: Little, Brown and Co., 1971.

———. "The Diffusion of Innovation Among the American States." *American Political Science Review* 63 (September 1969):880-99.

Walton, Richard E. "Advantages and Attributes of the Case Study." *Journal of Applied Behavioral Science* 8 (January 1972):76-86.

Willbern, York. "Administration in State Governments." In *The Forty-Eight States: Their Tasks as Policy-Makers and Administrators.* New York: American Assembly, 1955.

Winch, R. F. "Heuristic and Empirical Typologies." *American Sociological Review* 12 (February 1947):68-75.

## Bibliographies

Beyle, Thad L., and Crowe, Edward W. *State Government Reorganization: A Working Bibliography.* Chapel Hill: Department of Political Science, University of North Carolina, 1978.

Chase, Karen A. *Reorganization of State Government: A Selective Bibliography.* Berkeley: University of California Institute of Government Studies, 1968.

The Council of State Governments. *Selected Bibliography on State Government, 1952-1972.* Lexington, Ky.: The Council of State Governments, 1972.

———. *State Executive Reorganization Clearinghouse: Documents on State Executive Reorganization, No. 5* (cumulative), May 1974.

Jones, B. Crichton. *State Government: A Selected Bibliography.* Washington: Center for Governmental Studies, 1970.

Rogers, Everett M., and Thomas, Patricia C. *Bibliography on the Diffusion of Innovations.* Ann Arbor: Department of Population Planning, University of Michigan, 1975.

Tompkins, Dorothy. "Organizations and Reorganizations in State Government, 1958-1959: A Bibliography." *California Public Survey* 11 (1959):185-95.

Weiner, Grace. "Surveys of the Administrative Reorganization of State Government: A Bibliography." In *Manual on the Use of State Publications,* edited by Jerome K. Wilcox, pp. 92-100. Chicago: American Library Association, 1940.

Winsten, Richard. *Reorganization of the Executive Branch of State Government: A Selected Annotated Bibliography.* Albany: Legislative Reference Service, New York State Library, 1974

## Dissertations

Blue, Leonard. "The Governor and Executive Organization." Ph.D. dissertation, University of Pennsylvania, 1902.

Fellers, Raymond. "The Political Limits of Executive Reorganization." Ph.D. dissertation, New School for Social Research, 1973.

Gottlieb, Anita F. "State Executive Reorganization: A Study of Hallucination, Supposition, and Hypothesis." Ph.D. dissertation, George Washington University, 1976.

Mattos, Alexandre M. "The Pattern of Public Administrative Reorganization in the United States: 1945-1955." Ph.D. dissertation, University of Southern California, 1962.

Tipermas, Marc. "Jursidictionalism: The Politics of Executive Reorganization." Ph.D. dissertation, Harvard University, 1976.

Wood, Robert C. "The Metropolitan Governor: Three Case Inquiries into the Substance of State Executive Management." Ph.D. dissertation, Harvard University, 1949.

## Data Sets

Burnham, W. Dean. *Partisan Division of American State Governments, 1834-1974.* Data set from the Interuniversity Consortium for Political and Social Research.

Hofferbert, Richard I. *Socioeconomic, Public Policy, and Political Data, 1890-1960.* Data set from the Interuniversity Consortium for Political and Social Research and updated at the Center for Social Analysis, State University of New York at Binghamton.

## Interviews

Carlson, Richard. Director of research, the Council of State Governments, Lexington, Ky. Interview, April 26, 1977.

Carter, James E. Interview with Neal Peirce, consulting editor, *National Journal.* March 6, 1975.

Gulick, Luther H. Interview, November 30, 1976.

Hallet, George H. New York State Charter Revision Commission for New York City. Interview, September 13, 1976.

Macchiarola, Frank J. New York State Emergency Financial Control Board. Interview, September 14, 1976.

Martin, James L. National Governors' Association. Interview, February 16, 1977.

Martin, James W. Interview, April 27, 1977.

Nicholson, Judy. The Council of State Governments, Lexington, Ky. Interview, May 12, 1962.

Uslaner, Eric. The University of Maryland Department of Political Science. Interview, January 16, 1978.

## State Government Documents and Consultant Reports

*Alabama*

Legislative Reference Service. *A Governmental Reorganization Commission for Alabama.* Montgomery: Legislative Reference Service of Alabama, 1949.

————. *The Reorganization of Alabama's State Government.* Montgomery: Legislative Reference Service of Alabama, 1950.

*Arizona*

Arizona Legislature. House Government Operations Committee. *Governmental Organization.* Phoenix: The Committee, 1973.

Office of the Governor. *Governmental Reorganization: A Report to the Thirty-First Arizona Legislature.* Phoenix: The Governor's Office, 1973.

Staff of the National Social and Rehabilitation Services Demonstration. *The Movement Towards State Executive Reorganization: A Key Issue.* Tucson: University of Arizona, 1972.

*Arkansas*

Department of Planning. *A Preliminary Evaluation of Governmental Reorganization, Parts 1 and 2.* Little Rock: The Department, 1971.

Legislative Council. *Summary of Recent Efforts to Reorganize Executive Departments of Government in the Various States.* Research Report No. 144. Little Rock: The Council, 1970.

Milam, Max. *Administrative Reorganization in Arkansas.* Little Rock: Arkansas Program Planning Project, 1968.

Office of the Governor. *Arkansas State Government: The Development of Executive Management.* Little Rock: The Office, 1974.

*Survey Report and Recommendations of the Arkansas Governmental Efficiency Study Commission.* Little Rock: Arkansas Governmental Efficiency Study Commission, 1967.

*California*

California Assembly Committee on Governmental Organization. *Report on Executive Reorganization Plans One and Two of 1970.* Sacramento: Assembly Committee on Governmental Organization, 1970.

Gardner, Neely. *Report to California Governor Edmund G. Brown by Deputy Director's Conference.* Sacramento: State of California, 1966.

Governor's Committee on Organization of State Government. *The Agency Plan for California.* Sacramento: The Committee, 1959.

Hurt, Elsey. *California State Government: An Outline of Its Administrative Organization from 1850 to 1936.* Sacramento: California Department of Finance, 1937.

————. *California State Government: The Independent Agencies, 1850 to 1939.* Sacramento: California Department of Finance, 1940.

Interim Committee of Twenty-Five of the California Conference on Government and Taxation. *Final Report of Committee on State Reorganization.* San Francisco, April 1941.

### Colorado

Colorado Committee on Government Efficiency and Economy. *General Information and Summary of Reports.* Denver: The Committee, 1969.
_____. *Reports of the Committee on Government Efficiency and Economy.* Denver: The Committee, 1969.
Colorado Legislative Council. *Constitutional Recommendations of Colorado Committee on Government Efficiency and Economy.* Denver: The Council, 1969.
_____. *Legislative Recommendations of Colorado Committee on Government Efficiency and Economy.* Denver: The Council, 1969.
_____. *Organization of State Government.* Research Publications No. 162. Denver: The Council, 1970.
_____. *Organization of State Government.* Research Publications No. 179. Denver: The Council, 1971.
_____. *Organization of State Government.* Research Publications No. 198. Denver: The Council, 1972.
_____. *Report to the Colorado General Assembly: Reorganizing the Executive Branch of Colorado's State Government.* Research Publications No. 171. Denver: The Council, 1967.
Management Services Office, Colorado Department of Administration. *Colorado State Government Organization.* Denver: Management Services Office, 1970.

### Connecticut

Commission on State Government Organization. *Report.* Hartford: The Commission, 1950.
Committee on the Structure of State Government. *Better Organization for Better Government.* Hartford: The Committee, 1976.
Public Expenditure Council. *The Structure of Connecticut's State Government.* Hartford: Public Expenditure Council of Connecticut, 1968.

### Delaware

The Governor's Task Force on Reorganization of the Executive Branch of Government. *Cabinet Department Reports.* Dover: Governor's Task Force on Reorganization of the Executive Branch of Government, 1969.
_____. *Final Report on Cabinet Departments.* Wilmington: The Task Force, 1970.

### Florida

Booz, Allen, and Hamilton. *Organization Study of the Executive Branch of State Government.* Tallahassee: Booz, Allen, and Hamilton, 1969.
Legislative Auditor. *Outline Charts: Executive Reorganization by the 1969 Session, Florida Legislature.* Tallahassee: Legislative Auditor, 1969.
State Planning and Budget Commission. *A Proposal for Reorganization of the Executive Branch of Florida State Government.* Tallahassee: The Commission, 1969.

## Georgia

Office of Planning and Budget. *Reorganization and Management Improvement Implementation Notebook.* Atlanta: Office of Planning and Budget, 1972.

————. *Reorganization: Providing Better Services for All Georgia Citizens.* Atlanta: Office of Planning and Budget, 1972.

## Idaho

Executive Reorganization Staff, State Planning and Community Affairs Agency. *The Executive Branch of Idaho State Government.* Boise: The Staff, 1971.

————. *Executive Reorganization in Idaho: An Overview.* Boise: The Staff, 1972.

Legislative Council. *State Government Reorganization.* Research Publication no. 3. Boise: Legislative Council of Idaho, 1966.

Legislative Executive Reorganization Commission. *An Explanation of Executive Reorganization Legislative Proposals.* Boise: The Commission, 1974.

————. *A Tentative Proposal for the Reorganization of Idaho State Government.* Boise: The Commission, 1973.

State Planning and Community Affairs Agency. *The Executive Branch of Idaho State Government.* Boise: The Agency, 1971

## Illinois

Commission on State Government. *Report.* Springfield: The Commission, 1965.

————. *Recommendations on Management, Organization, and Functioning of the Executive Branch. Report of the Commission on State Government to the Governor and General Assembly of Illinois.* Springfield: The Commission, 1967.

————. *Management, Organization, and Functioning in the Executive Branch.* Springfield: The Commission, 1969.

*Report of the Efficiency and Economy Committee.* Springfield: The Committee, 1915.

Sixth Illinois Constitutional Convention. *Proposal Number 1, Committee on the Executive.* Springfield: Sixth Illinois Constitutional Convention, 1970.

## Indiana

Commission for the Reorganization of the Executive Branch of Indiana State Government. *Executive Reorganization in Indiana.* Indianapolis: The Commission, 1968.

*Report of the Committee to Make A Survey of the Boards and Commissions of Indiana.* Indianapolis: The Committee, 1925.

*Report of the Indiana State Committee on Government Economy.* Indianapolis: The Committee, 1935.

## Iowa

Governmental Reorganization Study Committee. *Report to the Sixty-Fourth General Assembly.* Des Moines: The Committee, 1971.

Institute for Government Research of the Brookings Institution. *Report on a Survey of*

*Administration in Iowa.* Des Moines: Committee on Reduction of Expenditures of Iowa, 1933.
*Report of the Joint Committee on Retrenchment and Reform.* Des Moines: The Committee, 1914.

## Kansas

Commission on Executive Reorganization. *Reorganizing Kansas State Government for Maximum Effectiveness and Economy.* Topeka: The Commission, 1971.
Ernst and Ernst. *Kansas State Government Executive Branch Reorganization Program.* Topeka: Ernst and Ernst, 1969.
Kansas Legislative Council Research Department. *State Administration Reorganization.* Preliminary report prepared for the Committee on Municipal Government. Topeka: Kansas Legislative Council, 1937.

## Kentucky

Office of the Governor. *Governor's Reorganization Reports.* Frankfort: Office of the Governor, 1972–74.
*Report of the Efficiency Commission.* Prepared by Griffenhagen and Associates. 2 vols. Frankfort: The Commission, 1924.

## Louisiana

Public Affairs Research Council. *The Executive Branch: Committee Proposal No. 4.* Baton Rouge: The Council, 1973.
_____. *Powers of the Governor and Gubernatorial Succession.* Baton Rouge: Public Affairs Council of Louisiana, 1965.
Reorganizational Study Commission. *Final Report of the Reorganizational Study Commission.* Baton Rouge: The Commission, 1962.

## Maine

Governor's Task Force on Government Reorganization. *Toward a More Responsive and Effective State Government.* Augusta: The Task Force, 1969.
Institute of Public Administration. *State Administrative Consolidation in Maine.* Report submitted to Governor William Gardiner. Augusta: The Institute of Public Administration, 1931.
Savage, Philip M. *State of Maine Governmental Reorganization: A Summary of New Departments and Agencies Approved by the 105th Legislature, June 30, 1971–July 7, 1971.* State Planning Office, Executive Department, State of Maine.
State Planning Office. *State of Maine Governmental Reorganization.* Augusta: State Planning Office, 1971.
_____. *State of Maine Governmental Reorganization: A Summary of New Departments and Agencies Approved by the State Governmental Reorganization Project, May 1971–July 1973.* Augusta: State Planning Office, 1973.
_____. *State of Maine Governmental Reorganization: A Summary of New Departments and Agencies Approved by the First Special Session of the 105th Legislature, March 1972.* Augusta: State Planning Office, 1971–72.

*Maryland*

Commission for the Modernization of the Executive Branch of the Maryland Government. *Report.* Baltimore: The Commission, 1967.

Department of Legislative Reference. *State Government: Eleven New Departments Created in 1969 and 1970.* Annapolis: The Department, 1971.

Governor's Executive Reorganization Committee. *Executive Reorganization: A Comprehensive Plan for Maryland.* Annapolis: The Committee, 1969.

_____. *Modernizing the Executive Branch of the Maryland Government.* Annapolis: The Committee, 1967.

_____. *Summary of 1970 Reorganization Legislation.* Annapolis: The Committee, 1970.

Griffenhagen and Associates. *Report on the Organization and Administration of the State Government. Part 2, A Plan of Administrative Consolidation.* Annapolis: Griffenhagen and Associates, 1921.

Reorganization Commission of Maryland. *Plan for the Reorganization of the Administrative Departments of the State Government of Maryland and for the Reduction in the Number of Elections in Maryland.* Annapolis: The Commission, 1921.

*Massachusetts*

Office of Planning and Program Coordination. *Modernization of the Government of the Commonwealth of Massachusetts.* Boston: The Office, 1968.

_____. *The Management Problems and an Approach to Their Solution.* Boston: The Office, 1969.

Legislative Research Bureau. *Report Relative to Executive Branch Reorganization.* Boston: Legislative Research Bureau, 1965.

*Michigan*

Milliken, William C. *Departmental Reorganization.* Memorandum. Lansing: State of Michigan Executive Office, 1971.

State Library. *Major Recommendations of Present State Agencies in Planning for Reorganization under the New Constitution.* Lansing: State Library, 1968.

*Minnesota*

Constitutional Study Commission. *Executive Branch Committee Report.* St. Paul: The Commission, 1972.

Governor's Council on Executive Reorganization. *Report.* St. Paul: The Council, 1968.

_____. *Executive Reorganization for the Improvement of State Government, State of Minnesota.* St. Paul: The Council, 1968.

Office of the Governor. *Report to the People on Executive Reorganization from Governor Harold LeVander.* St. Paul: Office of the Governor, 1970.

Loaned Executives Action Program. *Final Report.* St. Paul: The Program, 1972.

*Missouri*

Governor's Loaned Executives Action Program. *Final Report.* Jefferson City: Governor's Loaned Executives Action Program, 1975.

Governor's Task Force on Government Reorganization. *Toward a More Responsible and Effective State Government.* Jefferson City: The Task Force, 1969.

State Reorganization Commission. *To Make Missouri Government Manageable: Proposed Plan of Restructuring the Executive Branch.* Jefferson City: The Commission, 1971.

_____. *For a Trimmer State Government: Final Report.* Jefferson City: The Commission, 1972.

## Montana

Commission on Executive Reorganization. *Executive Reorganization: Final Report.* Helena: The Commission, 1970.

_____. *Report to the Montana Legislative Assembly: Executive Reorganization.* Helena: The Commission, 1970.

_____. *Explanation of Senate Bill 274: The Executive Reorganization Act of 1971.* Helena: The Commission, 1971.

Constitutional Convention Commission. *Constitutional Provisions.* Montana Constitutional Convention Occasional Papers Report no. 7. Helena: The Commission, 1969.

Montana Executive Reorganization Office. *Reorganization Guide.* Helena: The Office, 1971.

_____. *Reorganization in Review: Report to the Montana Legislative Assembly.* Helena: Montana Executive Reorganization Office, 1972.

## Nebraska

Constitutional Revision Commission. *Report.* Lincoln: The Commission, 1970.

Management Analysis Study Committee. *Nebraska Surveys and Recommendations.* Lincoln: The Committee, 1968.

*Nebraska Civil Administrative Code, Chapter 190, Laws of 1919, as amended* by Chapter 210, Laws of 1921.

Nebraska Legislative Reference Bureau. *Chart of the Administrative Organization of Nebraska.* Lincoln: Nebraska Legislative Reference Bureau, 1937.

## Nevada

New York Bureau of Municipal Research (Institute of Public Administration). *Nevada and Its Government.* Supplement to *Nevada State Journal,* November 20, 1924.

Office of the Budget Director. *The Need for Reorganization and Proposals for Reorganization.* Carson City: Office of the Budget Director, 1963.

*Report of the State Survey Commission to the Governor and Legislature.* Carson City: State Survey Commission, 1925.

## New Hampshire

Citizens' Task Force. *Reports of the Consultants.* Silver Springs, Md.: Macro Systems, 1969.

_____. *Report.* Concord: The Task Force, 1970.

Institute for Government Research of the Brookings Institution. *Report on a Survey of the State, County, and Town Governments of New Hampshire.* Washington, D.C.: Institute for Government Research, 1932.

## New Jersey

Governor's Committee on Economy and Efficiency in State Government. *Report of the Committee.* Trenton: The Committee, 1963.

Governor's Management Commission. *Survey Report and Recommendations.* Trenton: The Commission, 1970.

Institute of Public Administration. *Organization and Administration of the State Government of New Jersey.* Trenton: Institute of Public Administration, 1930.

*Report of the Joint Legislative Survey Committee of New Jersey.* Trenton: The Committee, 1925.

## New Mexico

Governor's Committee on Reorganization of State Government. *Interim Report.* Santa Fe: The Committee, 1967.

————. *Final Report.* Santa Fe: The Committee, 1970.

*Report of the New Mexico State Reorganization Committee.* Santa Fe: New Mexico State Reorganization Committee, 1952.

## New York

Committee on the Executive Branch. *Proposals for Mandated Departments.* Albany: The Committee, 1967.

New York Bureau of Municipal Research. *The Constitution and Government of the State of New York.* New York: The Bureau, 1915.

New York State Assembly Standing Committee on Governmental Operations. *Executive Branch Reorganization.* Albany: The Committee, 1973.

Report of the Secretary to the Governor of New York. *Proposed Reorganization of the Executive Branch of New York State Government, 1959.* Albany: The Governor's Office, 1959.

State of New York. *Record of the Constitutional Convention of 1915: Unrevised.* 4 vols. Albany: J. B. Lyon and Co., 1915.

## North Carolina

Governor's Committee on State Government Reorganization. *Report.* Raleigh: The Committee, 1970.

————. *Report.* Raleigh: The Committee, 1971.

————. *Report.* Raleigh: The Committee, 1972.

Governor's State Government Reorganization Staff. *Quarterly Reports on Progress of Reorganization of State Government.* Raleigh: The Staff, April through October, 1972.

Institute for Government Research of the Brookings Institution. *Report on a Survey* of the Organization and Administration of the State Government of North Carolina. Washington, D.C.: Institute for Government Research, 1930.

*The Reports of the 1953–1955 Commission on Reorganization of State Government.* Raleigh: Commission on Reorganization of State Government, 1956.

State Government Reorganization Study. *State Government Reorganization in North Carolina.* Raleigh: State Government Reorganization Study, 1970.

State Planning Division, Department of Administration. *Fundamental Approaches to Government in North Carolina.* Report no. 112.01. 2 vols. Raleigh: The Department, 1970.

_____. *North Carolina Government Functions Model.* Raleigh: The Department, 1970.

## Ohio

Council for Reorganization of Ohio State Government. *Survey Report and Recommendations.* Columbus: The Council, 1963.

*Report of the Joint Committee on Economy in the Public Service.* Columbus: The Committee, 1929.

## Oklahoma

Commission on the Reorganization of the State Executive Department. *An Analysis of the Twenty Executive Departments in the First Proposal.* Oklahoma City: The Commission, 1972.

_____. *The Executive Director's Report to the Commission on Guidelines for the Reorganization of the Executive Department.* Oklahoma City: The Commission, 1972.

Volunteer Executives. *Reorganization.* (Report to the Oklahoma Special Commission on the Reorganization of State Government). February 5, 1976.

## Oregon

Executive Department. *Organization of Oregon State Government.* Salem: Executive Department, 1975.

"Governor McCall's Major State Government Reorganization Proposals." Press release. Salem: Office of the Governor, 1968.

Management Seventies Task Force. *Oregon State Government for the Seventies.* Salem: The Task Force, 1968.

_____. *Summary of Recommendations and Status of Implementation as of October 1, 1970.* Salem: State of Oregon Executive Department, 1970.

*Report of the Consolidation Commission of the State of Oregon to the 1919 Legislature.* Salem: The Commission, 1919.

## Pennsylvania

Bureau of Systems Analysis, Office of Administration. *Plan for the Reorganization of the Executive Branch.* Harrisburg: The Bureau, 1969.

Governor's Commission for Modern State Government. *Final Report.* Harrisburg: The Commission, 1970.

*Report of the Commission for the Consolidation of State Government.* Harrisburg: The Commission, 1922.

## South Dakota

Bucks, Dan. *Executive Reorganization in South Dakota.* Pierre: State Planning Bureau, 1974.

Citizens' Commission on Executive Reorganization. *Staff Documents.* Pierre: The Commission, 1971.

_____. *Achieving Responsible Government.* Pierre: The Commission, 1972.

_____. *A Plan for Responsive Government in South Dakota.* Pierre: The Commission, 1973.

*Executive Reorganization Order of 1973.* Pierre: State Printer, 1973.

Griffenhagen and Associates. *Report on Reorganization of the Executive Branch of the State Government of South Dakota.* Chicago: Griffenhagen and Associates, 1954.

Legislative Research Council. *Proposed Amendments to the South Dakota Constitution.* Pierre: The Council, 1970.

_____. *The Administrative Organization of South Dakota State Government.* Pierre: The Council, 1972.

Office of the Governor. *Implementing Responsive Government.* Pierre: Office of the Governor, 1974.

_____. *Loaned Executives' Final Recommendations.* Pierre: Office of the Governor, 1974.

## Utah

Commission on the Organization of the Executive Branch. *Report.* Salt Lake City: The Commission, 1966.

Government Operations Committee of the Legislative Council. *Selected Organizational Studies in Utah State Government: Clarification of the Lines of Administrative Authority in Three Major Departments. First report.* Salt Lake City: The Council, 1970.

Office of the Legislative Analyst. *An Analysis of Utah Departmental Reorganization and Consolidation.* Salt Lake City: The Office, 1968.

Office of the Legislative Analyst, State of Utah. *A Report to the Joint Budget and Audit Committee and the Planning and Goals Subcommittee of the Legislative Council.* Salt Lake City: The Office, 1968.

## Vermont

Budget and Management Division, Department of Administration. *State of Vermont: Observations on Reorganization.* Montpelier: Department of Administration, 1970.

Committee on Administrative Coordination. *Reorganization of the Executive Branch: Report to the Governor.* Montpelier: The Committee, 1969.

_____. *Report on Uniform Administrative Districts for State and Local Government.* Montpelier: The Committee, 1970.

State of Vermont Executive Department. *Vermont State Government Reorganization: The Time Is Now.* Montpelier: State of Vermont Executive Department, 1968.

## Virginia

Commission on State Governmental Management. *First Interim Report.* Richmond: The Commission, 1974.

———. *Second Interim Report: Recommendations on the Roles of the Secretaries.* Richmond: The Commission, 1974.

———. *Management of Virginia State Government: Tentative Recommendations of the Commission.* Richmond: The Commission, 1975.

Commission to Study State Government. *Report.* Richmond: The Commission, 1961.

New York Bureau of Municipal Research. *Organization and Management of the State Government of Virginia.* Richmond: New York Bureau of Municipal Research, 1927.

## Washington

Council for Reorganization of Washington State Government. *Survey Report and Recommendations.* Olympia: The Council, 1965.

Governor's Task Force on Executive Organization. *Report to Governor Daniel J. Evans: Recommendations for Improving Structure of State Government.* Olympia: The Task Force, 1968.

———. *Report to Governor Daniel J. Evans.* Olympia: The Task Force, 1970.

Washington State Legislative Council. *The Reorganization of Internal Management Facilities in State Government: Report of the Subcommittee on Simplification, Coordination, and Reorganization of Administrative Branches of State Government.* Olympia: Institute of Public Affairs, University of Washington, 1948.

## West Virginia

Governor's Management Task Force. *Implementation Progress Report.* Charleston: The Task Force, 1970.

———. *Report: Survey and Recommendations, West Virginia State Government.* Charleston: The Task Force, 1970.

Public Administration Service. *Administrative Organization of the Executive Branch, State of West Virginia.* Chicago: Public Administration Service, 1964.

## Wisconsin

Department of Administration, Bureau of Budget and Management. *The Organization of Wisconsin State Government.* Madison: Department of Administration, 1969.

———. *The Organization of Wisconsin State Government.* Madison: The Bureau, 1971.

Legislative Reference Bureau. *The Organization of Wisconsin State Government.* Madison: The Bureau, 1972.

Temporary Reorganization Committee. *Government Reorganization in Wisconsin.*

Madison: The Committee, 1967.

Wisconsin Legislative Council. *Staff Report to the Commission on Efficiency in Government on the Organization of Wisconsin State Government.* Madison: Wisconsin Legislative Council, 1963.

"Wisconsin: The 1967 Executive Branch Reorganization." Madison: *Wisconsin Blue Book,* 1968, pp. 366–78.

*Wyoming*

Griffenhagen and Associates. *Report Made to the Special Legislative Committee on Organization and Revenue.* Casper: Prairie Publishing Co., 1933.

Legislative-Executive Commission on Reorganization of State Government (Wyoming). *Report.* Cheyenne: The Commission, 1970.

_____. *Report.* Cheyenne: The Commission, 1972.


## U.S. Government Documents

Graves, W. Brooke. *Centralization of Government in Hawaii.* Legislative Reference Service Study. Washington, D.C.: Library of Congress, 1962.

Public Affairs Counseling (A Division of the Real Estate Research Corporation). *Factors Involved in the Transfer of Innovations: Summary and Organization of the Literature.* Washington, D.C.: U.S. Department of Housing and Urban Development, 1976.

U.S. Advisory Commission on Intergovernmental Relations. *Factors Affecting Voter Reactions to Governmental Reorganization in Metropolitan Areas.* Washington, D.C.: U.S. Advisory Commission on Intergovernmental Relations, 1962.

_____. "Modernization of State Government." In *Eleventh Annual Report,* pp. 12–13. Washington: The Commission, 1970.

_____. "State Reforms." In *Thirteenth Annual Report,* pp. 13–14. Washington, D.C.: The Commission, 1972.

_____. "State Government Modernization." *Intergovernmental Perspective* 3, no. 1 (Winter 1977):8.

U.S. Congress. Subcommittee of the House Committee on Government Operations. *Reorganization by Plan and Statute, 1945–1962.* Washington, D.C.: U.S. Government Printing Office, 1963.

# Index

Information on asterisked pages appears in tables or figures.